W9-CCN-861

50
FARRAR
STRAUS
GIROUX

THE SLAM AND SCREAM

THE SLAM AND SCREAM

and Other *Powerful* Strategies and *Great* Career Moves for Secretaries, Assistants, and Anyone Else Who Has *Had Enough*

Carole S. Fungaroli

THE NOONDAY PRESS Farrar, Straus and Giroux New York

Published simultaneously in Canada by
HarperCollins*CanadaLtd*
Printed in the United States of America
Designed by Jaye Zimet
First edition, 1996

Library of Congress Cataloging-in-Publication Data
Fungaroli, Carole S.
The slam and scream : and other powerful strategies and great career moves for secretaries, assistants, and anyone else who has had enough / Carole S. Fungaroli.
p. cm.
1. Secretaries—Vocational guidance.
2. Managing your boss. 3. Career development.
I. Title.
HF5547.5.F86 1996 651.3'74'02373—dc20
95-41504 CIP

Thanks to:

Byron Woods for reading every draft, repeatedly, and for calling me a peach-throwing monkey; Richard M. Laska for the ''overall poop, status-wise'' on the feds; John F. Edwards for the view from the other side of the desk; the Hsiang Foong dinner group (Glenn, Dennis, Nancy, Chris, John, Keith, Neil, and Peter) for brainstorming; and Leigh Palmer for her first name. John and Mike Foley and Jeanette Witter read drafts. Betty and Mike Foley provided assistance in the form of dead presidents. Sabura Woods, Mike Kelly, Charlotte Griner, Carol Bowman-Smith, and Patrick Harrison, onetime typewriter jockeys all, offered advice and suggestions. Rick Nakroshis, John Paul Mains, Robert Miles, Chris Hemedinger, and Michael Murphy helped with URLs and BBSs. Harold Lemon sent me a great BBS list. Neale Baxter remembered the feds and the 1960s. Rosemary Hanes at the Library of Congress tirelessly hunted Murphy Brown secretaries. Laurence Avery, Darryl Gless, and the English Department at UNC–Chapel Hill provided an academic setting in which to work productively.

To all the folks from rec.arts.movies and rec.arts.tv who helped me with the historical research: David Zobel, Michael Ritchie, Mara Jade, D. E. Holden, Alex Santoro, Carey D. Allen, P. Moloney, Steven Basford, Zeke M. Towson, Thomas Hamilton, George Swan, Christian Harris, Bill Livingston, Paul Kunkel, Matthew L. Marshall, Eleanor H. Goodman, Brian E. Bradley, Patrick Murphy, William H. Nolte, Lynne Kirste, Erika Grams, Claire Murray, Kay Cashman, Movie Fan, Marie Clear, W. Saul Caplan, Sandra Lee, Ulrich Plate, McNeal Maddox, Tim Carvell, Dan Simon, S. Pines, E. C. Sutton, Allen Kirshner, Betsy Brett, Murray Chapman, Gregory Byshenk, and all the anonymous or pseudonymous respondents.

Special thanks to Breck Richardson, Jr., for help with the television history; Peter Byrnes, popular culture expert, for guidance with television and film; and Andrew Burford for giving me the U.K. perspective. Red-tape thanks to *M*A*S*H* experts Connie Gunderson, Vic Kamhi, and Deborah Conroy.

CONTENTS

THE SLAM AND SCREAM

INTRODUCTION: Battling *"Twins Syndrome"*

Richard Nixon and Rose Mary Woods

I went to the movies one night in 1988 hoping for a little escapist entertainment. The movie was *Twins*, and Arnold Schwarzenegger and Danny DeVito played two brothers conceived in a laboratory experiment. Julius, the big, strong Aryan muscleman, was the successful result. Vincent, the short Italian petty thief, was an unplanned mistake. *Twins* was billed as a comedy—so why wasn't I laughing? Why did the movie disturb me instead? Then it struck me: I saw myself and my employer represented in this duo. Julius was strong at Vincent's expense. When Vincent asks Dr. Traven why he ended up the losing half of a "team," Traven explains:

> *"The embryo* did *split in two, but it didn't split equally. All the purity and strength went into Julius. All the crap that was left over went into what* you *see in the* mirror *every morning."*
>
> *Vincent: "Whoa, whoa . . . you're telling me . . . [t]hat I'm no good? You're saying that . . . I'm a* side effect*?"*
>
> *Traven: "You haven't got the brainpower to understand this, and I haven't got the time."*

How many times had I heard employers say this to administrative assistants? "We'd promote you, but we need someone who understands business," or "Don't bother reading that memorandum. You wouldn't understand it." Worse yet, "We would have given you a shot at that job, but we needed someone . . . (more educated, more experienced, more male, more like us). Maybe next time."

I realized that, just like Vincent, *I* felt like a side effect in the business world. Someone had sold me a bill of goods about a boss and an assistant being a "team," and I'd believed it. They said that, with good performance reviews and a can-do attitude, I could get a promotion someday. So I earnestly contributed my skills, intellect, and energy to help my employer become an economic and political powerhouse, but I gained little in return.

Forty years ago, feminism tried to address this "*Twins* syndrome" in the American marriage, and it succeeded in limited ways. Many women devoted themselves to creating "perfect" 1950s-style marriages; they decreased or eliminated their external market value as they took themselves out of the working world to put all of their energies into making their husbands successful.

What did they accomplish? Some found that their husbands went on in midlife to earn big salaries and marry trophy wives, leaving the first wife faced with a hostile job market and a world that had no place for her. As feminism challenged this model, insisting that women were sacrificing so their husbands could thrive, millions of couples restructured the dynamics of their relationships so that both partners could benefit.

In large part, though, the business world never caught on. Boss-secretary teams, the most exploitative of all the white-collar working relationships, still operate much as they did forty years ago. Women and men in support staff work remain observers on the sidelines, losing their market value while deteriorating both professionally and personally so that their employers can thrive in the marketplace.

But the assistants aren't getting anywhere. That persistent, internal voice that says, "There's a problem here," is right. This book is for people who are tired of being side effects, of having their gender, ethnicity, and good nature regularly used against them in a corporate environment which rewards aggression and where demanding people thrive. Many books have tried to assure the administrative assistant that she or he matters, that the system cares, and that lawsuits through the Equal Employment Opportunity Commission (EEOC) are useful. In overly optimistic, even rosy terms (or, on the other hand, in strident, negative tones), they have tried to make support staff feel wanted and important; in so doing they have lied.

Let's face it: many lawyers and executives in power feel they have "earned" obedient office help the way someone earns a new car or a tailored suit. These people believe—deeply—that their expensive educations and high salaries entitle them to a whole subclass of personal slaves. And guess who they turn to? Secretaries, administrative assistants, receptionists, and clerks are the most obvious candidates for servanthood. You may find yourself being held back because your boss believes that she deserves this higher social status, or that you should always stay several steps beneath her on the corporate ladder. If you try for promotions, these people may stop you, simply because they will feel more comfortable if you stay on your side of the social dividing line. They want to believe that you come from a different world.

This book understands that the corporate system is at best

neutral, or even configured against you. It can destroy you, not out of malice but rather because it is designed to further its own agenda without concern for the consequences. Frequently the system carelessly crushes those who aren't schooled in looking out for their own best interests.

So is happiness even possible? Can a clerical worker find satisfaction in a 9-to-5 job? I say yes, and I can teach you how to do it. This book will show you, chapter by chapter, how to recognize a dead end and escape if you're in one. If you're trying to work your way out of an assistant's position and you're sick of playing Vincent the Side Effect, this book will tell you what your next step should be. If you enjoy working as an administrative assistant but you just don't like abuse, it will teach you how to triumph. If you want raises and promotions, it will tell you where they are (and where they will never be). It will teach you how to find happiness in any office job.

Why should you read this book instead of the others on the market? Because it's the one that will tell you how to survive. Other books have come and gone, mostly because they didn't understand getting out. Some suggest that you learn snappy comebacks for sexual come-ons, that you placate aggressors, and that you sacrifice yourself so that your boss can get ahead in this world. Believe it or not, several manuals offer a *checklist for personal hygiene*, including such helpful hints as "Don't wear clothing fastened together with safety pins" and "Use an effective deodorant." The implication is inescapable: these books are written as though their readers are children. I don't know about you, but I was a grown woman when I found myself trapped, and all the well-pressed shirts in the world couldn't help me. This book cuts through the condescension and tells you what you need to know.

Many of these strategies are the same ones that executives use every day to succeed. It's time everyone had the same opportunity. This book is for you if you think you're just as intelligent as the people you work for. It's for you if you have ever been shouted at, abused, or intimidated at work. If you want a better, happier clerical job, or if you want to get in the promotional line for more responsibility and higher pay, come on in.

If the things you love are just your hobbies, and you do something you dislike for eight hours a day, forty hours a week, then you've got it all backward. Read this book and learn how to escape your rut, change your course, get promoted, and go back to school.

When you do, write me (in care of the publisher) or send E-mail (carole@Virginia.edu or carole@email.unc.edu), and tell me how it went, and what you're doing now. We'll celebrate together.

FROM THE TYPING POOL TO A PH.D.: Notes From a Former Office Worker With a Short Fuse and a Long Memory

Have you ever suspected that you were really someone else? Do you remember being in grade school and pretending you were a princess, a magician, or a rock star?

As a kid, I used to pretend I was a writer. I'd make believe it was *The Merv Griffin Show*, and Merv would introduce me right after Eva Gabor and just before Elliott Gould. I'd talk about writing books and act like it was easy.

Even after my twenty-first birthday, when I was a hostess in a resort restaurant in Florida (what people now refer to as a "McJob"), I'd secretly confess to people that I wanted to be a writer.

They didn't care.

Dining-room hostesses aren't supposed to be writers. They're supposed to be restaurant professionals. A waiter pointed this out to me late one night after work. We stood outside the restaurant on the marina, looking out over the Intracoastal Waterway. Boats sluiced by in the inky darkness, outlined with running lights, their motors humming. In the distance, a car door slammed. Late diners left the bar, laughing and singing. My friend said, "You'll never be a writer working here." He encouraged me to do what I wanted to do.

People had told me, however, that following dreams wasn't "responsible." So instead of listening to him, I moved back to Washington, D.C., and traded my restaurant rut for the office version. There I worked a few temp jobs while still insisting to anyone who would listen that I really wanted to write.

I planned to return to college in the fall, but a boss that summer offered me a position that at the time sounded too good to resist. I accepted, and fell into an overly long cycle of moving from one entry-level clerical post to the next.

From age twenty-two to twenty-four, I worked as a secretary for a direct-marketing firm in Old Town Alexandria, Virginia. Although my boss was a nice guy who is still a friend, he had quite a bit of trouble seeing me as anything other than the temp worker he'd hired. When an entry-level management position opened up, he filled it without even letting me know it was available. I roared into his office, furious for having been overlooked like that, and he expressed the deepest surprise. "I thought you liked what you did," he said. "It never occurred to me you might want that position."

The job went to a woman who'd been with the company less time and who didn't even know the department. She was, however, not the boss's assistant. What my boss didn't want to admit was that he didn't want to lose an excellent right hand. Promoting me would have deprived him of a devoted workhorse. I did not stay at that company much longer when I realized that my own boss and good friend would never help me get ahead.

Instead, I looked for a higher-paying position, and I found it with a Washington, D.C., law firm located in the famous Watergate building on the Potomac River in Georgetown. An employment agent took one look at my high test scores and two years of work experience and sent me to the legal world, where, she said, I could quickly move ahead once people learned of my research and writing skills. I began work as a legal secretary, hoping to be promoted to legal assistant or paralegal.

The promotions never came, but the verbal abuse did. The attorney I worked for screamed at me on a regular basis. He shouted his demands and berated me when I couldn't read his mind. Although he claimed to value me for my intellect and verbal talents, he insisted that I fetch his lunches, mediate telephone calls with his ex-wife and his girlfriend, take his shirts to the cleaners, and generally act as a hybrid between a butler and Bob Cratchit. I started seeing a doctor for ''inexplicable'' stomach pains.

When I complained about the abuse to the senior partner, he thanked me for my input, and did nothing, even though this lawyer often shouted at me in public.

From there I went to another rich downtown law firm, but this time I was smarter. When the abuse started (as it did on the second day), I marched into the boss's office and told him I would have none of it. He smiled, we chatted, and he offered me a promotion. Impossible, you say? Then you need to read Chapter 3 for more ''whaddya know'' advice about those amazing animals, lawyers.

Another employee who put up with this lawyer's verbal abuse had never been promoted. She was understandably resentful when he treated me better. So I asked her a few questions. ''Why do you tolerate his put-downs? Why don't you tell him 'no' when he makes inhuman demands?'' She responded that she had a child to think about. She was afraid of losing her job. ''I've learned to accept my lot in life,'' she said. ''I try to block out the work world when I go home. It's just hell when the alarm goes off at six a.m., though, and I know I have to face the shouting again.'' I still think of her, ten years older than I, sitting in that man's office listening to his ranting. Meanwhile, he and I made a deal that I would stay there only until something better came along. He never shouted at me again.

The ''something better'' was a stock exchange on K Street in the business district known as Washington's Golden Triangle. The money was excellent on K Street, especially at a financial institution before 1987's Black Monday, and I was happy to get a job offer with a nice raise attached. For once in my life (I was now almost twenty-five) I was earning a living wage and enjoying my 9-to-5 life.

Finding this job was no accident. I was well on the way to developing many of the principles in this book, and I used them to land a job that met my needs. The boss was a fair, reasonable person. The company offered excellent benefits, including a savings plan that enabled me to salt away enough money to eventually buy my own home. I worked there happily for three years.

Even though I liked my job, however, I saw a lot of people who hated theirs, so I began to interview them. This was a big company in the heart of the business district, and there were thousands of dissatisfied people trudging to the office in their putty trench coats wishing their lives were different. I kept notes about these characters for later use.

My notebook filled up and my job skills improved, but I couldn't get a promotion. The stock exchange had no plans to give me a shot at moving on, no matter how competent I was. Even though I published a financial directory on a regular basis, I had to train someone who knew nothing about this publication so that he could be my supervisor on the project. Although I was every bit as intelligent and motivated as the analysts who worked there, when I talked to their boss he said I couldn't get one of their jobs. The reason was simple: I didn't have a bachelor's degree.

I awoke from this long, gray sleep one event at a time. First, there was a trip to Europe. I was twenty-six, I'd always wanted to travel abroad, but I was beginning to accept that no one had any plans to take me anywhere. So I went to the Map Store in Washington, D.C., and bought a map of Switzerland. I don't know why I chose "the jewel of Europe" for my first foray, but it seemed elegant, picturesque, and *foreign*.

Like everyone else with a 9-to-5 job, I planned a two-week trip. After all, isn't that the most time off you're allowed to take in a year? (It wasn't until after I had traveled much more that I learned how American the fifty-weeks-on, two-weeks-off schedule really is.) According to the travel agents, a trip would cost about $4,000, including airfare, hotels, food, and interesting tours. I began saving my money, hoping to have enough in two years to make the trek.

Then I read some useful books, and I took a course in traveling alone from a school specializing in short evening courses. I learned all about discount airfares, hosteling in Europe, and living cheaply by shopping at European grocery stores rather than going to restaurants. My teacher explained why two weeks isn't enough: you're not over your jet lag, and you haven't acclimated to the new culture. She encouraged me to go for six months instead.

We compromised. I planned a two-month excursion backpacking in seven countries. The total cost was $1,500, including airfare. I could leave right away.

Now came the hard part. How would I tell my boss at the stock exchange? We had a fine working relationship, and I didn't want to quit my job just to run around the world. He would never let me leave for two months, would he?

Nervously, I made an appointment, walked into his office, sat down, and faced him. I told him that I wished to keep my job but this trip had become enormously important to me. Even though I had only two weeks of available vacation time, I wanted to take six additional weeks without pay, and return at the end of two months. I waited while he absorbed this news. Then I marveled when he agreed to my plan. He said we could hire a temp until I returned. He shook my hand and wished me a pleasant journey.

On that trip I went to England, France, Switzerland, Austria, Germany, Italy, and Holland. I traveled with a letter of introduction from US Servas, an international peace organization. I spent two nights each with various European families who wanted foreign visitors, at no charge. I cut my hair to an inch all over (at a London hairdresser's called the Zoo), and I lost about fifteen pounds of stubborn fat because I walked everywhere possible to save money. There I learned that the backpacking American abroad is an international cliché. The trip that had seemed so daring from my safe office in Washington seemed quite commonplace on the train platforms in Amsterdam.

You'd think that all this trekking would make returning to my desk impossible, wouldn't you? Well, it didn't. I came to appreciate some of the subtler points of job security and an office "family." At the end of two months I was ready to come home to a place where the toilets flushed in a predictable manner and where I didn't have to use a calculator every time I went to the market. I longed for a full wardrobe of clothes again, and evenings spent with friends I'd known for years. Once home, though, I decided it was time for a promotion, no matter what the stock exchange thought about it.

I accepted a quasi-promotion (called a "lateral move," since I made no more money and since I was no closer to the next level). This next job bumped me right up against that glass ceiling you've heard so much about. I went as far as a woman in that company could go if she didn't have both a college degree and the know-how to break into the mostly male management ranks. It wasn't very high up.

About a year later, hoping to locate that elusive promotional track, I left K Street to work for lawyers again. The employment agent promised me an excellent salary and scads of responsibility, with opportunities for advancement. However, my new bosses took one look at my mostly clerical résumé and tried to wrestle me back to word processing and lunch fetching. I wouldn't let them. Instead of allowing this cycle of entry-level jobs to go on forever, I returned to college, obtained a bachelor's degree at long last, and went on to graduate school in a field I loved. I worked my way through college at that law firm and others like it.

That near-decade of office work brought me in contact with an amazing array of people, all of whom had childhood dreams. I met a data-entry clerk who really wanted to sing Gospel music. There was a computer operator who loved science fiction and wanted to write genre novels. A clerk who was a little brown wren by day went home at night, changed clothes, and became a witty, charming man-about-town, knowledgeable about food, wine, and fine decor.

I expanded my notebook, adding these characters to others I'd collected over the years and in Europe: the Baptist pastor who dreamed of being a professional baseball player, for example. The secretary who loved to travel, and wished she could *be* the tour guide in her favorite countries, Israel and Greece. The couple who spent every vacation minute in France, working hard all year to afford the luxury of cruising down a river on a houseboat, enjoying café au lait and croissants in the early-morning summer sunlight. The bank programmer who adored geography and puzzles, and studied maps at home for hours in his spare time. The receptionist who wrote science fiction, and played Zork with me on the company's computer system just to stay sane.

All of these people had something in common with me. We believed, deeply, that it was more responsible to get up every morning and do something we disliked ("steady employment") than to take a risk and try something we loved, full-time. We all acted as though childhood dreams were the stuff of hobbies, whereas the real world consisted of boring, reliable work. Employment can't be fun and also be responsible, can it?

Of course it can. I learned something crucial while traveling. Most dreams are out there, they are achievable, and they await anyone who asks the most basic questions about his or her job. *Is this what I want to do? Is a two-week vacation all you get? Can you really go from administrative assistant to management or do you have to change tracks? Does my (writing, singing, painting, dancing, mapmaking) have to be just a hobby?* And, of course, *Who is this boss person telling me I "have" to do what he says, even if it's inappropriate?*

My memories of that European trip helped me decide to return to college. When I toured Oxford University, an undergraduate mistook me for a student. We enjoyed a beer together at a pub in Oxford's High Street, and I told him about my bad experience with school. He encouraged me to try again. Once back home, I reenrolled at a local university. There I earned an A in an English class (my first in a long time) and felt the satisfaction that came from doing one thing carefully and well.

Two years after going abroad, I was writing on a regular basis and earning excellent grades in college even though I'd once thought I was an academic "lost cause." Not bad for someone who barely stayed awake in high school and stumbled through a mercifully short first run at college quite a few years before. Through it all I supported myself by working full-time or almost full-time while taking a heavy course load. It was exhausting, and I can't say I recommend the frenetic pace, but I wouldn't trade the experience for anything.

A close friend from my first law firm saw my academic progress and decided that college looked pretty good. She went back to school a couple of years after I did, and she too had excellent success. When one of the lawyers she worked for asked her why she slaved so hard at work and school, she said, "Carole did it, and now I think I can too.'' He laughed. ''Don't base your life on what Carole does. She's *never* had a firm grasp on reality!''

What he meant was that I didn't know my place. He demonstrated, in that brief comment, the anxiety that many lawyers and other professionals feel when their ''servant class'' starts to move ahead.

Meanwhile, I had my sights set on graduate school, and my friend wasn't far behind me. I quit work in the summer of 1990 to start graduate study in English literature at the University of Virginia.

Talk about feeling like a fake.

My first day of grad school was horrible. I didn't understand a word anyone was saying in a literature seminar. I remember looking out my classroom window in Cabell Hall at a bus stop and thinking, ''I could just walk out of here, get on the bus, and go home. The lawyers would hire me back.'' Instead, I stayed in school, but dropped that particular class. *(True story. When I decided to drop the course, a classmate asked me why. The professor hadn't arrived yet, so I said to the assembled roomful of students, ''I just don't understand a word anyone is saying in here.'' Another woman looked up, smiled, and said ''Oh, thank heavens. I thought I was the only stupid one.'' A man chimed in with ''Yeah, me too. My notes are a mess.'' Years later I learned the truth. This professor was known for his impenetrable, confusing classes. Sometimes the emperor is naked.)*

And I survived. Surprisingly, though, it was that near-decade of ''wasted'' time working in Washington that helped me finish so quickly. Years of waking up at 6 a.m. and working a 9-to-5 job taught me consistency, dependability, and how to bring a task to completion. I was a fast, accurate typist (always useful when producing endless drafts of academic papers), and I already knew something about research. Those jobs working for Men in Identical Suits taught me time-management techniques. I had learned how to juggle several competing priorities at once—something any good administrative assistant understands well—and I could pace myself without burning out. You've probably developed most of these same skills on your job.

Oh, I stumbled now and then. For one thing, I spent the first six months of graduate school apologizing for not being ''one of them.'' Many of my fellows came from Ivy League universities, and they had all been star pupils in high school. Quite a few held prestigious fellowships with names like Mellon and Carnegie. I was deeply intimidated.

Then something clicked and I settled in. I stopped apologizing and pretending to be someone else. I got my own fellowships. I asked questions when I didn't understand something (amazingly, this is simply not done in the competitive jungles), and I didn't use words I couldn't define. I wrote papers in clear, readable prose, because every time I tried writing in grad-student babble the result was a blithering mess.

Ten years of working in offices had taught me a final lesson: how to be a professional. I applied these principles to graduate study and got out of there in just under four years with a doctorate in English literature.

And here's the final, ironic twist. My graduation date, two months after my thirty-fourth birthday, was right in line with the national average. Students who go directly from high school to college to graduate school spend an average of eleven years getting their master's and doctoral degrees. With hard work and a little professional coaching from my friend and grad school expert Rob Peters, I got mine in three years and ten months. This means I graduated with people who had stayed in school all those years I was working! It was as though I'd never taken time off to grow up, to travel, and to work. I entered a giant time machine and came out on the other side, right on schedule. My office skills gave me a competitive edge I needed in the academic world.

So why am I writing this book? Because I found the exit route, and guess what? *They lied.* The escape hatch isn't where you thought it was. You can't get to your boss's desk just by working harder. You can only do it by being smarter and knowing where they hid the promotional path.

As you well know, smart people frequently end up in servant jobs. Belligerent, pushy, even stupid people frequently get promoted. I have seen cases where a group of support staffers made their clueless boss appear competent. Intelligent older employees hired to do office work often served lunches and washed dishes. Meanwhile, eager young hotshots fresh out of their MBA classes waltzed in with no prior work experience and made four times the money.

What's worse, these college-kid bosses frequently acted as

though they were better than the people who reported to them. In my time in the trenches I was shouted at, insulted, berated, and (just once) fired. I had an attorney sit across the desk from me and ridicule my efforts at getting a bachelor's degree. I comforted more than one friend as she sobbed in the ladies' room after being screamed at. I've had people ask me "who I thought I was" simply because I would not call them Mr. or Ms. (or Dr.) So-and-so if they insisted upon calling me Carole. I've seen talented, capable employees training the people who would eventually be their bosses, and the only difference between them was a college degree.

Now that graduate school is over, I'm earning a living as a scholar, with a little help from the NPR station where I'm an announcer for a classical music program. I'm writing the books I always dreamed of, and I enjoy traveling abroad whenever possible. It's an excellent, fulfilling life.

But I can see how easy it would have been to miss this life, out of fear of changing course. I could have listened to the naysayers and stayed in that entry-level job cycle. Conventional wisdom would have kept me under an angry lawyer's thumb, doing something I hated and watching my life go by.

When I was an office worker, I didn't know there was an alternative to enduring sexism, verbal abuse, and petty office politics. Once I saw how it feels to be treated well, though, I became furious in retrospect. Although I'll never forget the people who were kind in those early days, I'll also never forget the ones who tried, for whatever reasons, to keep me and my colleagues "in our places." At points I may indulge in a little righteous anger, but the facts and names in these true stories have been sufficiently changed to protect the guilty as well as the innocent. If every abused secretary learns to "Slam and Scream," and if every petty office dictator finds himself or herself without anyone to do their bidding, I will feel that justice, in some small way, has been served.

Are you wondering what happened to my friend? You know, the one whose boss told her I didn't have a firm grasp on reality? Well, she's in graduate school right now and doing wonderfully well. She's studying for the profession she wants rather than the one society taught her to expect. Some of my other friends are still administrative assistants (because they want to be), but they're enjoying the increased responsibility and respect that comes from demanding fair terms in the best possible job. Our stories may sound atypical, or even exceptional, but they don't have to be. If you use the ideas in this book that you need, you'll find yourself telling your own similar story with more than a touch of pride.

Raymond Burr and
Barbara Hale in an
unguarded moment on the
Perry Mason set

(COURTESY OF *TV GUIDE*)

PHOTO: SHERMAN WEISBURD

TAKE A LETTER, MARIA: How to *Improve* Any Administrative *Assistant* Job

It's not the 1950s anymore, but little has changed in boss-secretary land. Assistants still ask themselves what they really mean to their bosses and the corporations where they work. ''What,'' they ask, ''*is* a secretary after all?''

✎ A Secretary Is Part of the Incentive Package

In the typical executive's mind, the personal assistant is a reward. A bonus. The icing. Most companies understand that the boss-assistant relationship is indulgent and inefficient, but they don't really care. When they promise their top executives competent, *personal* assistants, they offer a powerful incentive to sign on. It's not just a male phenomenon either; when women ascend to power status, they often adopt the same value system. As Ellen Goodman writes about the 1988 movie *Working Girl*, where Melanie Griffith's Tess climbs from typing duties to the executive suite:

> *In the last scene of the movie our heroine wins the symbol of success: The secretary gets a secretary. But the only progress she promises is that, as a boss, she'll get her own coffee. Solidarity forever. Hold the cream.*

Even movies that claim to speak for administrative assistants acknowledge that they are, in part, an executive's reward.

Executives consider the whole package of benefits when they are deciding whether to accept a new position. They think about salary, but they also ask questions about insurance, bonuses, investment plans, and support staff. It's possible that, as a private assistant, you are part of an overall "enticement package" to make an executive leave one corporation for another.

Once I viewed administrative assistants and receptionists through an executive's eyes I saw the truth: even the most competent, influential private assistants are about as important to the typical executive as a corner office or a solid-mahogany desk. Sharon Atkins, the receptionist in Studs Terkel's best-seller *Working* (Pantheon, 1974), puts it this way:

> *You're just there to filter people and filter telephone calls. You're there to handle the equipment. You're treated like a piece of equipment, like the telephone . . . just a little machine.*

Does anyone think about giving a copier a career path? Are there advancement opportunities for the computer? Of course not. Yet hundreds of applicants accept administrative assistant, secretarial, and receptionist jobs hoping the boss will promote them someday.

It almost never happens. When assistants do rise, it is seldom far. Bosses continue to view former assistants as "damaged goods," because they've worked in a devalued position. According to this old but durable model of office life, bosses prefer assistants without education or ambition. ''Shut up and type'' is more the rule than the exception.

Although Beth now has ''education'' and people pay for her opinions, they didn't want to hear them when she was an assistant. For example, one attorney snapped that he wanted none of her ''editorializing'' when she told him, politely, that the deli was out of Gruyère cheese. They had only Swiss, Muenster, or American in stock, and, in a burst of personal bravado, she recommended the Swiss. He nearly fired her. The moral? Secretarial work is supposed to be performed by the invisible in the service of the highly visible.

✎ What's Wrong with Being a Secretary or Administrative Assistant?

There's nothing wrong with the work you do. There is, however, something terribly wrong with how executives perceive it. Secretarial work has never recovered from its ''dumb blonde'' image. Although groups like 9 to 5 claim they are making progress, bosses persist in viewing assistants as less intelligent or motivated. Most employers commit the sin of overmanagement, taking away the interesting parts of an assistant's job and leaving him with the routine tasks, which bosses then explain in endless, condescending detail. I asked some former secretaries to list the biggest problem with secretarial or administrative assistant work. Here's what they said:

''It's dull.''	*Maya*
''I hated it. It was a yawn.''	*Chris*
''God, was I bored.''	*Steve*
''Boring, boring, bo-ring.''	*Charlotte*

Now that Charlotte is a manager, she offers her own administrative assistant a more interesting job. ''I'm not a micromanager. I let her figure out how to do what I ask, and she usually does it without additional instructions from me.'' She thinks that most managers don't mean to insult the assistant's intelligence but really don't know when to stop giving instructions. Most bosses have never been secretaries or assistants, so they seldom appreciate how dull it can become.

And the job isn't just boring; it can also lead to clinical depression. A study in *Women and Health* (June 1992) by Roberta Garrison and William W. Eaton entitled "Secretaries, Depression, and Absenteeism" shows that administrative assistants are much more likely to become clinically depressed than other working women. Missed work seems to be the most conclusive sign that you have this type of depression. If you're hitting the snooze button more and more or making up excuses not to go in at all, why not consult a therapist or psychologist? Your health insurance may cover at least half the cost, and you might be surprised to find out you're in this growing group of working adults.

✎ It's Not Just a Job—It's a Marriage

Have you ever heard the term "office wife"? Did it disturb you? It should have. Secretarial work has always been structured to make the personal assistant the "wife" of the boss, linking the two together in what I consider an inappropriate way. When the secretary is female, the boss often treats her like either a dim spouse or a bright child. Many people will assume that she is sexually available. When the secretary is male, people often treat him like "one of the girls," since the secretarial role is a feminized position. Some people will assume he is gay whether he is or not; others will conclude that he lacks ambition.

If you think these problems arise only when working for male bosses, think again. Working for a woman may be as bad, or worse. Many professional women avoid the clerical staff, whether because they worked their way out of those duties or because they never would have dreamed of doing them in the first place. Professional women climb a tough ladder to the top, and many only respect other women who have done as they did. Often they think of female assistants as "wasting their lives." One woman admitted she feels uncomfortable if she gets too chatty with the secretarial staff at her company: she has enough problems with her image, and she feels that talking to the secretaries would only hurt her more. "A client once mistook me for a secretary," she confided. "I was horrified, and also quite angry. Now I never

Are you handcuffed to your secretary?

venture near their work stations.'' Reactionary? Perhaps, but a lot of women feel this way. Although this can be a subtle problem, it's occasionally right out in the open; I've worked with women who were unable to hide their disdain for the clerical staff.

✎ Wives Don't Get Promotions; Neither Do Secretaries

In the standard office relationship, the administrative assistant fully invests himself in his boss's job. He puts all of his efforts into making his boss shine. But what's in it for him? Even the lowliest manager or mail-room clerk has a hope of promotion someday, but the administrative assistant is frequently stigmatized. Most firms hire new employees for the future: for how they can grow and what they can bring to the organization. Only in secretarial work do managers consider it a drawback to have an education, ambition, and to want to be president someday. Bosses everywhere expect their assistants to willingly stay where they are.

In one well-known management magazine, an article written for bosses, ''Making Your Secretary a Supersecretary'' (*Supervisory Management*, September 1994), admits this antipromotion bias. The author advises bosses to quiz secretaries about their career goals, and then subvert them!

> *Example: Your secretary wants to move up the corporate ladder. You don't want to lose a good secretary. Possible compromise: Let the secretary help create a training program for new secretaries and assistants, or serve as a mentor for new-hires.*

What kind of compromise is this? By telling the boss to ''let'' the secretary train others and be a mentor, the writer is really saying, ''Throw the secretary a bone so she or he won't bug you about promotions.'' The author then gives bosses detailed instructions for making the secretary as useful as possible, without the needless bother of offering that person either a raise or the hope of a better job someday.

If the secretarial world were seen as any sort of path to the top, more people would take it. Instead, it is perceived as part of the *boss's* path to the top. In the Introduction, I talked about ''*Twins* syndrome,'' in which the secretary puts a great deal of energy into strengthening the boss's professional image and becomes a weak ''side effect'' in the process. No other working relationship demands this of one partner. In every other employer-employee duo, the two work for their mutual professional advancement. With the boss and the administrative assistant, however, the assistant stays behind while the boss gets ahead.

✎ Can't I "Hitch My Wagon to a Star"?

Some assistants work for successful executives and enjoy the raises and perks that come from following this rising boss to bigger, better things. This policy of allowing an assistant's status to change with the boss's status can backfire, though. It's called ''rug ranking,'' a term that derives from the quality of the carpets in an executive's private office. Like fine rugs, the personal as-

LIBRARY OF CONGRESS

Rug-ranking compares you to carpets in the executive suite

sistant is considered a luxury. She or he receives higher pay and more benefits as the boss's status increases. But here's the flip side: if the boss gets demoted, the assistant does too.

A court found this policy unlawful, but this didn't make things better for assistants in the real world. In 1987 Elaine Truskoski challenged the "rug ranking" policy at ESPN, the sports television network. When the boss was demoted, Truskoski was demoted too, despite fine performance reviews. The court agreed that this wasn't fair.

So she won. But what did she really win? The court ordered ESPN to pay her attorneys' fees and to rehire her at her old salary of $29,800 a year. This long, costly confrontation took six years of her life, in exchange for which she won the right to return to the same place she was before the fight began. Secretaries' groups cite this as a victory. I view it as a sad comment on the legal system and the administrative assistant/secretarial profession.

Companies that practice rug ranking seldom advertise it, and most will try to deny it. One way to discover hidden rug-ranking policies is to ask, at interview time, whether you will have the opportunity to be promoted along with your boss. If the hiring officer says, "Oh yes, you'll get raises when she does," then you can bet the reverse will be true as well. My standard advice is to stay away from companies with rug-ranking policies if you plan on an administrative assistant career.

✎ Still Want to Be an Assistant? How to Make It a Better Job

Don't say I didn't warn you, but if you still think that administrative assistant work is for you, then by all means follow my ten tips for survival. You'll need the first five when you go looking for a job. The second five are survival hints once you start working.

Before You Accept a Job, Make Certain You:

1. Work for a boss, not a department. If you accept a position as a departmental secretary, everyone will think you work for them personally. Never accept a job working for an office manager: they are relatively powerless, and they will try to make you a model of efficiency to impress their superiors.

2. Only work for corporations that offer time-and-a-half pay for overtime. Companies that don't pay overtime will still ask you to work it, but for free. Some will claim to let you earn ''comp time,'' giving you an hour and a half of leave for every hour you work overtime, but don't believe them. Few employees ever get to take that leave, and it's hard to prove you've got it. Also, make certain your boss, not the office manager or a higher-up, will authorize your overtime. You cannot afford to work for a boss so powerless that he or she has to seek outside authorization when you work beyond your normal hours.

3. Remember that fully paid health insurance, dental coverage, and personal or discretionary leave (which is distinct from sick leave) are valuable parts of an employment offer. Never accept an offer without excellent benefits, since good ones are the same as cash. Companies offering poor benefit packages will skimp with you on everything else. See Chapter 6 for tips on how to shop for benefits.

4. Terminate any interview where the interviewer says they're looking for someone who just wants to be an administrative assistant and nothing more. Even if that's what you actually do want, by saying this they've shown you how backward they are. Similarly, ask how many of their executives are

women and how many assistants or receptionists are men. Stay away from offices where all support staff is female and all management is male. You'll be doing their dishes in no time.

5. Refuse the following duties under any circumstances, and make it part of your employment agreement that you do not have to perform them. (a) Don't agree to take written dictation: it's out of date, and it forces you to sit in someone's office waiting for them to organize their thoughts. There are more efficient ways to handle this that don't involve indulging the boss and inconveniencing the assistant. (b) Reject taking overflow typing from other personal assistants. Because you're new, the senior staff will dump work on you. You'll have begun your new job in a weakened position. (c) Refuse to cover the receptionist's station during lunch breaks. No one else in a corporation has to regularly "step down" to do a lower-level job, and neither should you.

On-the-Job Suggestions

1. Although you should work for only one boss, sometimes a higher executive will give you work to do. Ask your boss for protection to help minimize this as much as possible. Never do typing for a same-level or lower-level executive. If you work for more than one person, don't use the First In First Out (FIFO) system unless you want executives shouting at you. Make them decide whose work gets priority, and always defer to the higher-ranking executive, not the pushiest one. Let them fight it out among themselves.

2. Avoid doing work for nonexecutives. Refuse to do any typing for paralegals or summer staff, and keep to a minimum work you do for other assistants or the office manager. People who ask you to help them with their workload are showing the symptoms of a bigger problem. The more you take on, the more they'll give you, and they may never be able to help you in return. If someone can't promote you or return your favors, don't waste your time making them look better. If the office manager is your boss, then you didn't follow my "never work for office managers" rule. Consider changing jobs.

3. Do the tasks on your job description perfectly. Do nonprofessional tasks, such as washing dishes and making coffee, poorly. Example: Does your job include balancing the petty-cash account, but do executives keep sending you to fetch lunches? Then turn in perfect balance sheets that you've

triple-checked for accuracy, and be sure to goof up all lunch orders. Martine was a great researcher, and lawyers used to seek her out for these interesting jobs. However, the one time they told her to wash dishes, she left a greasy, poorly washed mess. They couldn't pull her off of kitchen detail fast enough. (Special hint: If the firm is really pushing kitchen work at you, "accidentally" break dishes. This never fails to get you out of there.) If you have to fetch coffee, make certain it is too cold, too strong (or too weak), and way too sweet. They'll get the picture.

4. If anyone ever shouts at you, insults you, berates you, or tries to intimidate you, confront them in private and let them know you'll have none of it. *Never* be polite to bullies, not even once. Scare them if you can. The "Slam and Scream" technique in Chapter 3 is too harsh for corporate executives, who might fire you, but I discuss a modified version of it in this chapter's next section, "How to Talk Back to a Briefcase."

5. Join 9 to 5, a clerical workers' organization, especially if you think you might need to sue your employer. It offers valuable legal services, plus generous discounts on credit cards, first-time mortgages, and more. Call 1-800-522-0925. Warning: This group acts as if all assistants are women and all bosses are men, and it sometimes offers strange advice, such as suggesting that you politely and sweetly respond to bullies. Your $25 annual fee will more than pay for itself in credit and legal services, however, and they have a great support line. Use it for what it's worth, and ignore the rest. Better yet, become an active member, and encourage them to update their image.

✎ How to Talk Back to a Briefcase

Corporate executives are much less prone to shouting matches than their legal brethren, so you'll need to use different techniques when confronting them over inappropriate behavior. My "Slam and Scream" method in Chapter 3 works with lawyers because they are born fighters who often respond only to confrontation. When you yell back at an obnoxious lawyer, you speak a language he or she understands.

When you bellow back at executives, however, they often clam up, refusing to continue discussions with you. They may even fire you in retaliation. Many executives go on the defensive, spending so much time protecting themselves that they never really hear what you're trying to tell them. Instead, you may have to show rather than tell how you feel about difficult office situations.

For example, let's say you're a twenty-five-year-old administrative assistant in a stock exchange, and one of the vice presidents, Carl, has told you to hold all of his calls. Now he's shouting at you for not recognizing an important CEO on the telephone and putting her call through. How do you respond? If he was an attorney, you could simply yell back, saying something like ''How was I supposed to know who she was? It's not like I ever met her. Give me a break!'' An executive would bristle at this, however, and he wouldn't forget it either.

Instead, recoil. If Carl says, ''How stupid can you be? That was one of our most important chief executives. You should have told her I'd speak to her right away!'' act shocked at his aggressive tone. Respond with ''Good heavens!'' and back away from him. If he continues shouting, say, ''Do you need a glass of water? You seem upset . . . really. Almost out of control.'' Continue to move away, and look as though he might have something contagious. Don't overplay the scene, however.

This should embarrass him, and that's what you want. Executives put an enormous amount of time into looking good in front of one another and in keeping their behavior consistent with the group norm. If you act horrified at an executive's display of temper, you are likely to humiliate him out of trying it a second time.

If Carl ever repeats his offensive behavior, go into his office, privately, and shut the door. Then say, ''I'm beginning to worry that we cannot work together happily here. If you continue to feel the need to shout at me in public, I'm going to have to file a complaint in writing, and consider seeking more suitable employment. Please decide what you want, and act accordingly.'' There are many ways to say this. In a sweet voice this sounds like placating pablum. However, if you say it like machine-gun fire, inflection down, and to the point, it will have quite an impact. Don't accuse him or go into details, and keep your voice at a moderate level, but don't be a patsy either, ameliorating the tension and smoothing things over. It is perfectly all right to let this moment be uncomfortable, as long as the mood doesn't become hostile.

If he tries to explain that he only wants you to start recognizing CEOs on the phone, you can say, "I do my best at this job, Carl, every day. But mistakes happen, and unless we can both learn to work with them when they occur, I suggest you find a more perfect assistant. Try a robot." *Never* apologize for your error, even if you were wrong. He'll take this as a sign of weakness. Keep the focus on his inappropriate outburst, not on what you did to anger him.

If the executive gets even angrier, don't be intimidated. If an executive shouts first, snap back one notch below the shouting, but still quite angrily. Pretend you're yelling at your spouse or boyfriend or girlfriend. This also works for sexual aggression: If someone comes on to you, show them they'll get more than they bargained for by tangling with you . . . be even *more* aggressive in return. Just be sure to keep all of your confrontations private. Look him or her in the eye and flash some fire. If an executive *really* loses it, though, throttle back. Look at them as though they are deranged. The resulting embarrassment should be entertaining to watch. If you are older than the person verbally attacking you, so much the better. Draw yourself up to your full height and let them have it, to the same degree that they have begun the confrontation with you.

This method works with women as well as men, and it's just as appropriate for your boss as it is for the highest executive in the corporation. Nobody, not the president, not the chairman of the board, and certainly not a middle manager, has the right to shout at you, even under pressure. They demonstrate admirable self-control with each other. Insist that they treat you with the same respect at all times, and act horrified when they have the poor manners to lose their composure in front of you. You are not in the office to "brighten up the place" and absorb their bad karma.

✎ Your Voice Is Your Best Protection

Have you ever talked to people who put a question mark on the end of every sentence? As though they're not sure of what they are saying? And they sound incredibly young and stupid? This is called an inflection-up speech pattern, and it can ruin you on the job.

Practice talking into a tape recorder, and drop your voice at the end of every sentence. Say sentences, even questions, as though you are delivering a statement.

Never speak in a baby voice or talk to lawyers and executives in a soft, placating manner. Save this for your sweetie at home. At the office, try dropping your voice about half an octave, as long as you don't sound artificial.

Think about a presidential address to the nation. Most presidents talk in simple, straightforward English, and they use inflection down at the end of each sentence. This makes them sound clear, forceful, and direct. It will work wonders for you at the office, especially in confrontation situations. The less you act like a subordinate, feminine (or, if you are male, feminized) geisha, the less people will think they have any right to shout at you or publicly berate you.

✎ Secretaries' Day Is Embarrassing for Everyone

"Raises, not roses" is a rallying cry at 9 to 5, and I couldn't agree more. April comes once a year to irritate both the boss and the assistant by emphasizing the social disparity between them. The two often go to an awkward lunch, over which they have little to say to one another. One boss may buy her personal assistant flowers, while another purchases a scarf or a bottle of perfume for his secretary. The staff may pitch in to send a big card, a plant, or balloons. Most assistants find this display embarrassing, because it is done for no one else in the firm. Even the few assistants who do tolerate it—and the very few who actually like it—consistently report that a raise or bonus would more appropriately show professional appreciation.

You can nip secretaries' day in the bud (so to speak) by telling your boss sometime around April 1 that you find it uncomfortable, and you'd prefer not to play along. Don't worry. Your boss hates it, too, and she or he will be relieved you said something. If someone in the office does give you roses, thank them, and then put the flowers out in the lobby ("so that everyone can enjoy them") instead of sticking them on your desk. This way you subtly change the focus away from your job, without hurting anyone who meant well. Who knows? Instead of $80 worth of roses, next year you might see that extra money in your paycheck.

✎ Can You Be a Good Employee and Also a Good Parent?

If you are a legal secretary or an administrative assistant with children at home, you may find yourself unable to obtain simple leave to care for them from time to time. Bosses who don't hesitate to waste hours of your time, who ask you to fetch their lunches and run their personal errands, or even help them with matters concerning their own children, may resent any extra time that you take to look after yours.

So what is an assistant with children supposed to do? My advice is sinister, but necessary. Hide them. Don't tell your employer you have children, because she or he simply does not care, and may well use it against you. If you ever bring your children to work, your bosses will resent it, even if they parade their own little angels through now and again. For them, pictures of children on *their* desks mean status. Photos of your kids on your desk mean guilt, and frequent scheduling burdens.

✎ But What If I *Need* Time to Care for My Children?

Many assistants must take time away from the office now and then to care for their children, and most bosses resent the intrusion. Ironically, though, these same bosses often let students take time off from the office to do something related to college.

An assistant I knew used this unfair situation to her advantage. Although she occasionally took time off to care for her children, she never told this to her boss. Instead, she pretended she was in night school, so that she could give her boss more plausible reasons for being out of the office now and then. When she had to leave work early for her daughter's school play, she said it was to watch a movie for sociology class. She even bought an academic calendar and put it on her desk, penciling in fake tests and school appointments when she needed to take the kids to the doctor or dentist. Ridiculous? Perhaps, but her bosses seldom denied her leave.

When Deborah was in college, she asked her boss if she could take a two-hour lunch to hear a poetry reading at a local bookstore. The boss not only said yes, but she went with Deborah. The day before, however, the same boss denied Pat, another assistant, a two-hour lunch so she could pick up her son when his school let out early.

Why did this boss go with Deborah to the bookstore on her long lunch, while forcing Pat to stay at her desk? It's clear. The boss respected education, not children. Her husband stayed home with the kids, so she had little sympathy for Pat, whose husband had to work full-time. Even though Pat and her husband divided the parenting tasks equally, this boss was far less comfortable letting Pat be a mother than she was letting Deborah be a student.

Because kids can make parents late for work, bosses think that working moms and dads devote less of their time to their duties, whether or not it is true. These working parents have to try harder than other employees to get to the office on time every day. I know it's a hassle, but even if it means putting your children in a preschool day-care program, get yourself in before the boss each morning. This way you will save up "generosity points" on the mornings when your daughter wakes up with a fever or your son misses the school bus.

When your kids make you late, call in immediately and let the boss know you've been delayed. Don't go on about your children's problems, and don't offer excuses, because you don't owe any. Get to the point, say what time you'll be in, and make a big fuss about making up all of the time on your lunch breaks. This may buy you valuable time later when your children have the mumps or when a typical school crisis forces you to leave during the day.

For pregnant secretaries, the prospects are even bleaker. My friend Evelyn sat in disbelief one day as her office manager fired her a few days following her announcement that she was pregnant. Ironically, the woman who fired her also was pregnant. Why didn't Evelyn sue the firm? At the time, Washington, D.C.'s Equal Employment Opportunity Commission office had a four-year backlog of lawsuits. All the EEOC office could suggest was that she should come downtown, fill out a form, and hope for the best.

She and her husband couldn't afford a private attorney, especially since the organization which fired her was a law firm with almost unlimited resources for fighting back. Besides, have you ever tried starting a lawsuit when you're four months pregnant? Evelyn had morning sickness, lower back pain, and exhaustion that prevented her from walking downstairs every morning, let alone launching a protracted, expensive lawsuit. After the baby's birth, there was even less money and time to think about suing.

Therefore I recommend treating both children and pregnancies as personal business that you don't need to discuss with the boss. *It's illegal for a boss to ask if you are pregnant, either at your hiring interview or on the job. It's also illegal for bosses to ask if you plan to have children.* Oh, they'll ask anyway. A lawyer recently told a candidate that he enjoys "breaking all the rules," and then he proceeded to ask if she was married. Refuse to answer these questions, even if your refusal terminates the interview. Announce pregnancies near the end of your term—whether the "evidence" has been obvious all along or not—and only to people who need to know; then take your full maternity leave. Companies and law firms will have a worse time trying to explain how they fired a seven-months-pregnant woman than they would with one who isn't showing yet.

Administrative assistants with children represent unwanted problems for most bosses, and few employers will stand up and cheer because you have kids. Instead, they will blame you. If you don't believe this, ask yourself why prominent members of the federal government feel so comfortable taking money and benefits away from working and welfare mothers.

They Can't Hide Their Prying Eyes

Here's a contradiction. How can you be invisible and visible at the same time? When you're an administrative assistant. You're invisible because you look like a piece of office equipment to most people, but you're also one of the first people anyone sees when they come inside the firm. You're exposed, usually sitting out in the middle of the room, with no walls around you to protect you from other people's prying eyes. You're the middle guppy in the clerical fish tank.

When Bob was an administrative assistant, his office manager used to tell him to clean under his desk, because everyone could see there. Well, one day he went into her office and looked under her desk. She had two shoe boxes, a pile of old newspapers, stock reports, a Doritos bag (way back there), and a dog chew. *A dog chew*: Bob never dreamed that she indulged. How could she keep a dog chew under her desk and expect Bob to clean under his? Because he sat out in the middle of the room, Bob had to be a model of cleanliness.

Stouffer's, the ''Lean Cuisine'' company, reports that 85 percent of all administrative assistants eat at their desks. Why? Because most assistants can't leave, even though many firms provide dining rooms. It's hard to go to lunch when your boss demands that someone ''cover'' your telephones and pressures you to stay available at all times. Eating at your desk ends up being easier than the alternatives. Jill never had time for lunch, so she sometimes hid sandwiches under her desk, on top of banker's boxes, or in the bottom drawer of her typing stand. The office manager frequently caught her anyway and told her to get rid of the food. Yet she could look right into her boss's office and see him eating pizza, subs, salads, and once even a steak and a baked potato, in comfortable privacy. What are you supposed to do?

✎ Clock Watching Can Save Your Lunch Breaks

Remember those typing classes in high school where the teacher told you that bosses don't like ''clock watchers''? Forget it. Administrative assistants and clerks must be clock watchers every day of their working lives. Many new employees compromise their right to a full lunch hour by working through it. They want to ''make a good impression,'' so they skip lunch to pitch in and get more accomplished. Often they eat at their desks while finishing up some extra typing or balancing the boss's checkbook. These people might just as well say, ''Go ahead, walk all over me.'' Eager beginners usually find that their enthusiasm comes back to haunt them later, when the boss-secretary relationship deteriorates and they're unable to take a peaceful break once a day.

Salvage your private lunches by starting a rigorous clock-watching schedule. First, consistently arrive at work at least five minutes before your boss, every day. Remember that the difference between five minutes early and five minutes late on any job is enormous, and that most bosses are impressed when employees are more punctual than they are. Set your alarm clock an hour earlier if you must, but always get into the office before the boss. Trish loved this early-morning time, and she used it to read the paper, drink coffee, even balance her checkbook. You don't have to work that early, you just have to be there. As Woody Allen put it, "Ninety percent of life is showing up." The boss will have no idea how long you've been in. All he or she will know is that when they get there, you're ready to go. You can start your working day at the normal time.

Then, when it's lunchtime, go to lunch, from your first day on the job. Never give up your lunch hour, no matter how busy your boss says she is. If your employers insist that you work through lunch because of a deadline, and you agree, mark the missed portion of lunch down as overtime, and charge the firm accordingly.

Bosses may complain that you don't have the proper attitude. They may cite their own performance, saying things like "I don't charge the firm when I work overtime" or "We all pitch in around here." Do not listen to this. Your bosses are compensated far better than you are. They earn higher salaries, enjoy better benefits, and have more personal freedom. Keep a desk diary and log every minute of overtime, even if you cut your lunch period by only fifteen minutes to type more letters. If you work an extra five minutes every day because the boss asks you to, tally this up and charge twenty-five extra minutes per week overtime. After all, this is how attorneys and consultants bill their time. You're treating them the same way that they treat their clients.

Eventually, this will work to your benefit. Before a boss asks you to work through lunch, she'll probably think it through, calculate the cost, and then decide it can wait until you return. Many bosses actually appreciate this clock-watching schedule, because they know what to expect. An attorney in Washington, D.C., says he has more respect for assistants who keep consistent, reliable hours:

> *The point is dependability, in terms of knowing when she will be at her desk. An established lunch is fine, and so*

are breaks. I just need to know when. It wasn't the hours that made me frustrated, it was the inconsistency. Anything that I can schedule, I can work with.

Assistants who practice rigorous clock watching are a relief for busy employers, who often live by their appointment calendars. Once a boss can schedule your breaks in and count on them, she or he may begin to respect you and your time more.

Similarly, you can benefit a great deal from working a full day, every day. Most support staffers can't wait to go home (who can blame them?), and they pack up earlier and earlier each evening to leave. If you work right up until quitting time, even if it means catching the next subway or train, or switching car pools, you will seem like a demigod by comparison. Bosses won't tally up your actual hours, but instead they'll go on general impressions. This extra fifty minutes per week (five minutes before your boss gets there and five minutes after hours to pack up for the night) will earn you amazing rewards in return. You will seem to be always available during working hours, and bosses will begin to respect your precision about lunch breaks.

Besides giving you adequate time to eat your lunch in a private place without distractions, this policy of clock watching will minimize the times that bosses will throw something on your desk at 4:45 that "absolutely must" go out that night. Resolve to charge your employer, in five-minute increments, for every amount of time you work past the end of the day. Don't let a "nice boss" talk you into relaxing this policy. If an employer gives you something to type at the end of the day that will keep you there late, a perfectly fair response is "Would you like me to stay tonight and work overtime to do this, or can it wait until tomorrow?"

Marty worked happily for three years at one job this way. Her boss knew that he could count on her to be there, ready to go, every morning when he came in. However, he also knew that she went to lunch every day for an hour, without fail, and that she was not to be disturbed during that lunch unless he wanted to authorize the overtime. Again, he knew that he'd better warn her early in the afternoon if emergency work was coming, and give it to her in increments, or she would charge him for the overtime if the work kept her at her desk past five.

If a boss ever barges in on you in the lunchroom to ask you to return to work, look horrified at the rude intrusion, and respond that you will tend to work after lunch. You should be minimally polite the first time, but if it happens again, show your annoyance. A third interruption will warrant a private, in-her-office discussion where you make it clear that your lunchtime is sacred. If these lunchtime interruptions are real emergencies, and you decide to return to work, always charge the overtime.

Bosses claim they "respect" assistants who pitch in a little extra time here and there without complaint and without charging overtime. In return (so they say), they don't mind when the secretary is late once in a while, and they pretend to be more generous about unexpected leave. Baloney. Most bosses exaggerate their own generosity. The typical boss gives the same leave to everyone, regardless of how much that employee works or doesn't work, and they often take advantage of those who work through lunch and after hours. Don't be lured into this "give-and-take" game.

If you watch the clock and follow a rigid schedule on your administrative assistant job, you will find that many of the usual boss complaints vanish. Executives and lawyers are less likely to try to take advantage of an assistant who maintains a faithful schedule and keeps an accurate log of hours worked. They'll go find someone else to bother, and you can get on with your work. You will be able to eat lunch in peace, and your work performance will actually improve because you will be getting adequate rest in the middle of the day. Be sure to follow this same policy for your break schedule, taking an announced break at precise times each day and doing so for the full time allowed by company policy.

✎ How Do You Move from Secretarial Work to Something Else?

Success in administrative assistant work is quite different from success in other areas, so choose your career path *before* you look for a job. If you wish to be an administrative assistant or secretary, there are excellent office procedures books and schools like Katherine Gibbs that can train you. Top-notch assistants earn decent salaries these days, but they can expect to remain assistants, or at best advance to office manager. If you hope for promotions, you will need to start over at another company, doing something promotable.

What's promotable? Anything that earns a corporation money. In management's eyes, assistants cost money, they don't bring it in.

✎ Money Is, Was, and Will Always Be the Bottom Line

Anyone who wants to rise in a company and earn more money has to affect that organization's revenue, its bottom line. Assistants are often poorly paid because companies do not consider their jobs "revenue-producing positions." If you bring in enough money for the company to more than recoup your yearly salary, you can almost be assured of making more money and getting a position of more responsibility someday.

Read Chapter 7 ("Preparing for Takeoff: How to Get Out If You Want Out") to learn about great new jobs for people with clerical backgrounds. We'll examine computer software specializations, Internet skills, customer service, copier repair, and paralegal work as possible alternatives to the "take a letter" blues. You may find these jobs rewarding in themselves. If you want to move up, however, any of these jobs can lead to better ones, because, unlike secretarial work, they are in the promotional line.

The rules to remember from this chapter are:

1. Secretarial work hasn't yet recovered from its sexpot image of the 1950s and 1960s. Don't be an administrative assistant or secretary unless you're willing to fight decades of sexism and prejudice, and stay where you are professionally.

2. If you have children, keep their care and maintenance your personal business.

3. Watch the clock, coming in early, taking all breaks and full lunches, and charging for even five minutes of overtime.

4. Consider a new job doing something promotable if you think you're in a "Yes, Mr. Drysdale" rut.

Administrative assistants and secretaries are much more important than most companies admit, and they deserve respect, responsibility, and raises. But most still don't enjoy these benefits.

If you are an assistant now, or if you think you want to become one, know what you're up against and fight with your eyes open. If you see yourself as a manager someday, then I advise you to turn to Chapters 6 and 7 and look *now* for other kinds of jobs on the promotional path.

LIBRARY OF CONGRESS

WELCOME TO THE SHARK TANK, CHUM: A *Brutal* Look at Law Firms

It's 10 a.m.
Do you know where you are in the food chain?
—Byron Woods

Law firms are lucrative places to work. You'll earn an excellent salary at the bigger firms in major cities, and you'll have dollar signs in your eyes when you look over the job listings and see what top firms pay at all levels of the clerical roster. With these firms offering top pay and fabulous benefits for the right employees, why aren't people lining up to work for lawyers?

Because they're *lawyers*, and lawyers are the most aggressive, bullying, argumentative, and manipulative people in the professional world. They're worse than stockbrokers. These people may be loving parents and concerned citizens by night, but by day they put on their Everlast trunks and come out fighting. With everyone.

In the eyes of an attorney, if you didn't go to law school then you're not "one of us," and nothing you do will make you part of their gang. I saw this played out to neurotic excess in a New York firm, where one of the partners insisted that the staff call her Ms. DiLeo while she referred to her administrative assistant and the paralegals as Mark, Janet, and Paul. When I asked her why, she answered, "I got mine"—meaning her law degree—"now let them get theirs."

Of course, people who rely on diplomas for their self-worth are insecure, but that's just part of the turf when you deal with lawyers. Some of these people were the littlest kids in their schoolyards—real bully fodder—until they learned to fight back with words. In high school they scrapped with each other on the debating team. In college, they mystified liberals and conservatives alike when they championed unpopular positions, writing provocative papers with titles like "Barry Goldwater: Misunderstood Pundit" and "Why the U.S. Should Have Stayed in Vietnam."

There are also the lawyers who argue passionately on behalf of causes, championing minority-held viewpoints against the prevailing system. Both types often sacrifice themselves on the altar of their careers, putting in long days, nights, and weekends to win fights for or against huge corporations. Many of their parents decided from the outset that their children would become attorneys. They grew up with Mommy and Daddy saying, "Isn't he a great little fighter?" and "Honey, if the teacher tries to punish you, we'll sue the school board!"

Now, along comes you. If you are typical of most people who did not go to law school, you try to avoid fights whenever possible. You're probably a reasonable sort who likes to be fair and who sees nothing wrong in giving a little to keep peace in minor conflicts. Perhaps your parents taught you that screaming isn't nice and that insulting other people never helps your case.

Prepare to be eaten alive.

Lawyers expect screaming and insults. They spend so much time hollering at each other and slamming down telephones that they forget the world doesn't operate this way all the time. When you, the mild-mannered Normal Person, come to work in the morning, they often think that screaming will be effective with you too. Even if you're cheerful and pleasant in the morning, that will soon change after you've tried working for a disgruntled lawyer five days a week, plus the inevitable nights and weekends that a big-firm job demands.

The money, however, is truly excellent, and I can't discount it. In the world of clerical work, nothing beats the big bucks of a wealthy law firm. Therefore, instead of telling you to go earn 30 percent less working for the Friendly Company, I'll offer you my survival skills for law firms.

While there are thousands of ways to be devoured in the legal shark tank, I know of one proven way to win, and only one. It's my Unbreakable Rule for working with lawyers, a four-word maxim that you should engrave in gold and hang over your desk:

ONLY WORK FOR PARTNERS

In the card game of law, partners are trumps. If you work for a partner you work for power. If you don't work for a partner, you have nothing. Law firms are little kingdoms which operate differently from any other structure (except academic departments at universities), and partners are the kings. If you can't work for a partner, then make that your eventual goal, and try to work for only one associate. If you can't work for only one associate, then work somewhere else altogether. It's only worth being an assistant or a paralegal in a law firm if you can tap into the power structure. To illustrate the importance of working for partners, I'll share a true story about a friend of mine.

✎ Our First Victim: Sandra's "Dream Job"

My friend Sandra took my advice and went to an elite employment agency in Washington, D.C., which immediately sent her on five job interviews. When she returned, she had two competing offers from major law firms, and she couldn't decide which to choose. Should she accept $32,000 as a private assistant to a senior partner in a large firm, where she'd have full responsibility for his billing accounts? Or should she take the $34,000 offer from a smaller firm which also included free parking (a major benefit in Washington, D.C.), where she'd type and do legal research for two associates?

Two thousand dollars more for the latter job seemed like a lot of money. A paid parking space was worth another twelve hundred by itself. The smaller firm was effectively offering her $3,200 a year more to answer to two associates rather than one big, intimidating partner, and she'd also do research, which would help her résumé. I suggested that she instruct the agency to negotiate on her behalf, giving each firm a chance to sweeten the deal. The big firm wouldn't budge, claiming that this was the highest initial offer they'd ever made to a personal assistant, but they assured her that the holiday bonus was a full 10 percent, meaning she'd get an extra $3,200 in December. The small firm blinked, and offered her an 8 percent annual bonus on top of their already generous opening bid. She went to work for the two associates.

Nine months later she called the employment agency and begged them to find her another job. The two associates, a woman and a man, drove her crazy, competing for her time and attention, forcing her to work inhuman amounts of overtime, and screaming at her whenever they weren't yelling at each other. She now saw a psychotherapist twice a week instead of once, and her insurance didn't cover the second $90 session. Worse, an eating disorder from her high school days reappeared. A recovering bulimic, she now found herself in the ladies' room at least once a day throwing up, wishing she could fly away to the sunny, calm Mediterranean. Or just about anywhere else, for that matter.

Sandra thought that an offer working for two associates for more money beat a lesser offer working for one partner, and she learned the hard truth: a partner beats everything. To understand why, you have to grasp the firm's overall dynamics, and that means understanding the finer points of piracy and life on the professional high seas. Those with delicate sensibilities, be warned: it isn't very pretty.

✎ The Birth of a Law Firm

Law firms are born when some partners in a firm decide to leave. Perhaps they become restless and turn on their own managing partner. Or maybe they fight a horrific group battle, suing one another, angling for control of crucial partnership votes, and striving to start a competing enterprise. Teams of disgruntled attorneys may decide to pool their intellectual resources. Often they lure away prime clients from other firms, all while earning a breathtaking amount of money. One attorney may practice entertainment law, a second copyrights and trademarks, and a third intellectual property cases. The three may join together into a new firm to represent musicians. Most new firms will try to entice clients—in this case perhaps pop stars or music publishing companies—from their former organizations.

In contrast to this mutiny image, we have the fish-eat-fish model where big firms sometimes move to buy little firms in one greedy swallow. Generally this happens "over the dead body" of one or two of the smaller firm's partners, who are used to power and don't want to work for someone else in an overly large pond. Some of the partnership will vote yes, hoping to receive generous draws as new partners in a richer firm. The others, afraid of losing personal power, will vote no. In these cases, the "yes" lawyers may band together to politically overpower their dissenting partners. In extreme cases they'll resort to personal attacks, smearing one another's reputations and digging up scandals to turn everyone against the naysayers. Again, as in a mutiny, screaming and threats are part of the scenario, along with stealing one another's files, diverting important phone calls, lobbying the undecided voting partners, and name calling when nothing else seems to work. A new law firm is born.

✎ What These Legal Conflicts Mean to You

In these battles, only partners survive. Associates have no voice in these mutinies and buyout deals, because they can't vote. Partners are owners who share profits. Associates are employees who draw a salary. Many associates earn bonuses tied to the firm's profits, but ultimately, the partners divide the profits among themselves.

On a day-to-day basis, this has enormous consequences for you as an employee, and it proves why you should only work for partners. Partners are "rainmakers" who lure in clients by promising them legal expertise. Associates, on the other hand, have to deliver on the promises that partners make. When a partner convinces a big client like Sony Music or Castle Rock Entertainment to entrust the firm with business, that partner doesn't actually sit down and write the client's complicated legal documents. Instead, the partner calls in the associates. These attorneys are generally younger, and may be recently out of law school. The partner divides the work among them. She might ask two of them to collaborate on a buyout agreement, and she might assign some articles of incorporation to a third.

If you work for one or more of these associates as an assistant, you'll type the myriad early drafts. As a paralegal, you'll spend hours in the firm's library, researching other cases and meticulously documenting each project's intellectual background. If you're lucky, later on someone will remember to order a pizza, or maybe Chinese food, because this crew will work through dinner tonight, tomorrow night, and the night after that.

While you're doing this, what will the partner's secretary and paralegals be doing? Nothing. They don't see these projects until they are complete and ready to show the partner. While you're helping an associate build his or her career by creating letter-perfect manuscripts, the partner's staff is enjoying a comparatively relaxing day in the executive suite, handling routine paperwork, cite-checking work that has already been approved at a lower level, and going home, usually at 5 or 6 p.m. Meanwhile, in the lower ranks, the associates continue to grind out long documents, shouting at you and each other, demanding impossible turnaround on changes, and insisting that everyone work until 1 a.m. if that's what it takes to finish.

Now and then a partner will work particularly late, or will come in on the weekend, but these are usually more junior members of the firm. The really big sharks already sacrificed enough early in their careers. Now it's their turn to spend weekends on the catamaran or shopping in the Bahamas. Extremely senior partners, a few of whom may be semi-retired, don't even come in to the office every day. As a perquisite or special benefit, the firm may hire a private assistant for these attorneys. This assistant draws a fine salary simply to be available should the partner want to organize a cocktail party or dictate some letters.

 A Partner Is Your Protection When Problems Arise

Besides the more reasonable workloads, working for a partner has the added benefit of giving you a powerful ally in office wars. Like giant compost heaps, law firms squeeze from the top down, creating a rotting mulch of mayhem at the lowest levels. If you're getting pressure from all sides and it's looking steamy in there, your partner can be your best friend. Tell her exactly who is pressuring you and why it's her problem. Be aggressive, arguing that other people in the firm are using you to work her over. Imply that she is not being treated with sufficient respect. Subtly question whether your partner is really powerful and suggest (if you can go this low) that the system is using sexist tactics to lock her out of power or emasculating him by taking advantage of you.

Then stand back and watch the fireworks.

Your partner will protect you because she views you as a status symbol. Only weak partners let the firm walk all over their assistants. In order to save face in front of her colleagues, your partner will stick up for you, insisting that she gives you enough work as it is and demanding that the firm hire more staff or some temporary help if they're really in a crunch.

Additionally, partners can give you raises and bonuses without seeking approval elsewhere. Associates must submit raise requests to the partners, and sometimes those requests will be denied. Partners are reasonably autonomous, especially with regard to their personal staff, so they can reward you without concern that a supervisor may object. Find a good partner, and you can negotiate discretionary leave, vacation schedules, and unforeseen personal matters directly with your boss. Associates may be criticized for how they "handle" their staffs; partners do as they wish without discussion.

How Lawyers See You

I've read that sharks, big cats, and other predators have terrible eyesight; in general, they rely on their sense of smell to isolate their prey. This is also true of attorneys. At the biggest firms the attorneys never really "see" you at all. Unless you have a law degree from the right school, you might as well be a spider plant

PHOTO: MICHAEL MALONEY, *SAN FRANCISCO CHRONICLE*

Josh Kornbluth contemplates life as a legal secretary in his one-person show *Haiku Tunnel*

THEODOR HORYDCZAK COLLECTION, LIBRARY OF CONGRESS

Glee club from the Washington School for Secretaries

for all the attention they will pay to you. Don't worry, however: this dismissive treatment is nothing personal. During the working day, lawyers don't notice anyone who doesn't smell like money (a paying client) or blood (an adversary).

Because new employees often haven't yet learned how invisible they are, many of them accept lower-level jobs working for young associates, hoping to climb the ladder when the top lawyers finally recognize their hard work and dedication. This often backfires, and here's why:

Suppose you take a job working for two associates with the hope that you can "prove yourself" and work for a partner someday. Most law firms will not promote you. Partners like to reward hardworking associates by giving them an efficient staff. This works to the partner's advantage, for he can then be assured that the associate can grind out tons of impressive-looking paperwork with maximum efficiency.

Let's say your name is John, and you've done a wonderful job for two years at the biggest firm in town. Now you have a chance to work for a senior partner who has already said how much he admires your productivity and intelligence. Will he hire you? His thinking may go something like this:

> *I need an assistant, and the office manager tells me that John is applying. But John does a great job working for my associates, and I have three big cases coming up this spring. I plan to dump tons of demanding paperwork on my staff until they holler for mercy. If I promote John, who will take his place and be the associates' slave? I'd better leave John right where he is, and call the employment agency. They'll only charge me $3,000 if they send me someone good, and then my associates won't resent me for taking away their workhorse.*

Don't be surprised when the office manager calls you into her office to tell you how sorry she is that you didn't get the promotion, but how pleased she is to offer you a $1,500 pay raise (the one you actually deserved last year). The partner decided that placating you with money would probably keep you from resenting his decision to hire someone else. If you threaten to quit, you may get an even higher offer. Sure, you can play this one and maybe even get a big raise out of the firm. But before you take the money, ask yourself: if you're working nights and weekends on those three big cases, when do you think you'll ever get a chance to spend it?

Better to work for the partner in the first place, and never find yourself sitting downstairs in personnel wondering why you can't seem to get anywhere.

✎ Fee-Paid Employment Agencies Can Find You Jobs with Partners

You may ask how you can work for a partner right away, without getting promoted within the law firm system. Don't only the best, most experienced, most mystically empowered people work for partners?

Not really. Normal people work for partners. The trick is in knowing how to find these jobs and grooming yourself to get one of the best ones. To work for a partner, you will need:

1. Above-average office skills. While shorthand is no longer essential, fast, accurate typing is. You should also know how to balance a checkbook, make airline and hotel reservations, send thank-you notes and professional announcements, and graciously greet important people with style and a minimum of fuss. Some of these skills require a command of "drawing room" English.

   If you're concerned about your style, contact a school like Katherine Gibbs in your town. Don't just look in the telephone book under "Secretarial Schools," however; some of the strangest places set themselves up as such. Get recommendations. You might even want to call a few law firms (anonymously), speak to the office manager, and find out which schools they respect in your area. Many business colleges now offer administrative assistant certificates.

2. A professional working wardrobe. You don't need to dress like a lawyer. In fact, you'll look silly if you try. However, do the administrative assistant profession the honor of not dressing like a secretary—that is, in Sunday-school dresses (too much) or corduroy trousers and running shoes (too little). Remember *Dress for Success*? You'll have to adapt the advice for the times, but it's durable, even after the go-go 1980s, and there's a chapter just for administra-

tive assistants. (*John T. Molloy's New Dress for Success*, Warner Books, 1988.)

3. An assertive, unapologetic working style. Partners can be meaner, grumpier, and more aggressive than associates, and you'll need to prepare for this. Deborah Tannen's *Talking from Nine to Five* (William Morrow, 1994) will help you get what you want from a partner on a daily basis.

The best employment agencies can help you assess your skills and personal requirements. Every major city has at least ten competing support-staff agencies. There are two kinds: the kind where the firm which hires you pays the fee, and the kind where you pay the fee yourself.

Rule 1 was "only work for partners." Rule 2 is only job-hunt with fee-paid agencies which charge you nothing. Remember that you want to work for a rich firm, not a poor one. Wealthy law firms are willing to pay agencies $3,000 to $5,000 for good employees. Firms refusing to pay the agency fee will probably be stingy with bonuses, raises, and employee benefits as well. Read Chapter 6 ("Put Down Those Want Ads: Where and How to Land a Decent Job") for detailed instructions on how to use agencies to screen prospective employers.

Once you pass their tests and begin to go on interviews, be insistent and tell the agency that you only want to work for partners. All of them will try to get you to accept jobs working for associates, frequently because the generous initial salaries increase their commissions. Also, some agencies practice the scattershot approach, sending everyone out everywhere and hoping some happy working relationships will result.

Perhaps you will need to sign up with more than one agency. Agencies want you to believe that you owe them exclusivity, but you do not. Shop around, and stay with the agency that responds to your needs. Emphasize, as often as you have to, that you want to work for a single partner. Be willing to consider one partner and one associate, but beware. These are sometimes highly productive teams that can drown you with work. The plum office job is one administrative assistant working for one partner, and a highly placed one at that.

✎ Don't Bother Reading the Want Ads

As I emphasize in Chapter 6, good legal jobs are seldom advertised in the paper, generally because the firm uses agencies, or its own employees snap them up. Attorneys who are too cheap to use agencies frequently run ads in the paper to save money. No one I know has ever found a good legal secretarial job through the newspaper, although they've interviewed for many. They may make sense if you want to be a waiter or a retail clerk, but for law-firm jobs they are a waste of time.

The best way to make yourself stand out is to go in with a personal introduction, to use an employment agency, or to approach a firm on your own (the cold-call method). Although I explore these topics in detail in Chapter 6, here are a couple of pointers just for law firms.

✎ How and When to Cold-Call a Law Firm

Lawyers are more responsive to cold calls than other kinds of employers because they are used to negotiating. They also admire people who are aggressive. You can use the cold-calling method outlined in Chapter 6 to great effect with them.

Kim, a student who needed flexible, high-paying work, found an excellent job this way. To start, she made a fanciful, exaggerated wish list of what she wanted from a part-time job. Her list said:

High salary (hourly wage equal to former yearly wage)
Full benefits
Work no earlier than 1 p.m., no later than 8 p.m.
Free to bring books and study when the workload is light

Then Kim started calling law firms, speaking to the highest-ranking person who would talk to her and asking for a job. She emphasized her legal experience and the convenience to them of having a part-time employee with the savvy of a full-time careerist. She continually emphasized her student status, something with which most lawyers could identify since they spent so many years in college and law school.

A downtown law firm just four blocks from her Seattle apartment needed a receptionist to come in during the late afternoon and stay after the regular staff went home. They wanted someone who could type legal documents when necessary, but mostly they wanted a professional voice/face on duty late in the day.

Kim insisted on a high salary, full benefits, and the right to bring her books to the office. They negotiated a bit, and she ended up making $15 an hour, with partial benefits (major medical insurance but no dental or optical coverage), and, yes, the right to bring her books to the office and study at her desk after hours. Her list hadn't been so ''fanciful'' after all. The hours were 4 p.m. to 7 p.m., with attorneys occasionally asking her to stay until 8 p.m. Often she found herself with little to do, so she was able to sit there and earn $15 an hour studying for exams.

✎ What If You're Still Unhappy?

Many people do all the right things (use an agency, negotiate a good deal, work for a partner, use the system ruthlessly), and they still find themselves unhappy on the staff of a law firm. Surprise, surprise. If you live in a jungle, you have to expect snakes. Law firms do not miraculously become benevolent organizations full of kind people just because you get yourself well placed.

Ofra remembers a former boss, Doug, who bothered her all summer long in a big D.C. firm. Doug used his administrative staff as servants, asking them to bring him tea throughout the day. When she suffered a momentary lapse of judgment and agreed to fetch his precious tea, he made a sexual comment about her. (''Nice tits'' was, I believe, the charming phrase.) Later he shouted at her when she gave him some bad news about a deal that was about to fall through. She was furious; she needed this job, at least for the summer, and Doug was one of the top four attorneys in the firm. If this was typical of his behavior, then it certainly reflected poorly on his partners as well, who generally shared his worldview.

She asked me for advice and we went to the library. We nearly fell down laughing when we read ''how to'' manuals that discussed strategies in the face of such egotistical people. One said that Ofra should use ''insistent, assertive'' language to state her wants and needs and should counter Doug's boorish comments in a polite yet firm way. Another book counseled her to ignore his come-ons and refuse to do anything helpful for him until his behavior improved. Who did these books think she was? Doug acted reprehensibly as a rule, and it was not her job to be a patient, "assertive" model of administrative calm and benevolence until he decided to act like a gentleman. He didn't deserve the honor, and she didn't deserve the abuse.

✎ Desperation Tactics: The Slam and Scream

If you find yourself miserable in a law firm because your partner is an oily bastard or because the associates are getting out of line, and if you're putting up with yelling and verbal abuse, for my money there's only one way out. I call it the Slam and Scream. Whether or not you keep your job, it will relieve your stress wonderfully, and more times than not it will actually put you in better standing with the offending attorneys.

When partners yell at you and associates insult you, take a minute, catch your breath, and ask, "Who *are* these people, and why do I have to be polite to them?" Of course, there is an old American work ethic that says you should be grateful for regular employment, but this has somehow mutated into a tolerant ethos that puts the full burden for being morally upright and socially appropriate on the administrative assistant or support staffer. My recommendation? Forget "I statements" and constructive language. Ditch your patience. It's not your problem if a full-grown attorney can't behave like an adult.

The first time a lawyer tries yelling at you, or commenting on your anatomy, execute the Slam and Scream. Walk into their office when they are alone, shut the door so firmly it nearly slams (don't quite let it shake the walls), and let them have it. *Caution*: I believe in fighting fire with fire and shouting back at shouters. Never, however, initiate a Slam and Scream with someone who hasn't made the first aggressive move. The following scenarios show when the Slam and Scream may be necessary and what it can do for you.

✎ The Usual Scenario: Margaret Faces Norris

Imagine that you are twenty-four-year-old Margaret, working in a top law firm in Washington, D.C., for the nuclear energy division. You spent all last weekend, from Friday to late Sunday afternoon, working ten- and fifteen-hour days, to help two associates put together an appeal package for a big nuclear power plant that was hit with millions of dollars in fines. You typed faster than you thought humanly possible and sat in one position for hours at a time, taking only occasional breaks to use the bathroom. You lived on Diet Coke and cheese crackers until another one of the lawyers finally remembered to order some takeout Chinese food. You also managed to take your associate's shirts to the dry cleaners, field several phone calls from his irate and suspicious wife who didn't believe her husband was really working all weekend, and mediate a near-walkout when the summer law clerk threatened to quit because he was tired of being insulted by a testy, overworked staff. You're proud of yourself, and deservedly so. Yes, it's nice that you earned time and a half for all that overtime, but let's face it, you make less than $30,000 a year, and your bosses make over $100,000, so although you're happy to collect your paycheck, you still expect something in the way of thanks.

Now, it looks as though you will get it. Norris, the associate who headed the project, has just called you into his office for a closed-door session. Will it mean a raise? Probably not, but you'll appreciate it if he just says, "Good work." You walk into his office. He motions you into a chair and you sit. Then he gets up and closes the door so you can talk privately. You're wondering what he will say first. He sits down, and looks away from you. Then, speaking directly to his cactus plant because he cannot look you in the eye, he says, "I'm afraid we're going to have to have a talk about your performance around here. This weekend was the last straw. I'm saying these things to you personally, because it's better than writing them into your personnel file, but I'm afraid that's what I'll have to do if things don't change."

What? You are stunned. You look at him for a moment, but he won't meet your gaze. He's looking just beyond you.

"First there was the sociology textbook. Now, I know you're hardworking, but reading at the desk is unprofessional and we can't have it in the office. It creates the wrong impression. Then there was the eating at your desk. We provide staff members with a dining room on the third floor, which we expect you to use. I don't want important clients walking in here and seeing Chinese takeout boxes. Also, I know you're a boisterous young lady and you have a vibrant social life, but you took three or four personal calls within my earshot, which means there must have been twice as many when I wasn't around.''

As you sit, nearly nailed to your chair, you feel them starting. The tears. You swore you'd never cry in front of a lawyer, but here they come anyway. How can he say this to you? You fielded five phone calls from his suspicious wife, and you also know that he's juggling a present and a former girlfriend, whose calls you screen. It was his shirts you took to the dry cleaners on Friday, and you had to argue with the shop to provide the one-day service they supposedly guaranteed. And what were you supposed to do about eating? Absorb the food through your flesh? One of the attorneys down the hall ordered takeout for everyone—two hours after you'd already felt faint from hunger—and the staff were all eating in their offices. You couldn't take a break and go eat in the dining room: there were thirty pages of reports to be faxed and you only had until 10 p.m. to get everything done. So you ate some kung pao chicken at your desk while you plowed through the typing. That whole package went out at 9:45 sharp without a single mistake in it, and this chucklehead is sitting here complaining that you left a little white carryout box on your desk?

All of this is what you think. What you say is ''What was I supposed . . . ?''

He interrupts you. ''What you are supposed to do is simple. Now, I feel you are a fine employee with potential. But the rules are the rules. One. No eating at your station. Two. No personal phone calls during business hours. Three. Get the schoolbooks off your desk, and don't let me see you reading them in your lap just because it isn't busy around here. There's plenty of filing to be done when we're not pressing you to do something else.''

Here come the tears. You try to stop them, but you know that your eyes are just awash. ''May I . . .'' you say, hoping that he will excuse you so that you can save a shred of dignity and go cry in the ladies' room. Instead, he wordlessly hands you a box of tissues from the credenza behind him. You dab at your eyes, but that only makes it worse, and now your nose is starting to run.

As you sit there, crumpling a pink tissue and wanting to die, he waits a long, almost interminable moment, and then says, ''I think we understand one another now. This doesn't have to go into your file if you step up the performance out there, okay, sport?'' Then he finally looks at you, with a dazzling smile that says, ''Friends?''

No, you are not friends. This is the office where you work as an administrative assistant, a legal secretary, or a paralegal. This attorney would love for you to believe that everyone's on the same team. It simply isn't true. Rather, you are their co-worker, and in their eyes you are inferior. The sooner you understand this, the sooner you can stop empathizing with them and insist upon the kind of treatment that you deserve.

✎ Rerun: Margaret Benefits from "Slam and Scream" Tactics

Now let's go back to you, playing the role of the twenty-four-year-old sniffling Margaret, still trapped in Norris's office. We'll rewind the film and send you back in for a second shot at the conversation. What you'll see is how the whole situation could be turned around with a simple Slam and Scream. This isn't a made-up scenario. I played this scene, both ways, in real life. Each time, the results were just what I've described.

Norris has just called you into his office for a closed-door session, but this time you're a different employee. Instead of hopefully wondering if you'll get a raise or some thanks for a job well done, you know better. This hotshot has been chewing up his law clerks all weekend, and you had to step in just to keep one of them from walking out in the middle of a project. This attorney is thirty-two years old, fresh out of law school and about ten years younger than most of the partners he works with. You know enough, from having read this book, to see that he is nervous, aggressive, and his job intimidates him. This weekend he's had to prove himself to the nuclear energy division, and he's terrified. The easiest target for him to take out his frustration on and level his attacks at is you, because right now you're convenient. Therefore you go into his office knowing full well there may be some sort of confrontation. But you're ready.

You walk into his office. He motions you into a chair, but you say, "No, thanks, I'll stand. I've got a lot of work piling up out there, and one of the senior attorneys just gave me something to type." Now, of course, no one really just gave you anything to type, but you know that he's terrified of senior staff, and so you use it when you need to. He goes to close the door, but you hold it open. "Anything we say can be said with the door open, can't it?" He shrugs and moves away from the door. He starts to sit down, but then realizes that he'll be shorter than you if he does, so he stands too. But he wasn't planning on this. *Whatever you do in his office, you know that you must not sit down.*

He fidgets, and then launches into the prepared speech that he makes to the carpet since he still can't look you in the eye: "I'm afraid we're going to have to have a talk about your performance around here . . ."

You interrupt. "Good. That was a great negotiation package and we all did a fine job. I'm glad you realize that."

"Well, yes, it did look sharp when it went out, but that's not what I want to discuss. It's about some problems I've noticed in your work habits . . ."

"You called me in here to say that? I saved your butt this weekend and you know it. If that's all we're discussing, I'm going out to get some work done."

He tries to stop you. "Sit down."

"I told you, I'm not sitting. Unless you care to thank me for something, I'm busy."

"I can have you fired for insubordination."

"Right. And you can train someone else to do your bills and field phone calls from who knows who." Of course, you know better than to ever mention either his wife or his girlfriends by name. That would take the fight to another level and you might really get fired. Keep it professional.

"Look, I don't want to argue with you. We just need to lay down some ground rules around here. Like those Chinese takeout food cartons on your desk . . ."

"What?"

"And the sociology textbook . . ."

"You're kidding me, aren't you? Go on, what else? Spit it out!"

He's getting angry now. "Oh, not just the textbooks, lady, but the personal phone calls all bloody weekend long."

"Is that all?"

"Isn't that enough?" he asks.

"No, come on, I want to know what you really think. Let's hear more."

"That's really all. I . . ."

Now is when you go for the big move. You push the door shut. Make sure that people outside can hear the door close hard. Keep standing!

"You can bet that's all," you say, your voice rising, "because let me tell you something. I broke a date Friday night to stay here and help you out, and it was with a guy I really liked. And about the Chinese food, if you or your fellow associates had remembered that you have human beings working for you, you might have ordered dinner at six o'clock instead of eight-thirty. I was starving to death, but do you think I could do something about it? That report had to get faxed by ten p.m., and I was about to faint from hunger."

"I don't have to listen to this," he says, and he starts to use his intercom. He's bluffing. You really raise your voice and let him have it.

"I know the nuclear division, and I do my job well. Clearly you and I have gotten off on the wrong foot, because instead of thanking me for sending out an error-free negotiation package on time this weekend, you're in here arguing about Chinese food boxes! Did they teach you this in law school?"

At this point you would think that he'd yell, "You're fired!" right? Wrong. Instead, he starts to laugh. Yes, instead of shouting back at you and being the jerk he's been all weekend, he laughs. At first it's just a little chuckle, but then this scene really gets his funny bone. Keep standing and open the door.

He'll try to be pleasant now, but don't be fooled by that. Remember: this is not your friend. Now he's just trying to get in the last word. Step out of his office, go back to your desk, sit down, and start working on something for someone else. If he comes out and tries to be pleasant, rebuff him. After all, you're still stinging. For the rest of the afternoon he should feel a bit "cold-shouldered" for having started something with you.

So what happened? Why did the subordinate, polite Margaret

the Good end up in miserable tears in our first scenario, while her Evil Twin Margaret triumphed over the lawyer in the second one? In the second scene Margaret was simply using law-firm survival skills, of which the Slam and Scream is an integral part.

Notice, however, that I said law-firm survival skills, not corporate-office survival skills. They're different. Read the previous chapter for rules about abusive corporate executives. The Slam and Scream might get you fired anywhere except a law office. If it does get you fired, ask yourself if that really matters. Isn't your mental and physical well-being worth it? Wouldn't it feel good just once to tell one of those attorneys how you really felt? Chances are, however, that you will not be fired. In fact, many attorneys pay attention only to people who holler at them. Listen to the way they talk to one another. They shout. They negotiate. They whistle loudly in the halls and compete over everything from the football pool to the Sony contract. By entering this fray, you become visible, possibly for the first time, because you are now finally behaving like a recognizable life form to them.

Of course, many legal secretaries don't feel comfortable with confrontation. I didn't either, and I don't pretend this will come naturally to you. You can be an actor, though, and play this role when you need it. One great tip for shy folks is to practice the Slam and Scream at home. Have your spouse, significant other, or friend play the role of your boss, and try this maneuver, over and over again. Practice saying out loud the things I've suggested. The more you put these strong words into your own mouth in private, the easier they will be to say in front of an aggressive, loudmouthed attorney.

✎ Should You Stay or Should You Go?

Many lawyer-staff relationships settle down after the Slam and Scream phase, because attorneys respond to shouting. One law professor agreed fully with the Slam and Scream method. He added that only a few "incurable bullies" would actually fire an employee for such assertive behavior. You'd be better off getting away from such brutes anyway; if you get fired, you can seek out a better, saner job. Chances are, however, that the attorney will respect you more for your willingness to fight on your own behalf.

You may ask, however, what this behavior has done to you in the process. Who are these people, and why are you becoming one of them?

Many big law firms resemble soap operas seething with interoffice intrigue: in short, an outtake reel from *L.A. Law*. In my experience they were filled with Napoleonic attorneys having affairs with the staff and each other, rife with pecking-order employees who consistently sniped at each other because of the intense internal pressure. Office managers became Gulag sergeants, treating their staffs with coldness and indifference because they had hardened, over the years, from the kind of treatment they received from above. The "good firms" were merely paternal, still admiring college and law school diplomas more than personal character, integrity, and perseverance.

Freelancer Barbara Rosen, writing for *ABA Law Practice Management* (July–August 1991), lists some top reasons why legal secretaries quit their jobs. Under the provocative title "Things Your Ex-Secretaries Didn't Tell You," she cites "shabby treatment" as the number one reason for walkouts. Number two on the list is, predictably, low pay, followed by lack of a promotional path.

Small-town law firms may be different. I worked for one briefly as a researcher, and there the folks generally spoke kindly to one another and everyone went home at five. In the metropolitan firms, however, money and power combine with a particularly noxious kind of class-conscious one-upmanship. People often sell their souls. It starts slowly at first, and generally builds, but sooner or later every relationship devolves to the strong devouring the weak. The Slam and Scream works, but it is a sad situation to find yourself in. If you'd rather get along with your co-workers, you may decide that the generous money in law firms isn't worth watching yourself turn into someone unrecognizable over the weeks, months, and years.

Good luck in your law-firm job search. Please remember the three major points of this chapter, for they can one day save your professional life.

1. Only work for partners.
2. Use fee-paid employment agencies to get the best jobs. Never pay a fee to an agent.
3. When all else fails, Slam and Scream. Lawyers (and only lawyers) often respond to this.

Always remember that no matter what time it is, you are pretty far down in the food chain in most law firms if you're not an attorney. Be sure to read Chapter 8, on sexual harassment, and always cultivate a good relationship with your employment agent so you can get a better job if your firm mutinies or if your partner becomes impossible to work for (Chapter 6 tells you how). Don't ever worry about leaving a lawyer ''high and dry'' by moving to another firm. Loyalty is a fiction in big-city law: *they'd* cut *you* loose in a minute if they had to. So watch yourself, and look out for your own best interests at all times.

Recommended Reading

Explaining the Inexplicable: The Rodent's Guide to Lawyers, by the Rodent (Pocket Books, 1995). $16.00.

Fawn Hall

ASSOCIATED PRESS

YOU CAN'T FIRE ME, SLAVES HAVE TO BE SOLD: Your Federal and State *Government* at Work

Radar, what's the situation on the overall poop, status-wise?
—Henry Blake, M*A*S*H

Remember Radar O'Reilly from the movie and television series *M*A*S*H*? Day after day he toiled, banging out forms in triplicate on an old Underwood typewriter, keeping up with the endless paperwork that threatened to shut down the unit. Radar was the only efficient thing about Colonel Blake's office. If it weren't for him, the 4077th would have drowned in a sea of regulatory violations.

One day Radar walked in with a pile of forms for Colonel Blake to sign, and Henry actually took a moment to read them:

Henry: ''Radar, this doesn't make any sense!''
Radar: ''None of it does, sir. You just have to have the right number of forms.''

So it is with most government clerical jobs. Men and women who work for the state or the feds end up shuffling papers nobody understands. It's a problem as old as bureaucracy itself.

✎ How to Handle Government Documents: Drive a Forklift

Most people who work for the government, especially the military, report that Colonel Blake is an all too common stereotype and Radar is a little too uncommon. If you are a conscientious, hardworking person, and you get a government job, you may find yourself living the Life of Radar before you know it. The forms are so complicated, and they are written in such an arcane, confusing, and impenetrable manner, that you'll soon be considered a wizard if you learn your job well. People will begin to depend upon you, because you know so much about the rules and the doublespeak.

The government is so awash in forms that most state and federal employees spend their days doing only one thing: processing paper. Paperwork is the lubricant that makes the bureaucracy run smoothly. And you'll be the chief oil dispenser. As administrative assistant or clerk in one of these agencies, your job will involve more paper and less decision making than almost any other post.

Remember when Vice President Gore went on *Late Night with David Letterman* and smashed a government-purchased ashtray? To purchase that particular ashtray, the government required nine pages of specifications. Now multiply that by every telephone, desk lamp, and toilet seat in the government. Gore decided to illustrate the paperwork problem for President Clinton. In a ceremony on the White House South Lawn, he said, ''Mr. President, if you want to know why government doesn't work, look behind you.'' Behind them stood forklifts piled with stacks of government regulations. Business author and government employee Richard M. Laska puts it this way: ''In these circles, the definition of a weighty report is in terms of kilograms.''

Now, remember that someone—some clerk—had to type every page of those ashtray specifications. Each of those forklifts represented thousands of Radar O'Reillys, typing on Underwoods (or, these days, on outdated computers), getting the job done. If you're the clerk doing the typing, you'll soon know why Radar needed a teddy bear for comfort.

If you do your best, people will realize this and seek you out for more of the same. Just like in law firms, where the bosses reward hard workers with increases in responsibility, but not necessarily with accompanying raises or promotions, in government the good worker may suffer for his conscientiousness. Although many employees complain about this at nongovernment jobs, the feds seem to have a hammerlock on the syndrome. You will drown in forms while every incompetent clerk on five floors lets their excess work slush over into your area.

Wait—did I say incompetent? Heavens, the federal government would never let people who do a substandard job stay employed, would it? Indeed, it would: it has to. Firing regulations are so complex, and the opportunities to sue the government are so varied, that many agencies find it next to impossible to dismiss employees who don't do their jobs well.

✎ Incompetence Is an Equal Opportunity Malaise

Did you ever hear the phrase "That's good enough for government work," meaning the task was completed with a minimum of skill and effort? When I asked government workers why the do-nothings thrive, I received two different racist answers. Many disgruntled workers blamed the Equal Employment Opportunity Commission (EEOC), saying that "lazy" members of ethnic groups are routinely hired ahead of qualified whites to meet quotas and that they can't be fired for ineptitude. Other equally angry workers blamed history, saying that "lazy" white folks hang on for decades in jobs they've long since become ineffective at performing, because the old-boy system won't turn against them. They cite cronyism, and they point to Congress's status as the "Last Plantation," lording a long history of white power and privilege over a black majority in the beleaguered nation's capital. I believe that bureaucracy is primarily color-blind. It tends to be inefficient and to promote its own gluttonous survival no matter who staffs the ranks. Still, interracial problems persist, especially in major cities such as Washington, New York, and Chicago.

How these problems play themselves out differs from office to office. The most commonly reported hazard is a "chilly" working environment. Chilly describes the kind of discrimination that's not overt or even necessarily intentional, but you can feel it all the same. As the only black employee in an all-white office, you may find people talking around you rather than to you. If you're the only white person in a mostly African-American division, you may find yourself out of the social loop. At best, it's uncomfortable. At worst, it can keep you from making the kinds of contacts you need to have a happy professional life and get ahead. Being Italian, Latina, Catholic, African-American, Methodist, white, or some other arbitrary designation can be the wrong answer in the wrong office.

These problems arise more often in the government than in private industry because companies have many ways of hiring and firing whomever they want to. The folks who survive in a corporate environment have generally learned to get along. In government, however, people often get thrown together by "the system," not by any particular decision maker. If they squabble, tough. It's hard to fire troublemakers or even move them around once they have a job. Some describe the hiring process as trying to run through hardening cement. You just go slower and slower until you're stuck.

Racial conflicts aren't the only factors making government offices tense places to work. Sometimes you have the joys of dealing with class. As in "no class." Vernon Loeb and Lorraine Adams of *The Washington Post* write of the city administrator who tried to fire a secretary. The secretary's offense? She spit on a supervisor: a retaliatory tactic which I generally do not recommend. The personnel office wouldn't let the administrator fire her, however, because "it was her first offense and a reprimand would suffice."

A city council member added that the worst thing about being a boss was "the inability to hire, fire, compensate, and supervise employees because of the personnel system." In other words, if your government job stinks and your pay is low, there's usually not much you or your boss can do about it. If your co-workers spit, well, that's just part of the contract. When you finally realize that hard work will only make you contemptible in the eyes of your peers, you will have grasped the central problem with government employment.

The bottom line on bureaucracies is clubbishness. Whether the dividing line is race or something more subtle, such as how many years of service someone has in a particular division or what political party you support, as the new kid on the block you may find yourself in a nearly impossible working situation that you did not create and that you have little hope of changing. You won't be an invited member of these informal groups for years, if you can ever even join them at all.

So what's a new government employee to do? The government is the largest employer in America, and it doesn't make sense to simply say, "Don't work there." I say work smart. Before accepting a government job, invest as much time in researching whom you'll work with as what you'll do. Ask people who work there—people of your own gender and race, if possible—what life is like on a day-to-day basis. Most people really want to tell their stories, if only someone will listen. If you promise not to get them in trouble by repeating their confidences, you may learn important information about "chilliness," cronyism, and other persistent syndromes of government life. Some offices are much better than others, so investigate any division before you accept a job.

✎ The Saga of the Maniac Mailmen

In a normal office, people who have severe emotional problems tend to weed themselves out. They can't handle their jobs, so they disappear or get fired. In the government, however, they can stay, and stay, and stay. When the pressures finally become too much, they snap. Some walk into work and start shooting. "Going postal" is the new tongue-in-cheek term for a terrifying public problem: disgruntled employees with grudges and guns who lose control and seek workplace retribution for their miserable lives.

Big, heavily staffed organizations like the U.S. Postal Service (actually a semi-private organization), the Internal Revenue Service, the Department of Motor Vehicles, and the Department of Transportation are known for offering lots of jobs, many at entry level. Think twice, however, before you jump into one of these positions. You may enjoy your job, or at least not mind it too much, but you might find yourself working shoulder to shoulder with some mighty strange people. Some of them seem to love red tape and regulations. Others have a grudge against "the boss" and society in general. Some, especially in police departments, district attorneys' offices, and the prison system, choose this line of work because of the regimentation. The bosses in these organizations tend to be order givers, who like to issue instructions and have them followed to the letter. If you fit in, fine. But you may find yourself chained to some peculiar, antisocial co-workers as a condition of your job.

Why do workers "go postal"? Some pundits blame budget cuts that force workers to accept lower pay in quasi-military conditions (*Reed! Pick up those mail bags! Braun! Take care of that customer service line, on the double*). Others say that repetitive, detailed work in a tense environment under watchdog supervision eventually drives folks crazy. Still a third study cites the "you can't fire me" mentality of many workers who seek out government employment for the security. You'll get a different group of employees in a place where getting fired is darned near impossible than you will in, say, a Fortune 500 company where no one's job is secure. Whether consciously or not, unstable people may actually seek out the steadier work for the greater structure, even if the pay is much, much lower. They need someone to tell them what to do all the time, even if they resent it in the long run.

I'm not saying that working for the Post Office, the IRS, or the DMV will necessarily bring you in contact with deranged postmen flying over the building with AK-47s (like postman Alfred Hunter did in 1989 when he hijacked a plane and strafed Boston). It will, however, introduce you to some of the pettiest bosses and some of the most frustrated employees you have ever seen. The lower you labor, the worse it will be.

My answer? Work higher. Avoid the entry-level trap of accepting whatever you can get, no matter how lowly, just to get a job. By learning to reach above your head when applying for work, you may be surprised at what a good job you can actually find. Ask yourself, honestly, how much you enjoy doing repetitive work under close supervision. If a college degree is all that's standing between you and the better jobs, then resolve to do everything you can to get that degree. Read Chapter 7 for advice about returning to school while keeping your present job.

✎ From Flying Ace to Desk Jockey

Have you ever heard of the ''golden handcuffs,'' those invisible monetary chains that keep people stuck in jobs they hate because the money is too good to resist? Well, I've got another one for you. The working world has a ghoulish term for a job that's so comfortable no one ever leaves. They call it a ''velvet coffin.'' The body in this coffin just might be your boss!

Your taskmasters may be former military officers who saw action in wartime. After the war, Uncle Sam grounded them behind a desk, and let me tell you, they're not happy about it. Many of these folks are disappointed, because their military lives were more exciting. Some of them were fighter pilots. Others worked on aircraft carriers. Some saw action on nuclear submarines, and a few were even in space flight. When these professionals get bumped upstairs to a desk job, the government considers it a promotion, but many of them long for the life they left behind. They're comfortable, though, and they will hang in there until retirement. If you're a clerk under one of the residents of a velvet coffin, you may find yourself working for a frustrated, difficult individual.

I've never met anyone crabbier than a fighter pilot who loved flying but found himself sentenced to fifteen years at a top post in a federal agency before he could retire. Ford was a charming man, an affable host, and still an ace pilot on the weekends, but he was stuck in a forty-hour-a-week job that he hated. Never mind the salary, Ford wanted his freedom! But instead he had to think about his daughters, three of whom were in college, and his responsibilities. So every day he dutifully trudged downtown to the office.

Ford started drinking after work to unwind. First it was a pitcher of martinis with his wife and a few friends before dinner. Then it was the whole pitcher by himself. Soon he began to drink at lunch, and by the time he'd logged a decade behind a desk, he was drinking regularly on the job. The secretaries and clerks reported that he was a bitter, confused man. He had an affair with a lobbyist, and expected his administrative assistant to make excuses for him to his wife. He berated his children. He insulted the staff, and sometimes left for lunch and never returned. It took the combined efforts of three staff members just to cover up Ford's tracks of missed meetings, unreturned phone calls, and delayed responses to important memos.

But, this being the government, Ford never got fired. Instead, he languished, growing more bitter and cranky as the days went by. His wife quietly removed the weapons from their home in the fear that Ford might do something foolish when he was drinking. She cooperated with his secretary in covering up his problem.

Doesn't this sound like an old litany from Alcoholics Anonymous? Well, there's a twist.

Ford retired. His wife feared the prospect of having a crabby old drunk at home all day. She got quite a surprise. He actually got off the sauce when he found he didn't need it to medicate a frustrating job. They took vacations together again, and they bought a second home in the mountains. Ford joined the staff of a tiny flying school in West Virginia. Fifteen to twenty years after their births, he finally made friends with his daughters. He became good company. It's simple: he was free.

But before we get too misty-eyed, let's remember the other person in this little story: the administrative assistant who had put up with Ford's misery for the last couple of decades and was still too young to retire. When Ford left, his department reassigned her to a former submarine captain. Yes, the government gave her a raise, but so what? Once again, her boss was miserable, jockeying a desk and pining for the open seas. Soon he began to drink noticeably. All in all, she endured another decade of the same treatment before she could retire and get away from them all.

Some people report working for bosses who love their government jobs and who are challenged and happy. Okay, not really. But they do tell me that their bosses are nice enough, and that the work is tolerable, if not exactly thrilling. But for every one of these people, there are several more who say that they work for a frustrated boss who wants to be somewhere else.

COURTESY OF THE JOHN F. KENNEDY LIBRARY

Evelyn Lincoln proved that in government it's important to choose the right boss

Here's the point: life is too short to work for a bastard. Just as in private industry, if your boss is abusive, you need to stand up to him (or her) and prepare to launch yourself out of there if necessary. What should you do if you find yourself working for the Corpse from the Corps? Use my "how to talk back to a briefcase" tactics if you encounter verbal abuse on the job (Chapter 2). Then try using your boss's prestige and position to land yourself another job the next notch higher. The best way out, as always in this world, is up.

✎ How to Get Ahead as a Support Staffer in the Federal Government

Don't start your government life as an administrative assistant or a secretary if you want to be something else someday. Once the government, whether the feds or the state, gets you in personnel's computer system as a secretary, you'll never lose the role. Ten years from now people will try to track you into bigger and better secretarial positions rather than consider you for anything approaching management status. Here are five suggestions for getting a better start in government:

1. *Avoid the clerk-typist trap.* Anyone who can bang on a keyboard at 45 words per minute or more can land a job as a clerk-typist. These are sweatshop positions, requiring you to sit for hours in the same position filling in minute, complicated government forms. You'll be miserable, and you probably won't get promoted any higher than administrative assistant for your troubles. Remember my advice from the job-hunting chapters, and don't tell them you can type. *Never* put your typing speed or your office machines experience on your initial application form. The more you emphasize your other skills (research, writing, mathematics, budget, and finance), the less people will try to classify you as a machine operator.

2. *Work for a successful organization.* There's no point trying to get ahead by working for a department that is underfunded and poorly managed. Go to the library and do a keyword search in the newspaper abstracts on all of the agencies that interest you. Talk to people who work for other agencies and see how these places are perceived. A lower-level job with a thriving agency that can lead to promotions is better than a higher job in an underfunded division that might lay you off.

Jan wanted to work at the same state university where her husband, Maury, taught French. She took a job as an administrative assistant in the English Department. Earlier that same year, and unknown to her, the governor slashed the budgets of all state universities, and every employee had to take a 2 percent pay cut. What Jan didn't know was that her job had originally been two positions that her beleaguered department had combined into one higher-level slot. Jan endured low pay and long hours trying to handle what was once two jobs. Because she processed the department payroll, all the staff complained to her.

Jan was from out of state, so she got blindsided by the job merge and the salary decrease. If she had read the newspaper abstracts for the past year, though, she would have known that the English Department was in trouble. Remember that most federal and state organizations will make the headlines when budget problems arise. Many articles discussed the coming cuts, and three different local news items mentioned that the university's School of Education was the only well-funded program that year.

Jan didn't have much choice about where to work, for the university offered the only really interesting jobs in what was otherwise a very small town. But she could have picked a healthier department with more funding and had a happier, more financially sound start.

3. *Take as much time with your federal or state application form as you do with your résumé.* Many people see the federal application (formerly SF 171, now also Form 612), or a standard state form, and they grab a pen and start filling it in. No, no, no! This form is the most important one you will ever fill out with the government, and it has to be perfect. Consult Kathleen Green's article in Appendix A for detailed instructions on how to do it right. Although you will make many copies from one master form, create a different master for each type of job that interests you. And remember, don't write anything on that form you don't want to see again in ten years.

4. *Reach above your head.* Search the government job listings thoroughly for the highest positions you think you can handle, and then look a little higher. If you're an administrative assistant or a receptionist now and you want to switch, don't look for secretarial jobs. Look for something in the promotional line that makes or saves money for the organization.

You'll have to be brave and apply for jobs that look hard. Try applying for bigger jobs, and then work your way down if you keep hearing "no." If your job is pretty much at the bottom level now, then try reaching up two or more levels instead of just one. A "boardinghouse reach," where you grab for the biggest and best jobs you can think of instead of just the ones you think someone is likely to give you, will help you enormously.

5. *Be creative.* Study the government job listing resources carefully, and look at positions you never thought of before. If you enjoy being outdoors, you might like a job as a field inspector or technician. These jobs may not require as much retraining as you think. Look at every job you think you could do if you were properly trained. Then ask yourself how much training that job would require. If a job requires a bachelor's degree and you've never gone to college, see if you can enroll in school now and work your way into the job. Always think about jobs you could like if you were qualified, and then angle yourself into them by putting yourself on the path.

Remember that there is no disgrace in going on an interview and not getting the job. *People won't remember who you are.* Go forth confidently and try. If you mess up, try again somewhere else. Once my boss asked me to screen all of the in-house applicants for a clerical position. Fifteen people from within my own company applied for the job, and I met with eleven of them. Some of them were simply not qualified for the job, but they tried anyway, and that was fine with me and my boss. The job finally went to a woman who was mostly (but not 100 percent) qualified, since we had no perfect applicants. She had to take a risk to apply for that job, and the risk paid off. When you learn to trust in the short memory of the average interviewer, and when you realize that few people start out with all of the requirements for their particular jobs, risk taking will become much easier. (Consult Chapter 6 for details.)

6. *Once you have a job, look for another job*. The best time to job-hunt is when you're already comfortably employed. Since you know that the government is famous for letting people languish at the same level, it's up to you to start identifying your next step once you get a position. Feel free to change departments or agencies for greener pastures if you see something you like somewhere else. Read insider publications for the division that interests you, such as *Roll Call* (the semiweekly Capitol Hill newspaper for congressional staffers) or departmental bulletins, and learn where the good jobs are.

If you're afraid that this attitude is disloyal, don't worry. The government treats its employees like cattle, and employer loyalty is mostly imaginary. Members of Illinois representative Dan Rostenkowski's staff had their résumés out on the street long before his ethics violations were a matter of public record, and I don't blame them. Don't waste your time being tirelessly faithful to a system that can't and won't look out for you.

Does all this get-ahead advice mean no one should be an administrative assistant or a secretary? Not at all. Some people have found rewarding careers as government assistants. In general, however, these folks have worked for the rich and powerful in Washington, D.C., or they have reported to the top-level officials in their town, such as the mayor, the district attorney, or the chief of police. In the government, as anywhere else, support staffers are only as powerful as the bosses they serve.

Reporting to power, however, sometimes means going along with practices that are dubious or even corrupt. From presidential appointees (who are usually in office for four short but often exhilarating years) to university presidents, it's hard to get to the top of a political machine with entirely clean hands. If you report to one of these people, you can expect to learn secrets that you may have preferred not to know.

✎ You Are Who You Work For

In 1973, Rose Mary Woods, who "accidentally" deleted eighteen and a half minutes of tape for her boss, Richard Nixon, became the most famous government secretary.

Then along came Elizabeth Ray. The media didn't make as big a fuss over Ray's 1976 affair with Ohio representative Wayne Hays as it did over her qualifications for her secretarial job. Ray couldn't type. She proved that she could cash in, however, when she penned a 1976 novel, *The Washington Fringe Benefit.* She then went on to study acting in New York, and confessed to *People* magazine in 1980 that she hoped to earn a guest star passage on *The Love Boat.* This, for the clerical world, was stardom.

In the 1980s, however, Fawn Hall took the prize from both of her predecessors. Before a congressional committee, she wept with admiration for her boss, Lieutenant Colonel Oliver North. She described North as "every secretary's dream of a boss." As the news cameras recorded every loyal moment, Fawn Hall became a secretarial superstar.

Hall's "dream boss" ordered her to help him destroy incriminating documents. In her eagerness to help North violate the public trust, Hall sneaked papers out of his office by stuffing them in her boots and down the back of her blouse. She fed so many papers into the heavy-duty shredder that it jammed. Then she carefully retyped fake documents to replace the shredded ones. "Sometimes," she testified, "you have to go above the written law." Secretaries are expected to go along to get along. Had Hall refused to cooperate with North's orders, she would have lost her job. She'd have been branded a whistle blower, and they never last long in the government.

If you dream of working for the President, the governor, a senator, or another high-level official someday, you will first

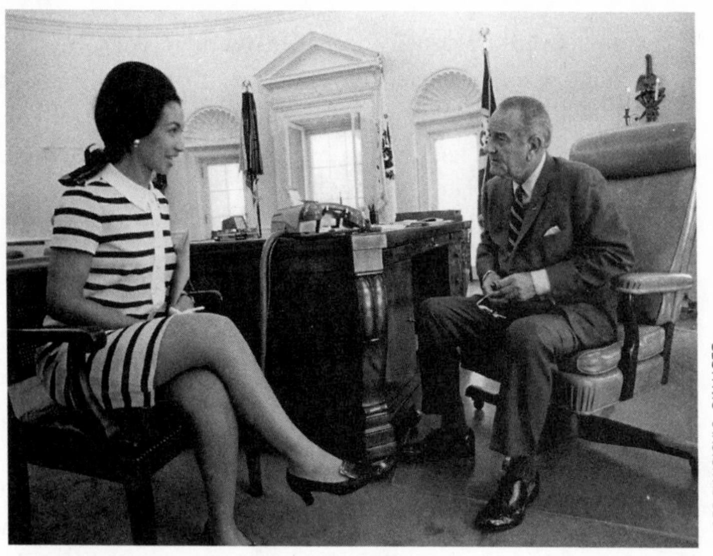

PHOTO BY YOICHI R. OKAMOTO, COURTESY OF THE LBJ LIBRARY COLLECTION

Geraldine Whittington and her boss in 1968

need to put in quite a few years of federal government service. Then you'll need to have an IQ high enough to run most major corporations. Every assistant that I found in a position of prominence and prestige got there the hard way: she or he made being a government secretary a career, and they fought their way to the top. There was no reason why the best of them couldn't have been earning three times their salaries in another profession.

If they didn't get there the hard way, something fishy was always going on. Nobody said you can't sleep or cheat your way to the top. You'll just have a tough time hiding it. And you'll find few rewards other than the dubious joy of knowing that you're helping a powerful person stay in power.

✎ Just Tell Him the "Big Guy" Sent Me

When Hanna Rosin was the assistant to *The New Republic*'s senior editor, Michael Kinsley, she knew the difference between working for an influential person and being one. Unfortunately, not everyone with whom she came in contact understood this distinction. She writes about her experiences dealing with secretaries who seemed to think that reporting to power was the same thing as wielding a personal sword:

> *I got close to George Stephanopoulos, Roger Altman, Tipper Gore and even the President. But . . . I had no real contact. I only got to talk to their secretaries.*

Rosin observed these top-level professionals with a mixture of amazement and amusement. She describes a nervous, subservient world, where personal goals become secondary to the demands of an important boss:

> *The aim is to challenge yourself daily to sacrifice your needs for the sake of the boss, right down to the last detail. If your boss doesn't want to speak to someone, you lie about his whereabouts. If your boss doesn't remember who someone is, you call that person and say you took an incomplete message. Most important, you slowly, if unconsciously, adopt your boss's personality.*
>
> *The secretary of one right-wing pundit was barely civil, addressing me only as Ms. Rosin in what I suspect was a fake British accent. . . . I was casual, sometimes belligerent, and I always threw in a wisecrack.*
>
> *But there are important differences between secretaries and assistants, and they often produce tension. Real secretaries perceived my informality as unprofessional. The wrath of important people hangs over their heads, so they didn't have time for my jokes. Will Mr. Kinsley keep his 7 p.m. appointment with* Washington Post *Chairwoman Katharine Graham? Mrs. Graham's secretary asked solemnly. I guess so, but I have no idea where he is. For security reasons, Roger Altman's secretary wanted Mike's birth date. That's easy. Did I know what he'd like to eat for lunch? she asked. Well, to start, he'd like confit of duck with a light plum sauce, then farfalle alla puttanesca and a crème brûlée for dessert. She didn't think this was funny. ("TLC: Tender Loving Care of a Good Secretary,"* The New Republic, *September 12, 1994.)*

Nobody will think *anything* is funny when you work for a high-powered politico or the top military brass. You'll deal with handlers who consider themselves personal friends of "the Big Guy" because they've been to his home once. You'll have to nod appreciatively when some yahoo shows you a picture of himself and the Great One, expecting you to understand that he has Access. You'll screen calls from fans, from enemies, from agents, and from your own acquaintances who think you can now do them favors.

Matthew Scully, a former speechwriter for Dan Quayle, wrote for *National Review* ("Air Force Two, Anyone?" January 18, 1993) about the typical hanger-on who confused knowing someone powerful with actually having power:

> *Nowadays the place is manned by a different breed of public servant. I think for instance of the guy who sat in the next office when I was assigned a temporary desk in the Office of Political Affairs. As the strategy man for the Southwestern states, he would accompany the President on trips to that region, and much of his time was spent on the phone haggling over which local big-shots would be allowed to ride on Air Force One: "That idiot—we let him on last time! . . . That a-- isn't stepping foot on the aircraft!"*
>
> *In between these delicate negotiations you could hear him complaining to colleagues about all those yokels out West begging for his petty favors. Meanwhile, his own office was adorned with three or four framed pictures of himself sitting on Air Force One, plastic cups and napkins from Air Force One, a model of Air Force One suspended from the ceiling, and—separately matted and framed—a seat-assignment card with his very own name and the words "Welcome Aboard Air Force One."*

Scully was almost seduced by the typical Washington power trip, but he caught himself just in time:

> *The same impulse nearly overtook me the other day when a memo arrived announcing our last chance to buy Air Force Two windbreakers bearing an embroidered vice-presidential seal, with order forms attached. Actually, the windbreakers are pretty snappy-looking—Dan Quayle himself wears them. Suddenly I saw myself, a few months from now, striding jauntily into a room, where an awed Republican temptress approaches to inquire how I came into this impressive raiment, her delicate hand reaching timidly to touch the official seal. ("Oh, just something from my White House years.") Only one somber fact pre-*

vented me from ordering two or three of them: I have never been Vice President.

This is precisely the point: When you work for a big shot, you are not a friend of the big shot, nor do you share in said big shot's power or salary. All you get, really, is the lifestyle equivalent of an Air Force One napkin holder or an Air Force Two windbreaker.

To offset the low pay, however, you'll enjoy being overworked. Now, perhaps your boss will be such a superstar that you won't care. Fawn Hall worked ten- and twelve-hour days to accommodate Oliver North, all in the name of duty. She bought into the lie that a secretary is part of the team and that her job was to make life pleasant and easy for her boss. Even her code name, "Sunshine," betrayed her role as the sweet, obedient servant. (North's was "Blood and Guts," which almost always translates into a higher salary in the secret language of the office.) Hall was so convinced of her importance as a member of North's "team," that she nearly went to prison on his behalf.

✎ No Tea Dances on *This* Disco Floor!

If you want to work for the feds in any sort of high-level capacity, you'll probably need a security clearance. The lower-level clearances, such as confidential, are easy to get: I got a confidential clearance through a temp agency by filling out a form and showing a valid passport. I think I could have been an arms dealer or a spy or a bomb builder needing to know how airplane wings are assembled: it didn't matter.

If you want a higher-level clearance, however, which you will need for anything interesting and important, you'll have to pass this simple test.

1. Have you ever seen a psychiatrist or psychologist?
2. Are you gay?

If your answer to either of the above is "yes," then go to the head of the unemployment line: you just failed.

The government claims that its bias against both psychiatric counseling and homosexuality is rooted in its fear of spies. People who "tell all" on the psychiatrist's couch, the argument goes, are more likely to disclose secret information that can render them vulnerable to blackmail. Likewise, those who engage in "sexual misconduct" (the government's term for everything from rape to consensual gay sex) are considered more likely to be blackmailed by the enemy.

History says this isn't true, but try telling that to the FBI agent who's busy calling your friends and family to learn your secrets.

Many people have been denied promotions and clearances in the government because of the psychiatry problem. One secretary found herself unable to obtain a top-secret clearance simply because she'd admitted to consulting a psychologist during a divorce. Many higher officials do not seek the help they need when they need it because they fear being denied or losing clearances.

The high-level security clearance, with its accompanying background check, has also helped weed out gays and lesbians from the federal rolls, New regulations say this isn't supposed to happen, yet traditionally homophobic institutions like the FBI and the CIA are still known to select against gays and lesbians when it comes to promotions and clearances. The government has never developed a clear policy on this kind of screening. It's neither legal nor illegal, and this "gray area" gives individual administrators a lot of room to select against gays without doing anything that can get them successfully sued.

A background check is a basic first step to a higher-level government job, and some of these can be thorough. If you live an openly gay lifestyle at home, even if you keep your sex life private at the office, you may be denied a security clearance.

A group of gay men in San Francisco were denied security clearances by DISCO, the Defense Industrial Security Clearance Office. They decided to sue, but the High-Tech Gays, as they called themselves, lost the suit. A *New Yorker* editorial (February 15, 1993) tells why:

> *On appeal, the court agreed with the government that the discriminatory practices had a "rational basis." The government's evidence that the discrimination was rational—that gays were more likely to be approached than heterosexuals—came in part from testimony at the court-martial of Sergeant Clayton J. Lonetree, a marine guard*

> *at the United States Embassy in Moscow who spied for the K.G.B. Ironically, nowhere in its opinion did the court mention that Sergeant Lonetree was recruited as a spy by his Soviet lover, a woman.*

Wayne Hays, Wilbur Mills (the representative who cavorted in a Washington, D.C., fountain with stripper Fanne Fox), and Clayton Lonetree notwithstanding, the government is more worried about gay sexual activity than any other kind.

If you believe the latest headlines, homosexuality is no longer being used as a basis for denying security clearances. If you believe the gay people who work for the government, however, the rules are changing for the better, but it's still a slow, uphill battle. Clerical staff won't benefit from these changes for quite some time.

If you do apply to the government, never reveal personal information, even if you are asked. Remember that there is nothing magic about a form: you don't have to fill in a box just because it is there. If a prospective employer asks you about your sexual orientation, refuse to answer it. My standard answer is: "I am a moral person committed to upholding the responsibilities of my job. I do not discuss my personal life with others." Likewise, if they ask you about psychiatric counseling, never say you've received it. Instead, answer that in times of trouble you seek the support of friends or your clergy, or give some other truthful response. Keep the rest of the truth to yourself.

✎ How to Apply to the Federal Government and Get a Decent Job

Your initial application form for the government will follow you for most of your working life, so you'll need to fill it out right the first time.

I cannot overemphasize the importance of this. One government attorney is currently seeking a new assistant. He has an excellent record of working well with his staff. Yet he's still looking after a month. The problem? Few of the applicants took adequate time to properly fill in their employment application.

You wouldn't believe the SF 171 forms I've seen. Some of them were handwritten in pencil. One was covered in white-out. They show me that the preparer didn't care enough to present herself or himself at their best.

I think at least some of the preparers did care. However, they didn't understand this form that would follow them throughout their government careers. Like so many applicants, they probably grabbed a handy writing utensil and starting filling in blocks, perhaps while waiting in the personnel office. They didn't know that, by doing this, they were guaranteeing themselves a merry-go-round of jobs at the lowest rungs of service.

Read Appendix A (page 233) if you want to find out how to apply to the government the right way.

✎ Find Government Jobs at Home, Using the Internet or a BBS

Once you have a résumé package prepared, you'll want to look at the listed computer bulletin board (BBS) job resources for possible positions.

Besides the boards Kathleen Green lists in Appendix A, the FedWorld BBS contains listings on nearly all civil service jobs nationwide. It is updated daily, and the information is available twenty-four hours a day.

If you have a link to the Internet, just type:

telnet fedworld.gov

to go straight to FedWorld. You'll have to provide your name, address, and phone number for a system-user ID. Be sure to write your ID and password down somewhere, because FedWorld will not provide you with a new one if you forget.

Once inside, you may find it a little confusing, but be patient: all computer BBSs are alike at some level. Learn this one, and you'll know them all, especially for the government. Be sure to read the introductory documents that will arrive automatically when you sign up. You can return to the main menu from anywhere within the system by typing:

/go main

If you get lost, type this command to get back ''home.''

You can search jobs by state and also by title. It took me a couple of tries, but soon I was able to find all of the writer-editor positions in Alaska, for instance, by using their system. FedWorld also has a ''gateway'' to other systems, such as the Office of Personnel Management's ''OPM Mainstreet'' (912-757-3100).

If you don't have an Internet connection, you can call FedWorld directly from your modem at 703-321-8020 or you can find it on the World Wide Web (http://www.fedworld.gov).

There are lots of federal government bulletin boards, telnet, and gopher sites to keep you busy. If you want more, send E-mail to hotlist@jobnet.com, and Harold Lemon will mail you his big list of job-hunting resources.

✎ So What's the Bottom Line?

Some people are happiest working for a secure employer in a job they know is unlikely to go away. These folks plan to work at one company or organization for decades and move up within the ranks. If this sounds like you, then you may want to put a lot of effort into looking for a federal or state government job at the highest level for which you qualify.

If, on the other hand, you value personal freedom and independence over steady, year-after-year security, or if you have a low red-tape tolerance, you will want to avoid the government and look for a job in private industry, or with a law firm, where you can earn more money and move quickly on your career track.

If you choose government work, remember the central points of this chapter:

1. Get yourself out of the clerical rut unless you envy Radar O'Reilly. The clerical shackles are among the hardest to shed. Try to find a job with responsibilities other than typing, filing, and answering the telephone.

2. Research any prospective agency thoroughly and know everything you can about the job before you say ''yes.'' Consult newspaper articles for the past two years (ask a reference librarian how) and talk to employees in prospective departments about working conditions.

3. Work at the highest level you can, but look out for corruption. Unethical bosses will not hesitate to use you to help them break the law. Keep your eyes open and remember that if you think you smell something fishy, you're almost always right.

To work at your highest level, you will probably need a bachelor's degree from a four-year college or university. The bachelor's degree has replaced the high school diploma as the minimum required education level for the most challenging, interesting jobs. Read Chapter 7 for ideas about going back to college while keeping your present job.

With a diploma and a job-hunting strategy, you'll be able to avoid the pitfalls of being near power without having any. Then you can look forward to a rewarding career in government, on your own terms.

LIBRARY OF CONGRESS

FEELING WHIPLASHED?

How *Clerks* Are Making Financial Barons *Rich*

Did you ever play crack-the-whip on ice skates, or have you ever swung a real bullwhip around? The kids at the end of the whip at the skating rink get thrown off. But if you're holding tight to the handle of an agile bullwhip, or if you're the center person on the ice rink, you don't move much; you're safe.

Financial organizations of all types—whether banks, savings and loans, brokerage houses, stock exchanges, or government-run agencies like the Federal Reserve Board and the Securities and Exchange Commission—fall somewhere on an invisible bullwhip.

At the wild end of the whip are the companies that ride the ups and downs of the international markets: stockbrokers like

Merrill Lynch or Charles Schwab are right at the outside edge. They invest not just their clients' money but their own as well, and they are likely to shrink or grow according to the fortunes of the various markets. Recently, trader Nick Leeson single-handedly brought down one of the oldest and most respected banks in England, Barings plc, through his wildcat speculation in backed investments called derivatives. Leeson was so famous, his face appeared on T-shirts; the disaster inspired a game called "Lose Your Bearings" that allowed participants to lose play money in the markets. (*The Wall Street Journal*, March 27, 1995.) For all its age and venerable reputation, Barings was still positioned as close to the end of the whip as other investors, and was all too vulnerable during wild trading. Crack! A British institution fell, in a matter of months.

Exchanges like the New York Stock Exchange (NYSE) and regulatory agencies like the Securities Exchange Commission (SEC) are close to the whip's base. They are usually secure, at least as financial markets go. Many companies lose or gain fortunes every day on the NYSE, but the exchange itself keeps going even when the stocks that brokers and buyers trade there drop or rise precipitously. It will be there no matter what. Likewise, the country may be in a depression, a recession, or a golden phase of prosperity, but as a regulatory board, the SEC continues all the same.

In between the stock exchanges and the brokerage companies lie just about every other financial organization you can think of. Take mortgage companies, for example. These may seem very secure to you, until you think about what's underneath them. They ride a market just as brokerage companies do. If the Federal Reserve Board lowers interest rates significantly, millions of homeowners who bought thirty-year mortgages when rates were high may choose to refinance. They'll get a new loan at a low rate and pay off the old, higher-rate loan. Often this is bad news for mortgage companies, who may have purchased loans from other mortgage companies on the basis of their possible future value. A paid-off loan brings in less money than a long-term loan at full interest.

Banks are another example. Many banks act as mortgage lenders and are therefore affected when interest rates decline. Banks are also tied to the stock market, derivatives trading, commodities, and the fortunes of the average depositor. Banks sell loans, certificates of deposit, and other products. When the markets change, banks' fortunes change. However, they don't ride the markets the same way that brokerage houses do; they are closer to the middle or top third of that whip. They'll feel the fluctuations of a wild market, but they won't fly up and down as much as the brokers. Remember the savings and loan scandal? Small investors lost faith in S&Ls and lined up for blocks to withdraw their money before it was lost. Before that, many folks thought S&Ls were closer to the whip handle. When the wild ride started, they found out just how speculative the American banking system can be at times.

✎ You Live at Another Whip End Too

Why am I spending all this time on a whiplash analogy? Because the whip goes more than one way. As a secretary, an administrative assistant, a file clerk, a receptionist, or some other support staffer, you're on the end of a different whip every day, even if you don't work for a financial company. If your individual company's fortunes go down, chances are you'll be the first to feel it, because you'll take a pay cut or be laid off. The support staff is always the first to go when times are tough at the office. The president, the CEO, the owner, and the other big players in your company are safely tucked away at the handle of the whip. Oh, they'll feel the rise or fall of the business's fortunes, all right, but they will probably continue to draw a paycheck even if things get bad. You'll go flying out the door, and pronto.

Now, let's say you get a new job working for a major brokerage company. The firm seems wealthy, and your bosses are happy. Business is booming: they're making money, buying themselves new cars, and giving you incentive bonuses. You might even get that last credit card paid off. It looks like a rock-solid job with a marvelous future.

One problem. It's September 1987. On Monday, October 19, one month from now, the Dow Jones Industrial Average is going to drop 508 points in one day. Perhaps your company doesn't go out of business. Maybe it doesn't even suffer as badly as the other brokerage houses in your city. But, as a whip-end company, it's going to take a big hit at the closing bell. As a whip-end employee, you'll be the first to go. When your boss hands you an envelope containing your two weeks' severance pay, she says, "Good luck. Let me know if you need a letter of reference."

Later, your friend who works for a stock exchange meets you for a consoling drink. You tell him that you're out of work. "Wow," he says, "that's really tough." To himself he thinks: "And my bosses are asking me to work all the hours of paid overtime I want this week. When the market took a plunge, we got incredibly busy, and it looks as though we'll stay that way for weeks!" Even though your friend is a whip-end employee, just like you (all clerical staff are whip-enders), he's better off, because he works for a whip-handle financial company. The stock exchange keeps standing. Your friends at the banks probably still have their jobs too, although bank employees suffer greatly for their place near the middle of the whip: banks traditionally underpay their employees to make up for having to have so many at all times.

✎ "Secure" Companies May Only Protect Their Executives

The higher you move up in a company, the closer you get to the safety of the handle. Executives generally negotiate for security as well as salary when they sign on with a new firm. One deal, the "golden parachute," guarantees an executive a generous payment of cash and other considerations if her or his employment is terminated for any reason.

When the Fourth Financial Corporation of Wichita, Kansas, fielded buyout rumors in April 1995, it offered "golden parachutes" to eighteen key executives. The chairman, the vice presidents, and other managers would receive severance payments of one and a half times their base salary, plus insurance coverage, bonuses, fully vested stock option and retirement plans, and other goodies for up to two years if they were fired or otherwise forced out. (*The Kansas City Business Journal*, April 28, 1995.)

What about their administrative assistants? Why, they'd receive lovely cardboard boxes for emptying their desks, beautiful severance checks for two weeks' pay (suitable for framing), plus a tearful goodbye from the boss, who's trotting off for a consoling dinner and drinks at a fancy restaurant she could still afford. But continued salary for a grace period or fully paid insurance benefits? For assistants? You must be joking.

As a whip-end employee, you can be fired or laid off almost without warning, either because of mergers, acquisitions, and closings or simply because a company decides it needs to "downsize." Ask the secretaries at IBM who just lost a third of their salaries; they'll tell you that the whip-end employees always feel the financial strain first, hardest, and most irrevocably.

So why on earth would anyone want to work on two whip ends by being (1) an administrative assistant at (2) a brokerage house? You're twice as likely to lose your job through no fault of your own. What's worse, brokers are not known for paying their administrative staffs very well, so you may have no savings to fall back on. After all, just like banks, brokerage houses need lots of clerks to keep things running. They can't cut all of the jobs, or they'd go out of business. Therefore they hire as many people as they can for as little as they can. When the markets start spinning, they let a few clerks fly off the end, and they make the other ones work harder: more hours for the same money. If the markets improve, fine. They can always give out bonuses or hire a few more people. Stockbrokers and banks earn huge fortunes on the backs of their clerical staffs by underpaying them and forcing them to live with the constant threat of layoff.

Therefore I don't recommend working for a stockbroker unless you are getting an *exceptionally* good deal: high pay, good benefits, generous employee investment plans, the works. Your company would have to pay you so well that you could afford to save up money on the side, just in case you got laid off. I'm willing to bet, however, that most brokerage houses and investment companies won't offer you that kind of a deal. There is such a thing as working for a good broker, but you'll have to do some research (explained below) to find out where any particular broker stands.

✎ Work for Whip-Handle Financial Companies to Make Money

Companies that process money make money. If you want a clerical job that helps you get ahead financially, work for a private whip-handle financial company. Sure, the bank down the road may offer you a secure job, but banks are famous for paying their clerks and their managers as poorly as possible. You could also work for the SEC or the Federal Reserve Board, but they're government, not private, and government agencies are not known for their generous salaries or major benefits.

Instead, look to private organizations like stock exchanges or other businesses that make money off the markets without riding them up and down too severely. To get you started, here's a list of the major American stock exchanges, with addresses and phone numbers. If you live near one, you might want to cold-call them for employment opportunities that lead to advancement. For example, you could start as a statistical clerk, and go to night school to complete your bachelor's degree. This combination would make you easily promotable to stock analyst. Remember to read the job-hunting sections (Chapters 6 and 7) first, though! You'll want to look for a job in the promotional line that makes or saves money for the organization. Secretarial work, while important, does not directly do either of these, and therefore it's a poor choice for promotion.

American Stock Exchange, Inc.
86 Trinity Place
New York, NY 10006-1881
212-306-1000

Arizona Stock Exchange
2800 North Central Avenue
Phoenix, AZ 85004-1007
602-222-5858

Boston Stock Exchange, Inc.
1 Boston Place
Boston, MA 02108
617-723-9500

Chicago Stock Exchange, Inc.
440 South La Salle Street
Chicago, IL 60605
312-663-2222

Cincinnati Stock Exchange
36 East 4th Street, #906
Cincinnati, OH 45202-3810
513-621-1410

Midwest Stock Exchange
440 South La Salle Street
Chicago, IL 60605-1028
312-939-4338

NASDAQ Stock Market, Inc.
1735 K Street NW
Washington, DC 20006-1500
202-728-8000

New York Stock Exchange, Inc.
11 Wall Street
New York, NY 10005
212-656-3000

Pacific Stock Exchange, Inc.
301 Pine Street
San Francisco, CA 94104
415-393-4000

Philadelphia Stock Exchange, Inc.
1900 Market Street
Philadelphia, PA 19103
215-496-5000

Some of these are small shops. The Arizona Stock Exchange only had eleven employees in early 1995. Others, such as the NYSE and NASDAQ, are much larger. Although employees tend to stay put at comfortable organizations, these companies may have openings. If not, keep checking regularly through the year.

I'm not saying that stock exchanges have no volatility whatsoever. I'm just saying that, in times of financial crisis, they're much more stable than stockbrokers or even mortgage companies. Plus, they tend to treat their employees better because they need a steady base of knowledgeable folks to run the shop year-round.

✎ Work Where? In That Madhouse? Are You Kidding?

A noisy floor full of screaming traders waving pieces of paper at each other and shouting "Buy! Sell! Kill!" is the most famous and persistent image in most people's minds when you say "stock exchange." But that's not accurate. As stock markets become increasingly computerized, the trading frenzy is limited to rapid computer action, not a kamikaze market maker surrounded by hysterical traders. When the National Association of Securities Dealers began offering an Automated Quotation System (another name for computerized stock trading, called NASDAQ) for stocks that didn't trade on the New York Stock Exchange, it changed the rules of the game.

Since the markets open and close at precise times each day, there isn't much work to do when the exchange stops trading. Stock exchanges and companies that base their activity on the market's hours are actually rather calm places to work. The workload is predictable and doesn't follow the seasons. Even law offices have busy times and slow times, but the stock exchanges keep a relatively steady work flow all year round. I worked at the NASDAQ stock exchange on Black Monday in October 1987, and it got mighty busy then. Otherwise, however, the job was steady and predictable. The staff rarely changed; many of my former co-workers are still there almost a decade later. I'd been at other companies where mass layoffs occurred. Nothing of the sort happened at NASDAQ.

✎ How Does an Investment Executive Compare with a Lawyer?

Many investment executives are the spiritual opposite of lawyers. People who like arguments, confrontation, and negotiation become attorneys. People who like making money in a clean atmosphere where all you fight are the numbers on the page become investment professionals. The exceptions to this rule are stockbrokers—born gamblers who can be as boisterous and uncouth as the wiliest attorney—but then I've already told you to stay away from them unless you're as aggressive as they are. Investment professionals range from the quiet speculator, such as one stock exchange manager who also bred racehorses on the side, to society's ultraquiet ''bean counters'' such as accountants and market analysts. If you work for one of these folks, you can assume, with few exceptions, that they will prefer office harmony to shouting and near-fisticuffs explosions.

It was boring? Not really. I enjoyed following the market's activity and learning about international investments such as commodities futures. I spoke to brokers long-distance on the phone every day—which is where I wanted to keep them—so I experienced the colorful side of Wall Street culture without having to work for difficult bosses. When one broker yelled at me, ''Hang on, doll, I gotta go to the toilet,'' in the middle of a phone conversation, I was able to laugh about it. Had I worked for this charming fellow on a daily basis, however, I might have lost my mind.

✎ Learn Where a Financial Company Sits on the Whip

If you want to work for any financial company, learning where it resides on the invisible market whip will help you decide whether to stake your financial life on its future. Ask these questions about any prospective company:

1. Is it over ten years old?
10+ years = 2 points
5–9 years = 1 point
1–4 years = 0 points

2. Has it made national headlines for financial trouble in the last five years?
No = 1 point
3–5 years ago = 0 points
Last 1–3 years = −1 point
Major trouble = disqualify (subtract all points)

3. Is its primary income tied to the fluctuations of an investment market?
No = 2 points
Mortgages and loans = 1 point
Stocks, bonds, commodities, etc. = 0 points
(If you're not sure, ask. Most companies will tell you, and you'll sound smart for inquiring.)

4. Is it generally well spoken of by financial newspapers and magazines such as *The Wall Street Journal, Barron's, Forbes, Money, Fortune*?
Yes, more than one favorable mention = 2 points
Mentioned once = 1 point
Not mentioned at all = 0 points
One negative press item = −1 point
Multiple bad press = disqualify (subtract all points)

5. Does it offer its employees investment opportunities such as mutual funds, stock options, or employer-matched savings plans?
Yes = 1 point
No = 0 points

6. Does it pay competitive or better wages than similar jobs at nonfinancial companies?
Yes = 2 points
Same = 1 point
Less = 0 points
Much less = disqualify (subtract all points)

Score:

10+ points. Congratulations, this company is probably at or near the snug base of the handle. Get a promotable job if you can and do your best to stay there.

5–9 points. This is an acceptable middle-of-the-road choice, but look to see where the points are spread. If it received a "disqualify" in any category, stay away. Otherwise, go ahead, but proceed with caution.

3–4 points. It's not worth it. Keep looking for a company that is able to take better care of its clerical staff. If you're really hot for the job, I certainly can't stop you, but keep your eyes open at all times for signs of financial upheaval.

0–2 points. Don't say I didn't warn you.

✎ How to Work for a High-Points Company

The best way to find a job at a high-points company is to identify winning organizations first and then look for the jobs. Start with the financial journals and newspapers and learn which companies are best. You can find "best company" ratings in many magazines.

I'll use my most recent computer search as an example. At the library, I used *Business and Company ASAP*, a popular newspaper and magazine abstracts database from InfoTrac, to search major articles in the last five years. A reference librarian can help you if you don't know how to do this. Then I used two keywords, "best" and "rating," for my search. Both of these words commonly appear in headlines about good companies. I eliminated the words "best-sellers" and "restaurants" to weed out the most common irrelevant articles. My search line looked like this:

best and rating not best-sellers not restaurants

You can read the instructions on searching, or "Boolean searching," to learn how to construct other useful search phrases.

This search left me with 308 articles from major newspapers and magazines on the best of everything from American cities to mutual funds. It didn't take long to use the computer to glance at the headlines of 300 articles. I slowly scrolled down the list until I saw this article (item 23):

> Money, *June 1995, volume 24, number 6, page 126. "The Best Bank in America" (USAA Federal Savings). Author: Vanessa O'Connell.*

Money magazine rated United Services Automobile Association (USAA) Federal Savings in San Antonio, Texas, the best of 427 banks in 1995. The article went on to discuss how banks are earning record profits right now, but they're not passing these profits on to their customers. *Money* thought USAA Federal Savings did the best job during 1995 of sharing its profitable condition with investors. If a savings and loan is good to its investors, it is more likely to treat its employees properly too.

Now, *Money* magazine is just one opinion. Other magazines may feel differently. After you find a thumbs-up article, look up all the articles about that company. When I looked up USAA Federal Savings in the same database, I learned that the Bank Administration Institute and *American Banker* magazine gave USAA high marks as well. USAA did not earn any negative press that I could find. Some employees did get laid off when it moved the credit card center from Tulsa, Oklahoma, to San Antonio, Texas, but First Data Resources, whose parent company is American Express, stepped in and offered all of them immediate jobs.

Then I looked up USAA's company profile on InfoTrac and learned that it was founded in 1983 (over ten years old) and that it has 544 employees in its one office in San Antonio, Texas. This seemed a bit small, until I counted seven other USAA companies, including an investment management company (480 employees), a travel agency (200 employees), and others such as financial services, life insurance, and real estate, all in San Antonio.

Of course, this information only helps if you live near San Antonio, but that's how the system works. You start with the best, and then look within the best to see what's in your neighborhood. Or, conversely, you start with your neighborhood, and then rank all of the major corporations that interest you from best to worst. This can take you as little as an afternoon in the library, and you can save yourself years of heartache and many, many dollars.

Let's say, for example, you're an African-American woman in Greensboro, North Carolina, and you want to look for a good job in a new city with a thriving black business community. You can read the "best of" lists to learn that *Black Enterprise* magazine found Washington, D.C., Atlanta, Chicago, Los Angeles, and Philadelphia to be favorable cities for black professionals to start a career. Then you can check the *Los Angeles Business Jour-*

nal (all on this same big list of 300+ "best of" articles) to learn that customers ranked Peat Marwick and Price Waterhouse as the best public accounting firms in Los Angeles. Information like this could be the basis of your first cross-country job search, and a move to a financial company in an exciting city.

Let's say, however, that you'd rather stay in Greensboro, or in the state of North Carolina. Then you can consult *Business and Company ASAP*, which I mentioned before, to learn about opportunities in Greensboro, Charlotte, Raleigh, Durham, and other major cities. Just type in "Charlotte, North Carolina" and hit "return." The database will give you articles about Charlotte, a list of Charlotte's major businesses, and even addresses and phone numbers. You can search for articles on the companies that interest you, one by one, until you learn which ones earn the best ratings.

Call all of the public libraries in your area to find out what kinds of databases they have. Most libraries are computerized to some degree by now, but they don't all offer the same resources. The reference librarian can help, though. Tell him or her that you want to research the best companies first, and then within those best companies you want to learn which ones are located where you'd like to be. Ask for InfoTrac and *Business and Company ASAP* by name, but use whatever you can find if these aren't available.

If there's a major university near you, call there as well. Many universities offer excellent library resources. Although most of these are for the use of professors and students, you can usually sit in the reference room and use the databases. Call before you go and ask about policies. If nobody asks you for an ID, then act like you belong there and you might be able to work undisturbed for hours.

✎ Use a Financial Company Job to Pay Debts, Buy a Home, and More

If you choose a thriving financial company that offers savings plans, use them fully. Some employers offer *matching funds savings plans*. If you join one of these plans, you can invest a percentage of your income (usually a maximum of 12–15 percent), and the company will add matching funds of, for example, 5 percent. This is free money which companies offer employees, but most employees, especially the clerical staff, don't take advantage of it.

A survey of clerical workers nationwide showed that most workers earning under $30,000 a year do not take advantage of matching funds plans, or 401(k) plans, because they think they can't afford to live without all the money from each paycheck. Most of these employees did not understand exactly how much these plans could earn for them over time.

If your company offers a plan like this, invest the most you are allowed to, even if it means struggling to pay the bills at home each month. These plans will work very hard for you, automatically taking a portion of your income each month and combining it with extra money from your employer. Some financial companies manage these plans as mutual funds. This means your savings can earn additional revenue in a big-money fund that you could never afford if you were only a private investor.

There's only one catch. If you take your money out of this fund too soon, you lose the matching funds and you may pay a penalty. Resolve that you will leave your money in the fund until you can legally remove it without penalty. I used one of these funds properly, and saved up an entire down payment to buy my first home when I was twenty-seven. It took only two years. These funds work, and if you find a company that offers them they can change your financial life.

Once you get fully invested in a plan like this, or in another payroll savings plan, you can start calling banks and mortgage lenders to learn about low down payment loans to first-time home buyers. For as little as $3,000 to $5,000 down, you may be able to buy your home instead of renting it. Quite realistically, you could save money, buy your own home, and live completely debt-free even on a modest salary simply by working for a wealthy company that offers superb benefits and employee savings plans.

Stock options are another benefit that few employees take full advantage of. Companies like Chemical Bank and PepsiCo regularly offer employees shares of stock in lieu of cash bonuses. Starbucks Coffee offers all of its employees "bean stock," allowing them to purchase a share of the company's profits. Some companies offer employees a choice: a certain amount of cash, or a certain, sometimes higher, amount of stock. Time after time, clerical workers opt for the cash because they trust it. Taking the stock, however, can be a very smart move.

The company doesn't give you stock certificates; rather it puts your stock shares in an account. Every payout period (perhaps quarterly) you then have the opportunity to receive a check for the amount of money that stock earned, or to receive more stock, sometimes in small amounts that you wouldn't normally have the opportunity to buy. Employees who choose to accept more stock each time can watch their little stock accounts turn into substantial nest eggs.

If you want to learn how to use your company's 401(k) plan, savings fund, and stock options to their full effect, just look up the subject in *The Wall Street Journal* and other financial papers. Typing "stock options" into a business database will lead you to many articles on how to take the best advantage of the benefits your company gives you.

Books

Lewis J. Altfest, *Lew Altfest Answers Almost All Your Questions About Money* (McGraw-Hill, 1992). $19.95.

John Bogle, *Bogle on Mutual Funds: New Perspectives for the Intelligent Investor* (Irwin Professional Publishing, 1994). $25.

Kal Chany and Geoffrey Martz, *The Princeton Review: The Student Access Guide to Paying for College* (Villard Books, 1994). $14.

Gerri Detweiler, *The Ultimate Credit Handbook* (Plume, 1994). $10, call 1-800-255-0899.

Barry Dickman and Trudy Lieberman, *How to Plan for a Secure Retirement* (Consumer Reports Books, 1992). $24.95.

Pamphlets

The Consumer's Almanac. Learn about your credit report. Write to the American Financial Services Association, Consumer Credit Education Foundation, 919 18th Street NW, Suite 300, Washington, DC 20006; enclose a check for $2.

How to Shop for a Loan and How to Shop for a Home. Available from Great Western Financial, call 1-800-492-7587.

Money Matters (AARP, 1993). Consult this before you hire a financial adviser, a tax preparer, or other professionals. If you're living alone, you might also want to request *A Single Person's Guide to Retirement Planning* (AARP, 1992). Write to the American Association of Retired Persons: AARP Fulfillment, 60 E Street NW, Washington, DC 20049. A good guide for older employees.

✎ Be a Smart Benefits Shopper

You should ask about these benefits before starting the interview process with any company. Call the benefits office at any company which interests you, *whether or not they have job openings*, and ask the following questions:

1. How can I learn about the full benefits package for clerical employees?
2. How long does someone have to work at your company to earn these benefits? (Most companies make you wait at least three months to a year, but some make you wait longer.)
3. Does your company offer payroll deduction savings plans in addition to straight benefits?
4. What are the opportunities for employees to purchase stock or additionally invest in the corporation?

Don't rule a company out just because it doesn't offer stock plans, however. Simply find out what else it offers that might add up to similar savings for you. Some companies help pay for child care. Others offer assistance with first-time home buying, to encourage their employees to settle down and stay.

You will probably be surprised at the difference between companies and their benefits plans. Employees at the more generous companies may earn as much as a quarter of their salary *more* each year in valuable benefits than the employees at the cheapskate firms! If you'd like a quick-and-easy guide to finding some of the best firms overall, read Robert Levering and Milton Moskowitz's book *The 100 Best Companies to Work For in America* (Doubleday/Currency, 1993). You can compare benefits packages at the best firms with the stories you hear from personnel managers in your town. Plus, one of these companies may be just down the street!

Financial companies can be great places to work, if you take the time to study them before accepting a full-time job. If you get a promotable job at one of the good ones, you could find yourself safe, secure, and happy, forty hours a week.

Two Chapters About Freedom: An Introduction

THEODOR HORYDCZAK COLLECTION, LIBRARY OF CONGRESS

Crystal City, Virginia, sits on Route 1 between Arlington National Cemetery and Old Town Alexandria, right next to Washington, D.C. It looks like the 1950s idea of what the future would be: all fountains, parking decks, and escalators. Trees, grass, and flowers are used sparingly, if at all. It is a monument to concrete, chrome, and glass.

Crystal City is a self-contained work world. Everything there is designed to make staying at the office an easier proposition. You can even live in Crystal City . . . if you really want to.

This throwback to the future is full of ''Beltway Bandit'' companies which fulfill government contracts for, among other things, top-secret aircraft, military weapons, and product designs. To give you an idea of its futuristic image, the President held a conference on a National Identity Card there.

One of the tens of thousands of employees in Crystal City was a woman who had fought her way out of clerical work but who couldn't seem to get any further. She was pretty, if you could see past the weariness that outlined her like a haze. She had chocolaty-brown hair that flipped under at the shoulders. She wore sensible navy or gray suits and low-heeled shoes. Her nails were clipped short to a neat, businesslike length. She didn't wear perfume, and her makeup was subtle enough to be almost unnoticeable. If there had been an manual for how to dress in camouflage in the city, she might have been the prototype for ''female attire.'' I might never have even remembered her had it not been for the 3:30 train.

Crystal City is zigzagged with trains. It was built—or rather it ''sprang up,'' like mushrooms—on the side of an old Arlington train yard, next to National Airport. If you are lucky enough to have a window in your Crystal City office, you get to look out over about a quarter-mile of train tracks before you see the tiny ribbon of the Potomac River off on the horizon, just beneath the light gray sky. People with offices on the tops of buildings see less train tracks and more river. People on the lower stories, however, just see a long, flat stretch of brown metal rust.

She had an office on the ground floor. When she called me in to talk that afternoon, a train went by, and it chugged just past her window. We saw the Chessie System with its sleeping cat and cars marked ''Southern Serves the South.'' The train's endless gray, black, red, and yellow cars loudly defied the sleek efficiency of the Metro, of the airplanes, of Crystal City itself. It lumbered through, making such a deafening clatter that we couldn't talk until it was out of sight. Instead, we just stood at her window and watched it roll by.

When it was gone, the ensuing silence surrounded us, and we didn't speak. She looked down, coughed, and shuffled some papers. I sat quietly, waiting for either her further instructions or my cue to leave for the day. Then she looked out the window one more time, at the wake of the now vanished train.

''Sometimes,'' she said, in a soft voice that was not quite a whisper, ''I think I'd like to get on one of those trains. I'd like to go somewhere else. Anywhere at all.''

We were silent for a few moments more, and then she blinked a little and turned to me. ''Now then,'' she said, ''about this afternoon. I don't really have any further assignments for you. It looks as though I'll be staying late again, but that doesn't mean you have to. Go on home. Have a great afternoon.''

I went home that day, and eventually the short-term job ended, as they all do when you're working your way through school. But I never forgot her wistful gaze at the disappearing train.

The next two chapters are about escape. They're about finding the life that everyone talks about ''getting'' someday. And they're dedicated to that woman, whoever she was. I hope she got out. If she didn't, I hope she's reading this now.

PUT DOWN THOSE WANT ADS: Where and How to Land a Decent Job

LIBRARY OF CONGRESS

Wartime stenographers

"Someday," said Ellen, "I'm going to quit this job, if I can just find something else."

When asked what he did for a living, Ira said, "Well, I'm a receptionist for now, but I'm looking around."

"I'm an administrative assistant," explained Shandra, "but that's just a paycheck until a better job comes along."

"This is a transition period," insisted Jane. "I'm really *interested in doing something with my history degree."*

Sound familiar? Sure it does. Most people in clerical jobs are looking for something else to do. Everyone that I talked to said they wanted to find a different job, hopefully sometime soon.

But here's a scary thought. Ten years from now, most of them will still be doing the same thing, because they don't know how to see themselves doing anything else. When I asked each of these people what they were doing to look for a new job, they all said, "I'm checking the want ads." When I asked if they hoped to find their dream job in the want ads, most said, "No, but at least it will be better than *this*."

> *CAREER GIRLS' CONFERENCE. Career opportunities for young women will be explored during a 3-hour seminar to be held at the Hilton Hotel. A fashion show is included and M.C. will be popular radio personality Charlie Van Dyke. Talks will be given by representatives of H. Liebes fashion department, TWA hostess employment, Barbizon School of Modeling, and White Collar Girl and Strictly Secretaries agencies.* (San Francisco Examiner & Chronicle, *May 17, 1970.)*

✎ You Know You Have the Right Job When You Don't Have "Manic Mondays"

If you're hitting the snooze button a few times and groaning each morning, dreading the thought of another day at work, then you have the wrong job. Remember that old Billy Joel song, "Piano Man"? *Nobody* liked their job. There was a waitress practicing politics serving Bob, the real estate novelist. Could you imagine Billy singing

And then there is Buster
An insurance adjuster
Who loves it and makes it his life!

Funny, I can't either. For every Piano Man who is true to himself, there are a hundred people who have the wrong job title after their names.

Even though it may seem as though everyone hates their job and nobody wants to get up on Monday morning, for some people quite the opposite is true. There are people who wake up eager to start a full day at work.

I'm not exaggerating; a surprisingly large number of people love their work. What we have to do now is help you present yourself as the right kind of person to get a job that you too can enjoy.

✎ You Are Who You Say You Are

To find the right job, you're going to have to present yourself as the right person to do it. And you can, for in this world, to a large degree, you are who you say you are. So what if nobody knows you? That's a plus! Embrace your own anonymity and use it to your advantage. With thousands of people in every city looking for employment, you can confidently represent yourself to your best advantage without worrying that someone will know what, if anything, you're not mentioning.

I'm not talking about falsifying your record or embellishing the truth. Instead, I'm talking about choosing which true facts to emphasize, which ones to tell, and which ones to keep quiet about. Sometimes the difference is merely in the words you choose.

Let's imagine two different one-sentence descriptions. One says, "Economics student, A average in his major, expert at two computer database systems, has worked steadily at three jobs in ten years with increasing responsibility." The second one says, "Man over forty, only has a high school diploma, B-average student, some database experience, fired from third job because of work/school conflicts and currently unemployed."

Which man would you hire? It doesn't matter whether you

chose the first or second one: they're the same guy. Sentence one hits the highlights, though, and sentence two is absolutely, painfully honest. I'd take highlights over "honesty" any day.

Being unknown gives you protective anonymity. If you apply to a radio station as a disc jockey trainee, how do they know you've never thought of doing such a thing before? You can say that being a deejay is a lifelong dream for you. If you sashay into an investment brokerage house and announce that you'd be a super salesperson, someone's just likely to believe you.

I'm not saying "lie." I'm saying "assert." Walk into a company full of strangers, and tell 'em what you want. If you goof up, don't worry. They don't know you, and if you fall flat on your face, I guarantee they'll forget after five minutes. Then you can start over with a new group of strangers, and keep trying until you get it right.

Yet I still hear friends who ought to know better talking in grim tones about their "employment record" or their "work history" as though these terms really meant something.

What employment record? There is no mystical, Big Brother-ish employment file out there identifying you as one person rather than another. Some offices may keep personnel files, but these are for their own use. They are not allowed to show them to outsiders. Face it: your only "employment record" is the one in your own head. If you start representing yourself as a winner and write the past to prove it, people will believe you.

Some people, however, still insist that they are what they do. While I was writing this chapter, Leroy (whose dream was owning a sports car repair shop) said, "Look, I'm a stockbroker. How could I stop now and train to be a mechanic?" Ann asked me, "How can I explain to a sales interviewer why I was a secretary for fifteen years?" as though they were going to know anything about her that she didn't tell them herself.

Your life story isn't stamped on your forehead. As much as anything else, your résumé is a picture of who you believe you are.

✎ Promote Yourself, But Avoid the Impostor Syndrome

As I've already mentioned, the job-hunting field is filled with peculiar and even misleading books. I read one that seemed reasonable and well balanced, until the author assumed a hushed tone and started whispering that if you don't tell the absolute, 100 percent, total truth about your past, "they" will come after you and ruin your career. He cited horror stories in which pathological liars were ultimately exposed and arrested, thereby making national headlines.

His examples, however, lacked one small ingredient: perspective. Obviously if you say you made straight A's at Harvard and you've never even been to Massachusetts, someone's going to catch you. Sooner or later, some vice president will walk into your office and offer you the secret Harvard honors handshake. You're toast.

But no one is going to stand up in a meeting where you're a new manager and shout, "What? Her? She used to type and take dictation at DiLeo, Wolff, and Finch. She's a fake. Off with her head!" Fear of just such a scene is called "impostor syndrome," and women and men who try to achieve something higher than life has taught them to expect are most vulnerable to it. Impostor syndrome starts when you sit down to compose a résumé, or when you're imagining what you want to do rather than what you are doing. It starts with "Oh, I could never do that," and, unchecked, it usually ends with giving up: "I'm just a (secretary, receptionist, file clerk, bank teller) with no hope of leaving this behind."

If you got off to a slower start than some of your high school counterparts, it can be hard to believe you'll ever catch up, let alone surpass them. When you see old buddies finishing college, going to law school, getting married, and buying Mazda Miatas while you're still driving a faded lime-green Pinto and answering phones for an insurance agency, it's easy to feel as though this will always be the story.

And when you do start figuring out what you want, "impostor syndrome" can set in, saying, "What? You? Get real, pal. You drive a Pinto. You'll always drive one. Accept yourself, and move on."

Do you fear that when you're sitting in an interview with some great boss at the perfect job, a sign will appear over your head that says:

Beware: Pinto Driver
It used to be his mom's car, but she took pity on him.

> *It's got lots of exterior rust, and a cracked black vinyl interior.*
> *Loaded with petrified french fries between the seats.*
>
> *Extreme loser.* Do Not Hire.

A lot of people feel that these invisible ID tags follow them around. Don't worry. It happens to almost everyone who moves ahead. The highest achievers sometimes experience impostor syndrome every day, especially when they receive awards, give speeches, or earn diplomas. Successful people are simply those who continue on in spite of it. The higher you move up, the more prone you'll be to it, so get used to it now.

✎ Why the Want Ads Won't Move You Up

> *BLITHELY GREET, TYPE for this financial district company. Use your cheery self and enjoy phones, people, and being busy.*
>
> *GROOVY GIRLS. Exciting new cosmetics firm needs sales reps for Bay Area. We train. High earnings potential.*
>
> *(Both from* San Francisco Examiner & Chronicle, *May 17, 1970.)*

I've got some bad news. There aren't any dream jobs in the want ads. Pick up the newspaper only if you want another job just like the one you have now, because that's all they advertise there.

What exactly are want ads anyway? The short answer: nothing more than a long list of things other people are willing to offer any stranger who wanders by. They're the jobs nobody else claimed. Businesses have many better ways to fill vacant positions, so they turn to the want ads only as a last resort. "MAID. Apply in person. Uncle Tom's Cabins." (*The Des Moines Register,* September 2, 1951.)

Ask yourself a few questions. If a job in the paper is so great, why doesn't the boss offer it to his best friend or to his nephew? Why doesn't the agency keep it a secret and make people compete for it?

I'll tell you why. Here are the most common reasons that people run ads in the newspaper:

1. The job is entry-level. This is true of most newspaper listings.
2. Nobody in the know at that company wants to touch this particular job.
3. The boss is too cheap to hire an employment agent.
4. The Equal Employment Opportunity Commission says that the company has to interview a certain number of minorities and women before giving the job to someone else. So, even though the company already knows whom it wants to hire, it has to pretend to conduct a fair and open job search.
5. The company has a policy of firing everyone who doesn't earn a certain level of sales commissions. It hires new people all the time, hoping to find one super salesperson out of ten.
6. The ad is actually a front for a sales pitch. Have you seen those "Postal Employees! Earn $30 an hour!" kinds of ads: the ones with the 1-800 or 1-900 phone numbers on them? Forget it. When you call, they'll ask you to pay them $50 or more to teach you how to fill out a federal employment application form.
7. The ad is actually a front for an employment agency; it's not a listing for a specific job. When you call, you'll be invited to come in for an interview, and the job you saw in the paper will be "unavailable" because it never existed in the first place. Most agencies use this tactic to fish for applicants who might not have called on their own. You'll learn to spot agency lingo such as "Super self-starter needed to keep a busy, high-powered exec on the go!" Companies don't advertise themselves this way. If it sounds fake, it is fake.

Even though their "want ads" are thinly disguised recruitment tools, however, employment agents *can* help clerical job hunters. It just depends on what you're looking for. Another section in this chapter has information on when you might need agents and how to use them to your best advantage.

By the time you weed out the phony ads, the "nobody in their right mind would do that" ads, and the ads for jobs that don't even remotely resemble something you want to do, such as

Animal lover needed to scrub dog kennels.

Exotic female models wanted to earn top $$$ with serious photographer.

Learn the poultry industry by hosing chicken parts off the walls at a slaughterhouse,

you're left with the ''useful'' ads.

This brings us back to number one on the above list: they're entry-level.

How much longer are you willing to accept an endless round of starter positions, in subordination to someone else who's doing the really interesting stuff?

I would bother consulting the want ads only if I wanted to wait tables or work in a retail store. Restaurants and retailers often rely on the ads because agencies don't usually meet their specialized needs and because turnover in their businesses is too high to justify agency fees.

> *THIS COULD BE YOU . . . You step off the gleaming new elevator onto a carpeted floor high above Park Ave. You walk in past offices of account executives, copywriters, TV producers, and artists—the busy creators of advertising so important to America's growth and well-being. YOU ARE A PART OF IT . . . A secretary to an important adman. Your desk is right in the heart of the advertising world, a valued member of one of the nation's top 4-A advertising agencies. (*The New York Times, *June 12, 1960.)*

✎ Why Don't Good Employers Use the Newspaper More Often?

Good employers avoid the paper because, in a tight job market, there are more efficient ways to find qualified applicants. First, employees in their own company usually apply for the choice jobs, or they recommend their friends for the positions. People who want promotions haunt their own personnel offices, waiting for something better to open up. Also, smart employees inside a company make friends with people up the ladder who may want

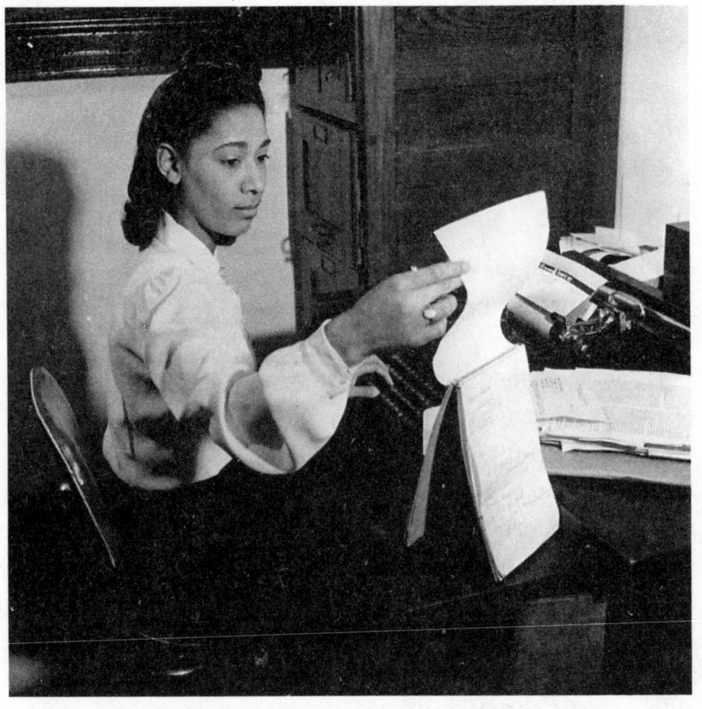

BY ALBERT FENN FOR THE U.S. OFFICE OF WAR INFORMATION, COURTESY OF THE LIBRARY OF CONGRESS

A New York government secretary tries to read her boss's handwriting, July 1942

to hire them someday. When upper-level managers have openings, they frequently offer them to employees they already know. Most jobs you'd want will never get into the newspaper.

Even if a firm doesn't already have someone in mind for a position, they usually won't resort to the newspaper. The best firms are selective, and they don't want to waste staff time sorting through the bizarre replies from people who answer newspaper ads.

Employers who do advertise in the paper have to screen tens or even hundreds of poorly prepared résumés and silly cover letters. This takes up staff time and costs more in the long run than most agency fees. Once a staff member, usually someone not very high up, selects the ''best'' résumés from the bunch, someone else will have to call all of those people to set up appointments.

Put yourself in a personnel assistant's place for a moment. Let's say you have ten résumés on your desk for a sales job that a local newspaper ad generated. Your job is to telephone all of these people and set up interviews. You call the first person, but he's already found a job as a clown at children's birthday parties, so he's no longer interested in being yours. The next person answers the telephone sleepily; she worked the second shift last night, and you called her in the middle of a good afternoon's snooze. She hangs up on you. The third person's answering machine takes the call, and you have to listen to him and three of his drunk fraternity brothers singing "Hail to the Redskins," but with lewd lyrics. You do write the lyrics down, but you keep going.

By the time someone answers the telephone, is interested in the position, and wants to come downtown to interview for it, you find that you and she don't have two hours without a schedule conflict for the rest of the week. Before you know it, you're ready to throw all of the résumés in the trash. It seems tempting to hire someone in-house for the job, even if you don't think they're qualified, just to avoid having to go through a second pile of applications.

Now do you see why employers don't bother?

Instead of slogging through the wrong part of the newspaper, making yourself fit their descriptions, only to have your résumé get lost in this motley pile, try turning things around. Create some favorable portraits of yourself with several great résumés, and then look for a variety of jobs that haven't even been advertised yet!

✎ Search the Trade Journals

Ads in the back of trade journals differ from generic want ads in that they are specific to a particular industry. They often cost more than newspaper want ads, so you can assume a bit more of an investment on the part of the company placing the ad. You can find jobs through trade journals, sometimes even in hard-to-enter fields.

The arts are a good example. Conventional wisdom might say there aren't any well-paying jobs in the arts. However, I picked up a copy of *American Theatre* and checked the classifieds in the back. Besides the casting calls, there were also listings of new shows that would need various assistants, and even an ad for an arts job bank. If you love the arts, you might just find an office job that beats whatever it is you're doing now. (Interested? Then write to ArtSEARCH, TCG, 355 Lexington Avenue, New York, NY 10017; or call 212-697-5230.) *ARTnews* magazine also has classifieds.

If you want a job in publishing and you buy a copy of *Publishers Weekly* or *Editor & Publisher*, you'll get an idea of what kinds of jobs are out there. *Architectural Digest* has a section called "AD-At-Large Inside the Design World," full of news on interior design and architecture. What better way is there to learn who the companies are and where to call to find interesting jobs?

There is no substitute for knowing all about a field if you want to break in. Use the trade journals to become an expert in the field that interests you, whether it's publishing, advertising, the stock market, or the arts.

Your specialized résumé sent to an organization in one of these fields, along with a brief letter mentioning that you read about them in a trade journal, should make you look savvy and knowledgeable to a potential employer.

Some journals have job listings and others don't. The best way to find out is to go to a full-service newsstand that sells hundreds of journals. Browse the ones that interest you, and look in the back. If you find ads, buy the journal. If you want more time to evaluate them than a few minutes in a store, check the periodicals section of a good public or college library. You'll find some journals at the newsstands, though, that the libraries don't carry. Check the back issues as well as this month's, for company changes taking place now may have been announced six months ago.

It's worth sending a well-crafted résumé package to several of these leads. You can also be assured that the person placing the ad won't be flooded with bad résumés, as they would from a newspaper listing. Most of the jobs are for managers and above, but now and then I see good job listings for support staff positions with real growth potential.

✎ Read the Rest of the Paper

As for newspapers, I have nothing against them. In fact, they're still a great job resource. Just stay away from the want ads. If you want a job in a corporation, read the business section cover to cover, especially on the day your major newspaper runs the most business news. In fact, don't just read one newspaper. Buy every newspaper in your area, and read all of the business sections. Make a habit of reading *The Wall Street Journal*, and a major regional paper such as *The New York Times, San Francisco Chronicle, Chicago Tribune*, or *The Washington Post*. You'll find job leads in the most unlikely places.

Does a headline say that a major corporation is moving into your town? Then now is the time to call their main office. Say you're from the region they've targeted, and you'd like to speak to one of their recruiters about job opportunities. If the receptionist transfers you to personnel, do what you can with them, and then call back and try to speak to someone who can really talk to you about a job. Don't worry that the recruiters are interested in talking only to big executives. They will have their hands full finding qualified employees at all levels, and you just might meet a particular need. You'll never know until you call.

When one of them asks for your résumé, don't make them wait for the mail to deliver it. Ask for a fax number and send it right away. Job placement expert Robert Half recommends mailing the follow-up hard copy in an 11-by-17 envelope so it doesn't get folded or bent. This will help your résumé stand out visually when it hits an executive's desk.

You may read about an executive being fired in a high-profile corruption scandal. If this happens, you can bet the company will give pink slips to all the employees who participated in the fraud or who sided with the person who got fired. What do you do? Call that company, without mentioning the recent unpleasantness, and say that you are interested in job opportunities there.

Mergers, rises in stock market share value, acquisitions, scandals: all of these common corporate events create upheaval and a need for new employees. These companies will probably never advertise their openings in the want ads, because opportunistic people like you will approach them, making such an effort unnecessary.

✎ Some Simple Homework Will Improve Your Chances

Be sure to study a company before you approach it cold. Go to your public library and search the newspaper abstracts for recent company news. Make sure you know why the company exists, what its major products or services are, and the names of its top executives. Be able to name at least two competitors. Read everything that the newspapers have published on the company in the last two years. If you use a newspaper abstracts database, this can take as little as an hour (ask the reference librarian for instructions). Then rush right in there with a specialized résumé crafted to show the new bosses why you are just the person they're looking for.

I once got a letter from "Doonesbury" cartoonist Garry Trudeau this way. He seldom grants interviews, but he gave one to *The Washington Post* when a play he wrote opened in Washington. In the article, he said he wasn't comfortable with authority, so he didn't even have a personal assistant to handle his mail. I knew that he lived in New York, and at the time I wanted to apply to graduate school at Columbia. So I wrote him a letter, care of his syndicate, offering to work as his assistant part-time while putting myself through grad school.

He wrote back a short note (on "Doonesbury" stationery), thanking me for the suggestion, but assuring me that he meant what he said about being uncomfortable with authority:

> *Belated thanks for your letter. After 16 years, I'm afraid I'm too set in my ways to consider your offer, but I appreciate your writing.*

(The note had a typo in the date.)

I sighed heavily at the crushing blow, and, to get a little sympathy, I showed it to a friend.

"See?" I said. "Garry Trudeau doesn't want me to work for him."

"Hey!" he responded. "That's a real signature! Trudeau doesn't do autographs. How did you get this?"

I shrugged. "It was right there in the 'Style' section of the *Post.*"

There are a million scoops waiting for the person who knows what to do with information. And who knows? In a parallel universe, Trudeau might have said "yes."

Of course, waiting for reclusive celebrities to offer you part-time work in the big city isn't a very practical strategy for making your résumé work for you. While you're busy reading the rest of the newspaper and checking those trade journals, consider the following suggestions. They might land you a job in this lifetime.

✎ Find Good Administrative and Bookkeeping Jobs with Employment Agencies

If you want to be a highly paid administrative assistant or a bookkeeper, then by far the best method for you to use is the fee-paid employment agency.

As I discuss in Chapter 3, many of the top law firms rely on agencies and they are willing to pay generous fees to find the right staff. Corporate secretaries and accounting staff can win big with agencies too, but you'll have to be careful. Many agencies will try to talk you into "going legal," since the money is so good. They'll get much higher commissions if they can pressure you into accepting a law-firm job.

Although this may seem like a good idea at the time, you'll only survive at a law firm if you are a skilled negotiator, if you can tolerate high pressure, and if you don't mind arguing back when necessary. Chapter 3 will help you decide if the legal world is worth the extra money.

Never pay an employment agent a fee, no matter what they promise you. The best agencies charge the employer a fee, not you. You can recognize them in the telephone book because they advertise this prominently. You'll know that your future boss doesn't skimp on money if you search only with fee-paid agencies.

Bookkeepers and accounting clerks who are not CPAs will want to use fee-paid agencies specializing in accounting personnel. Watch out, though. Some of these agencies also handle temporary help. You won't want to get lured into going on too many low-salary temporary assignments. You're a professional, not a temporary, and you risk creating the wrong impression if you let an agency send you to a company as a temp in the beginning.

✎ Isn't Temporary Work the "Growth Field of the 1990s"?

So many job-search pundits are convinced that temp work is the Next Big Thing; they're even devoting whole books to the subject. Temp work is considered a boom field, with more and more professionals accepting work on a temporary basis.

Speaking from experience, temp work seldom leads up the ladder if you're a clerical worker. First, office temporaries aren't "hired" in the same way payroll employees are, so they're never really welcomed into the fold. No one is individually responsible for your initial break-in period at the new company, and you're likely to feel like a permanent outsider. Second, many offices look down on temps, especially clerical ones. Since you have no power in the normal office structure, you may find yourself running errands and doing the work no one else wants.

Miracles do occur, however, and temps do get hired. In fact, my first real job was a summer temporary assignment that lasted. It was an entry-level job, though. If you're just starting out, temping may be a useful resource. If you're taking the next step, however, it could be redundant, and it could unnecessarily send you to lower-level work, reinforcing the wrong set of skills.

If you temp while you job-hunt, do so with a different agency, and don't go to companies where you hope to get a permanent job. Negotiate your time with the agency so that you are free to interview when you need to. There is nothing wrong with telling a temporary agency that you are job hunting and that you must reserve the right to block out time for interviews.

✎ How Employment Agencies Work

You will want to cultivate a good relationship with your employment agent so you can get better jobs down the road. A faithful employment agent can be your best resource if your company becomes an unpleasant place in which to work or if you gain new job skills and want to earn more money elsewhere.

Here are six things you can do that will make employment agents love you:

1. Dress appropriately for the kind of job you want whenever you go to your agent's office. Even if you have to wear the same suit on interviews that you wear to the agent's, show up in your best job-hunting clothes. You may feel like you're living in the same suit, but that's what dry cleaners are for. You'll see people in the agent's office dressed casually. Ignore them: your agent will too.

2. Study for the test. You'll be asked to take a grammar and spelling test. Study a good, basic grammar book, and focus on the mistakes you make most frequently. The test isn't all that difficult, but sometimes nervous applicants do poorly because they weren't expecting it. One trick to knowing what's on the test: take the test with one agency and learn how it works. Then study, and go to another agency to do better on the test. *Caution*: If you don't want to be a secretary, don't take a typing test, even if they insist. Lie and say that you can't type. If the agency tries to force you into taking a test, then the agent is probably going to try to coerce you into secretarial work. Keep looking.

3. If something happens and you're running late, call the agent, not the company. The agent will handle everything for you. Likewise, don't ever call an employer directly while an agent is negotiating for you. Do all of your communicating through your agent.

4. Never talk about job terms (salary, benefits, hours) during an interview. If the company offers you a job, defer to your agent instead of answering yes or no. This is tricky, but you'll come out a big winner if you can withhold your enthusiasm and let your agent negotiate for you. If an employer says, "You're hired," smile, thank her, and say that she'll need to tell your agent directly. You can certainly act pleased if you are, but if you give the whole thing away by saying you want the job, you may weaken your agent's ability to negotiate a good salary.

5. Don't let a boss hire you "around" the agent who got you the interview. Some employers want to avoid paying agency fees, so they'll turn you down for a job, and then call you a day later to offer you a different one. A really unscrupulous boss might even offer you a higher salary to take the job without your agent's knowledge. Just remember, this behavior means the employer is trying to weasel out of an agency fee. He is telling you in neon letters how cheap he is and how unethical. If a boss will do this to an agent, he'll do it to you too.

6. After starting a job, continue to do all of your talking through your agent until the "trial period" is up. Your agent does not get paid a commission until you've been on the job for a certain period of time, perhaps three weeks or a month. During this time, you and the boss have the right to terminate the agreement. Don't, however, just walk into the boss's office and quit. Call your agent and let him handle it.

Okay, that's how to get an agent to adore you. In a perfect world, this will ensure you a warm relationship with your agent. However, there are plenty of peculiar or even unethical agents out there, all mixed in with the good ones so you can't tell the difference until something bad happens. Here are four very important tips for getting pushy, rude, or belligerent agents off your back:

1. Don't sign any "exclusive" contracts. Agents will try to convince you that you can't work with them and work with someone else too. Simply smile, and say you're committed to finding a job with that particular agency and that you hope things will go well. If you do work with two agencies, don't tell them about each other. Set up interviews with all the agencies that look good to you, and then choose carefully on the basis of how they treat you, not on how hard they try to muscle you into a deal.

   Most employers use only one agency, but a few use two or even more. If you realize that two agencies with whom you work want to send you to the same company, decline with one. You'll be able to do this easily, since the agent will have to tell you which company you're interviewing with before you go. This is an unlikely scenario, however. Don't worry about it unless it happens, and remember, this is why you didn't sign any exclusivity agreements!

2. If you're unhappy on a job after you start, give your agent appropriate notice (as stated in your agreement) and leave, even if the agent tries to force you to stay. Beth had one employment agent call her at home and shout at her that she needed her to stay on a certain job after Beth had decided to quit. Well, it's true that the agent wanted her commission, but this was not Beth's problem. The boss was a bully, and Beth didn't find this out until after she started the job. Agents may try to strong-arm you to get you to stay until the trial period is over and they can collect their fee. Do not accept this; it's unfair to you and your employer.

3. Don't get caught up in the whirlwind of job-hunt fever. Some agents will try to rush you onto the market, especially if you have good skills and a professional appearance, and they'll monopolize your time, forcing you to mess up your present job to accommodate a three-interviews-a-day schedule. A forceful agent can intimidate a candidate into taking an unsuitable job. Many of these folks are desperate for big commissions. Ignore their flattery ("we really think you have

something special to offer''), and remember that they use the same canned lines on everyone else.

Use an agent to get a job. Don't get used by an agent. If you need time to think about a job offer or an interview, tell your agent that. If the agent ignores your pleas not to be called at the office, not to be bothered at home, or other restrictions, get away from him or her.

4. If an agent won't leave you alone, use call blocking. This is a marvelous telephone feature available in most states. For a mere dollar or two a month you can block up to twelve phone numbers from your line. When the annoying person calls, they will hear a neutral message saying you are ''not accepting calls at this time.'' What they won't know is that you've only blocked calls from them! Sometimes I think this feature was invented for people who couldn't take ''no'' for an answer.

✎ When Agencies Don't Work, Cold-Calling Might

If you are looking for jobs that agencies don't offer, cold-calling often works best. After all, most agencies earn their commissions from 9-to-5 clerical jobs, period. If you want different hours, or if you want to do other kinds of work, you'll have to be a little more creative.

Cold-calling takes practice. Make a list of your job requirements and then keep trying. Start by calling ten or fifteen companies that aren't very important to you, until you perfect your style. Then work your way up to the good places.

You'll get better at talking to the right people and selling yourself as a first-rate employee. At the first few firms you might not get past the receptionist. By the second ten you'll improve, though. Once you get the hang of speaking to the right person (usually the supervisor of the division where you want to work) and discussing what you can do for their organization that no one else can, you'll start getting interviews.

✎ Why Not Just Call Personnel?

Unfortunately, the personnel office is almost never the best place to get a job. Personnel offices are bureaucracies strangled by red tape and generally out of touch with the needs of the firm as a whole. Besides, they're so used to getting rushed by prospective employees that they've perfected a ''Go directly to hell, do not pass go'' response, and they're liable to use it on you, even if you are the right person for the job. Did you know the personnel department at IBM gets over a million unsolicited résumés a year? Personnel employees will usually advise you to come in, fill out a form, and then go home and wait for the phone to ring. Until when? Christmas? Armageddon?

Instead, talk to office managers for clerical work, and talk to lawyers or executives when you want something at a higher level, like paralegal work.

My friend Meg found a paralegal job this way. She wanted a higher salary than most paralegals (who are usually paid less than administrative assistants), so she started cold-calling. Instead of having to ask for more money than some vague classified ad offered, she found herself in the interesting position of being able to tell firms what her salary expectations were, since her job description didn't yet exist.

Don't forget your protective anonymity, however! I had to convince Meg that the people on the other end of the phone didn't know her and wouldn't remember anyway, so she couldn't possibly embarrass herself. She bravely began, refusing to be discouraged when the first twenty-five law firms said no. The twenty-sixth hired her. She found a job on the first afternoon she tried.

✎ If I Can Get a Computer Date, Why Not a Computer Job?

Lots of people are using the Internet to look for jobs. The good news is, there are plenty of on-line resources for this. The bad news is, most of them are even sleazier than the want ads. Amy Saltzman, writing for *U.S. News & World Report* (March 28, 1994), notes that many Internet offerings can range from mediocre to poor:

> *Online Classifieds . . . only offers a hundred postings or so. But it's an eclectic mix, mostly of nonprofessional*

positions ranging from chauffeurs, nannies and Avon sales reps to male dancers to perform with a Madonna impersonator.

Um, great. Really great. And they said the Internet was progress?

I've worked with the Internet every day for the past five years, and believe me, she's right. They ought to call it Inter-nut. It's loaded with pyramid schemes and once-in-a-lifetime opportunities for suckers who want to earn huge salaries and are willing to invest thousands of dollars of their own money.

Several job-hunt gurus advertise on the Net, and they claim that shy people can explore ''Cyberspace'' (beware of anyone who uses this term) and find their dream job even if they are terrified of actually talking to a live person. This is simply untrue, and it should give you a hint about the quality of the free advice you'll find there. To get a job you have to meet people. There's no anonymous way around this.

Still, it's worth a try as long as you don't break the bank. You can join Prodigy, America Online, CompuServe, GEnie, The Well, BIX, or other services which have such resources, and spend hours poking around in their job-search areas. Watch out, though, if you're paying for on-line time, because this can get mighty expensive, and end up costing you as much as a professional job search with all the trimmings. George used a major computer service one weekend and spent many fruitless hours exploring the ads. He was stunned to later receive a credit-card bill of over $200!

If you are a college student, call your school's computer center and find out how to use the Internet there. Nearly all colleges and universities give their students free Internet accounts. You can also find Internet services at some public libraries and major newspapers.

What will you find on the Internet? In many ways, you'll discover a lower-rent version of what you'd find in the newspaper. Agencies are all over the Internet like flies, and they're using the same tactics they use in the newspaper, just on an international level. When I saw three consecutive ads for legal secretaries in downtown Los Angeles, with three different types of firms, at three different salary levels, I smelled an agent. Sure enough, each of these three ads outlined slightly different qualifications and referred the job hunter to an L.A.-based agency. They were fronts for the agency itself. Although they might have represented real types of jobs, they weren't actual job listings. They were fishing lures. This is not illegal or even terribly unethical. It is, however, tiresome and misleading, since it makes a database appear to have many more opportunities than it actually does.

These resources are also filled with what Internet users call spam. Spam (whether used as a noun or as a verb, as in "spamming the Net") is an Internet term for junk mail: the same message posted everywhere, even where it doesn't belong. Spam can also refer to repeats of the same ad to the same list or group. The spammer wants to ensure that the message gets out, and he doesn't care whose time he wastes or whose resources he clogs up in doing so. I found the same job listings cross-referenced again and again. You can bet that if a newspaper ad generates too many résumés for one company to process fairly, an Internet ad spammed everywhere could easily generate many thousands more.

But I'm not saying, "Don't look here." In fact, I think a responsible job search should include a thorough Internet hunt. Don't spend a lot of money on it. Know what you're getting into, and don't go all goosefleshy when you get a hundred job listings from one keyword search. Minus the agency ads and the spam, you may find two or three leads in this bunch.

If you can get to the World Wide Web, you can type the following command lines in at the main prompt and find listings nationwide—in some cases even worldwide:

http://www.occ.com/occ/	The Internet's Online Career Center
http://www.occ.com/occ/NBEW/NBEW01.html	National Business Employment Weekly (through the Online Career Center)
http://www.careermosaic.com/	Career Mosaic "Jobs Offered" Database
http://www.jobquest.com/	America's Help Wanted!

http://www.resume.net	InterMarket
http://esc.state.nc.us/	North Carolina Employment Security Commission

Both the Online Career Center and Career Mosaic index the Internet's major job listings. You can search them by job title, keyword, city, state, or country.

If you don't have access to the World Wide Web and you still want to search for jobs, try Usenet newsgroups. Usenet is a reasonably democratic subset of the Internet that runs thousands of newsgroups with names like rec.arts.movies and soc.culture.italian. Once you have an Internet connection, you can join these discussion groups for free, and read the postings there to learn about local opportunities.

Here are some popular Usenet job-search groups to get you started. If one of them seems redundant, it's because newsgroups are set up on a surprisingly informal basis. Remember that these are all indexed by the World Wide Web resources above, so if you have access to the Web, use that first:

ba.jobs.contract San Francisco Bay Area contract jobs
ba.jobs.misc General discussion
ba.jobs.offered San Francisco Bay Area job postings
bionet.jobs Scientific jobs
biz.jobs.offered
biz.marketplace
biz.marketplace.international
can.jobs Canada
dc.jobs Washington, D.C.
ie.jobs
kw.jobs Jobs in Kitchener-Waterloo region, Canada
la.jobs Los Angeles
misc.jobs
misc.jobs.contract Discussions about contract labor
misc.jobs.misc General job discussion
msen.jobs.resumes.occ Online Career Center job information newsgroup
ont.jobs Jobs in Ontario, Canada
relcom.commerce.jobs
su.jobs Stanford University, Palo Alto, CA
tor.jobs Jobs in Toronto, Canada
tx.jobs Jobs in Texas
uk.jobs Jobs in the U.K.
uk.jobs.d Discussion group for U.K. jobs
uk.jobs.offered Jobs offered in the U.K.
uk.jobs.wanted Jobs wanted in the U.K.
umn.cs.jobs Computer Science jobs at the University of Minnesota

misc.jobs.offered
misc.jobs.offered.entry Entry-level positions only
misc.jobs.resumes Post your résumé here (*warning:* I don't recommend this. You never know if your boss reads the group!)
umn.general.jobs General jobs at the University of Minnesota
us.jobs United States
us.jobs.contract U.S. contract jobs

If you've never used the Internet before and you'd like to try, consult Chapter 7 for a list of books to get you started.

Local computer bulletin board services (BBSs) also have listings, although many of these are rapidly being replaced by World Wide Web sites. A computer BBS is run by an individual with at-home resources, and you can dial into it with your modem.

Harold Lemon maintains ''Harry's Job Search BBS List,'' with great information on finding BBSs nationwide. This information changes too often to list in a book, however. If you want the latest full list, send E-mail to hotlist@jobnet.com, or call the Online Opportunities BBS at 610-873-7170. If neither of these methods works for you (they should), send E-mail to hlemon@netcom.com and ask for the latest version. Send $5 to the address he provides if you want a list mailed to you or someone else. George Smith's Executive Connection also offers a BBS list. Send an E-mail message to employtext@execon.metronet.com, and ask for an updated copy by E-mail. Meanwhile, here are some others you might want to try:

Jobs USA	205-339-7823
National DP Jobs	212-727-9046
Office of Personnel Management, Philadelphia	215-580-2216
JobFinder BBS	315-428-3373

✎ Networking: Tell Him Louie Sent Ya!

Networking got a bad name in the 1980s and deservedly so. When I think of networking, I think of an anxious yuppie with a bow clipped in her hair, passing out business cards at a cocktail party and collecting cards of her own. Either that or I see Leisure-Suit Larry pointing his finger like a gun at people and saying, ''Buddy, *you* are a heavy hitter! Did anyone ever tell you that? And *I* need a job. So let's grab lunch and talk career-a-mundo.''

Although there's nothing wrong with consulting everyone you know about possible openings at their companies, this can accidentally lead to a "bad fit" by putting people in the uncomfortable position of finding you something rather than the right thing.

A friend of mine encountered this during a long period of unemployment. Her uncle found her a job with the federal government. He pressured her to take it since she'd been job hunting for so long, and he hinted that she'd be ungrateful if she refused and made him "look bad." Although his efforts on her behalf were generous, he went too far. Also, she was miserable in the position simply because it wasn't hers. Someone handed it to her, and it never did feel right. Plus, everyone in management knew that she got the job through contacts, over the heads of other qualified applicants. She never got promoted.

Networked jobs are often like borrowed shoes. For someone else they might be just the thing, but if they pinch, they'll pinch every day until you find something better to do.

Sometimes people who help you find jobs get offended if you don't like the jobs they turn up. "I gave Sarah three perfectly good leads," one woman complained, "and she didn't call any of them." What she didn't say is that she gave Sarah the names of three men who needed secretaries. Sarah was already a secretary. The only good lead the complainer knew about was a management interview she went on herself.

Then there's also the sticky problem of who gets "first dibs" on good leads. Why would anyone hand you a great job if they could take it themselves or pass the job along to someone who can do them a favor in return? It's the rare soul who does something out of simple goodwill.

You have to offer them an incentive. My personal favorite is cash.

✎ Do What the Realtors Do: Offer a Finder's Fee

Real estate professionals have offered finder's fees for years to get new house listings. I borrowed this idea, and I've gotten some of my best jobs, rental houses, and cars this way.

Sneaky? Yes. It also works.

First, you identify what you want to do. Be creative. Read the next chapter and try for something you'd really love. Then get the word out that you will offer a finder's fee to the person who leads you to a permanent job, and resolve to actually pay the fee (you only have to pay if you get the job). I have always succeeded with $175, but I've heard of finder's fees as high as a month's salary. Start the negotiations with a number that you feel comfortable with and see if it works. If you need to, gradually offer more.

Don't put yourself at risk by using your full name. Finder's fees work, but they can also attract unwanted attention from troublemakers. Only use your first name, or even a pseudonym, and give only your telephone number or an E-mail address. Then make up a flier similar to the one below:

> *Do you know of a great full-time job in the arts? Earn a FINDER'S FEE by telling me about it! I'll pay $175 to the person who can lead me to a full-time, permanent job at an arts organization, preferably in the main office. Art galleries or book publishing companies are especially welcome, but I will consider positions working for museums, theatrical groups, and similar places. Call Demetrius, 919-555-9999.*

One woman made her notice more effective by printing it on half of a self-addressed, postage-paid card. All someone had to do was write the job information on the bottom half of the card, where she left space, and drop the card in a mailbox.

Don't get caught passing out this flier or card at random. You'll only appear desperate, and your future interviewers might see you. Instead, mail the notice to arts organizations, or wherever it is you're trying to break in. Receptionists and secretaries will be the first ones to open the mail, and they usually want extra cash. If they hear of anything in their companies they may pass those tips on to you. If they do, and the job comes through, pay that fee. Anything less is stealing.

Once you get a lead, pursue it quickly, but don't say you found out about it through a finder's fee scheme. You can cold-call the executive and pretend that you've been calling many people, or you can ask someone in the firm to negotiate a formal introduction.

Of course, you'll get some weird, useless leads from this. You are under no obligation to follow them up. However, you are also likely to find out about wonderful jobs from people who know about them and either aren't qualified to apply or have too many qualifications. Many folks who already hold a job and are being relocated or promoted will tell you about the position before it is ever advertised.

A word of warning, however. Paying a fee to an employer to hire you is one form of an illegal kickback. Don't ever pay a finder's fee to someone for hiring you, and don't work for them either. Someone who doesn't understand the unethical aspects of accepting money from a potential employee will be a problematic boss in other ways as well.

✎ Special Resources for Single Parents and Older Adults

If you're a single parent, you might be saying, "Great. Just great. When am I supposed to find the time to do all this creative, positive-thinking stuff?"

Single parents of either sex have a tough time holding down a job, let alone looking for something better. When I went looking for good resources for single parents, I mostly found a lot of disconnected numbers, thanks to cuts in federal funding.

The Department of Labor's Work and Family Clearinghouse can give you information on job sharing, maternity leave, child care, and other important issues. Call 800-827-5335. If you happen to live in Columbus, Ohio, the Center for New Directions might be able to help. They run More Options for Mothers who are Single (MOMS), a twelve-week program on Saturday mornings that helps you explore new job opportunities. Even if you don't live in Columbus, you can call Sharon Sachs, the executive director, and see if she knows of special programs in your state (614-227-5331). Like all service organizations, MOMS is on a limited budget. Don't expect anyone to return your long-distance call; you may want to offer to contribute to the cause.

Older people can also feel stuck in dead-end clerical jobs. Several older people (especially women) I spoke to said they wished they'd had the same opportunities younger folks enjoy now. Two of them were over a decade away from retirement, but they were keeping their dull jobs out of fear of losing that security. If this sounds like you, the American Association of Retired

Persons can help you escape your rut. They offer a job-hunting seminar called AARP Works which they describe as useful for any midlife or older person thinking about changing careers or reentering the job force. Call the Washington, D.C. office, 202-434-2100. Someone will refer you to the area office in your state that oversees your local AARP Works group. You can also try calling Forty Plus, also in Washington (202-387-1582).

Whatever you do, don't let age discrimination or your own frustration keep you from exploring job opportunities, especially if you have years to go until you can retire.

> *SALESWOMEN under 40 years of age for our Retail Cigar Departments in fine Hotels in Chicago and thru-out the United States. Fascinating work: dignified surroundings, excellent starting salary, insurance and hospitalization plan. Must be a high school graduate. Submit photo with application.*
>
> *Up to $4,200 starting salary to man age 28 to 45 who wants a lifetime career. No travel. Should be married, well educated, must be well known in your community.*
>
> *(Both from* The Des Moines Register, *September 2, 1951.)*

✎ Multiple, Specific Résumés Will Get You Better Jobs

The résumé problem especially frustrated Ann, who had fifteen years of administrative assistant work behind her. Not only was she worried about what "they" would think of her past, she was terrified that her résumé would ruin any chance she had of changing careers. She wanted a sales representative position, and now she struggled to craft a résumé proving she could successfully handle sales accounts.

We both knew she could do the job. Even though her background was primarily secretarial, she had been an office manager in a large law firm, and most recently she had worked as a realtor. However, the real estate market in northern Virginia took a nosedive right after she started, so she limped along on rental commissions. To supplement her family's income she took a dull, part-time typing-and-filing job that just paid the bills. Now she had the chance to use her selling skills in business—something she was eager to do—and she felt that her past would hinder her.

I asked Ann to list all the jobs, with dates and work accomplished, on a sheet of paper. Then I gave her titles for everything she did according to her actual achievements. When I finished adjusting her résumé, the results startled both of us. In fifteen years, Ann had increased her duties and responsibilities to the point where she was smoothly running most of the offices in which she worked. She hired and managed employees, she did the bookkeeping and even handled complicated tax documents, and she had strong sales experience.

We used a functional résumé format so we wouldn't have to mention the words "secretary" and "office manager," and we eliminated any references to typing speeds and copiers. We graduated Ann to realtor as soon as she got her license.

We also eliminated the short-term jobs that she took during the real estate years, since they weren't important, and we made a big fuss over her volunteer position at a public radio station which gave her lots of responsibility and visibility, and taught her important fund-raising skills. Then we eliminated months, so that employment dates simply read 1981–1985 or 1991–1995.

Ann now looked like a woman with a growing career. So what if she'd made some detours along the way? With a little ironing, her record appeared seamless.

Now, for a special touch, we added the names, addresses, and phone numbers of three former employers who would vouch for her brains and determination. By putting her references at the end of the résumé (instead of using the weaker line "available upon request"), Ann showed that she was proud of her work history.

Think of your past as a detailed painting—a landscape as large as a museum wall. Now, let's say you have under five minutes to show someone that landscape, because that's a more than generous estimate of how long the typical executive will spend reading your résumé before she gets to the hiring stage. There's no time to talk about every detail in a picture that big. You can't possibly say everything about your life in that small amount of time.

Instead, you have to select, carefully, what you want someone to remember. What will you point out first? Second? Third? What would you rather not mention? You can't lie about what's in the picture, but you can guide employers to the things you want them to think about.

✎ Ann Liked Her First Résumé So Much, We Made Another

Working people learn—quickly—that you need several résumés, but most guides act as though you'll be writing only one. Plan on making a specialized résumé for each type of job you want. We made two different résumés for Ann. One highlighted her sales experience in real estate plus her contact with clients. It was tailor-made for the sales job she wanted. Her second résumé used the same progressive format, but it highlighted management skills. She used this to apply for several beginning management positions around town.

Don't stop at two either. Every time you see a new job that is completely different from the other work for which you've applied, take the few hours necessary to make a special résumé for it.

✎ Farewell to the One-Page Wonder

Get rid of the one-page résumé concept. This was the standard advice for college kids years ago, and it stuck. Now writers cite "evidence" that managers read only the first page and never go on. I don't believe it. Managers may glance at most résumés on the first go-round until they have a short list of qualified candidates, but then they read the good ones, sometimes in close detail.

Most interviewers aren't stupid. If you're forty-one years old, they know that you've done a few things in your full life and that you'll need a couple of pages to describe them. Use as many pages as you need in your first draft, and then pare down the résumé to only the best highlights for each version that you're going to show to certain employers.

If you end up with one comfortable page, fine. There's nothing wrong with a one-page résumé. Don't, however, perform a typesetting miracle to try to cram everything on one page if you need more. I'd be suspicious of a business résumé outside of upper management that went over two or three pages, but most working adults earn a second page of résumé space pretty quickly, and quite a few can justify using the top of a third page. Remember that white space can be effective (see the guidebooks listed below for examples); eating up the margins to make everything fit will diminish your résumé's visual impact.

✎ Don't Guess at Your Format. Ask the Pros

When it comes to format, you're going to need some help from a detailed style book. My personal favorite is Yana Parker's *The Damn Good Résumé Guide* (Ten Speed Press, 1989), which I appreciate for its clarity and honesty. It is aimed right at clerical people, and it's easy to read. There are other acceptable ones, though, such as Martin Yates's *Résumés That Knock 'Em Dead* (Bob Adams, Inc., 1993), and *The Smart Woman's Guide to Résumés and Job Hunting* by Julie Adair King and Betsy Sheldon (Career Press, 1993).

There are also many terrible ones, so watch out. Some of the most "respected" are poorly written, with just plain bad advice. You'll do best to start with the ones I've mentioned here.

Don't let the printed examples intimidate you. My biggest complaint with résumé books is their tendency to use examples where none of the applicants seems to need any help finding work. One book (not mentioned here) had samples only from people who went to Ivy League universities.

In many cases, though, the samples look intimidating simply because they are so well done. Once you rewrite your résumé according to a good guidebook's rules, you may be surprised at how much better you end up looking on paper.

Whatever you do, don't design your own résumé without consulting a guide. Writing a résumé is like putting out a press release. Nobody wants to have to work hard at figuring out your special format. If your résumé is weird, the typical office person will just throw it away. A good résumé should be transparent: it should be so clear that the person reading it gets a picture of you instead of focusing on your style.

✎ The Never-Evers

Despite what you read in other guides, you should not include any of the following information on your résumé:

1. Children, or any time off you took to raise them. They are none of your boss's business. As I pointed out in Chapter 2, bosses often view their employees' children as an unnecessary intrusion on company time. The best policy is simply not to discuss them. If you took some years off to raise children, fill in this gap with volunteer work and other important things you did. If you were the president of the PTA or the director of a school play, say so.

   Your style here can make a big difference. I've seen résumés that almost apologized for child rearing, while others proudly pointed to accomplishments during this valuable time. Use years to meld the time together, such as "1981–1984: Director, *Porgy and Bess, Oklahoma!* Chadsworth Elementary School, Tarsis, South Carolina; President, Chadsworth PTA; Reader for Books-on-Tape, Commonwealth Public Library," and a description of specific duties following each.

2. Age, height, weight, hair color. If the old-fashioned ads in this chapter aren't enough to convince you, remind yourself that discrimination on the basis of these unimportant characteristics is illegal. And no photographs, please, unless you're applying to be an actor.

> *TALL MEN: For some inexplicable reason the most successful $15,000 per year plus career education counselors we have been able to develop have all been six feet tall and over. WE NOW PLAN TO ADD TWO TALL MEN TO OUR PRESENT STAFF—QUALIFICATIONS ARE:*
>
> *1. Height: 6' and over*
> *2. Age: 28 and up*
> *3. Married with children*
> *4. Sole support of family*
> *5. Mature personality*
> *6. Desire to help others*
>
> (*The Kansas City Star*, February 26, 1967.)

3. Nationality or religion, unless it *really* matters. If you want to work at the Tunisian Embassy, you can say you are Tunisian, and you can always list languages spoken. Otherwise, no.

4. Marital status. They'll only use this against you, one way or the other.

5. Unemployment status. Let the future employer assume you're working, even if you're not. Don't lie about it, but certainly act natural if the interviewer assumes the best. You'll be more attractive to an employer if she thinks you already have a job.

If an interviewer presses this point and you have to tell, you can say something like "Oh, I'm sorry. I thought we'd mentioned I wasn't working now." State your reasons for leaving the job honestly and simply, and then move on to other topics. Be careful not to lie about this on your résumé, but don't state it outright either. Using years instead of months will make your résumé honest without announcing that you're not there any longer.

6. Getting fired. My reasons for eliminating this are a bit more complicated than the others. Time and again, job-search "experts" advise readers to tell all about their troubled pasts. "Honesty is the best policy," counseled one, "so be sure to own up to it if you were fired. Your prospective boss will appreciate your candor." Right. He'll thank you for giving him a good reason to move on to the next applicant.

If you get fired, people may sympathize, but they'll also secretly worry that your bad luck is somehow contagious. Bosses will assume that the firing was your fault. To prevent this, eliminate the following from your vocabulary forever:

I declared bankruptcy.
I was fired.
I flunked out of school.
I'm in a 12-step program.
I can't find a job.

These phrases and others like them turn people off. Once you stop mentioning your missteps and your woes, you'll be surprised how much more attractive you'll be to others and to potential bosses. You may confidently say that you left a previous job. You do not need to say that you had help finding the door.

7. Your arrest record. Tell your minister, not your boss. Don't check "yes" on a standard application if your infraction was minor or happened a long time ago. Felonies are different, however. If you have a serious crime or a prison record in your past, seek professional career counseling. And remember, if you've served your time, you've paid your debt. Avoid professions related to the felony (no convicted child molesters around children, please, or check forgers in banks), and then keep your past to yourself.

✎ Cover Letters? They're Not as Crucial as You Thought

Most clerical cover letters backfire, simply because they sound, well, clerical. Some people are born writers, and if you're one of those, then go ahead and write one. However, if you don't feel like Hemingway, it's best to skip this routine.

Cover letters are necessary only when someone can't see you in person. Since you're not going to be wasting your time sending out résumés in reply to newspaper ads, you've just eliminated much of the need for cover letters anyway.

Still, you'll have to put something on top of your résumé when mailing it somewhere. When you *must* use a cover letter, keep it as short as possible. Eliminate every filler phrase you can, especially boilerplate lines like "Enclosed please find," and "Please feel free to call me." Address the letter to a person whose name you have obtained by calling the receptionist and asking. Then write something like

> *I noticed in* The Wall Street Journal *(April 7, 1996) that your company will be expanding into the Southeast region, with a central office in Raleigh, North Carolina. I live in Chapel Hill, just a few miles away. The enclosed résumé presents my qualifications for customer service positions.*

That's it. Say "Sincerely yours" and get out of there. This brief, to-the-point letter will make you stand out in a crowd, since everyone else's will gush on about how "honored" they'd be to interview at the Bullwinkle Company and how much they respect its reputation. Yours will say, "Here I am, have a look."

After you're finished, try to show it to one or two people who hold professional positions similar to that of the person who will interview you. One way to find them is to call people you know from former jobs and fax them a copy of the letter for comment. Get their opinions. After all, the letter has to sound like who you *want* to be, not necessarily who you've been up until now.

Rather than trying to impress employers with unusual résumé formats and "original" cover letters, concentrate on presenting a professional, visually appealing package that makes people think more highly of you. Use 100 percent cotton bond paper and print your résumé carefully. Use a laser printer with a fresh cartridge.

Don't send photocopies. Although Jacqueline Kennedy Onassis was known for her lovely, light blue stationery, the modern office has not yet progressed to the point where colors other than white, cream, or a very muted oyster gray are acceptable.

If you are following your bliss and applying for jobs in the theater, the arts, or other creative places, you'll have room for a little individualism, especially in your choice of paper color. But beware: what's charming to you might seem tacky to a boss.

Still, I've seen some wonderful résumés on top-quality recycled paper, some of which even have a tiny symbol and a note to that effect on the bottom. The key here is to know your audience. You can try the recycled-paper résumé for conservation organizations, university departments, and politically liberal businesses. For law firms, Fortune 500 companies, and other conservative places, however, I'd stay with 100 percent cotton bond.

Now that you've embraced your anonymity and written a couple of résumés reflecting who you're *becoming* instead of who you *were*, you can use the better-than-want-ads methods above to identify available jobs.

✎ But What If I Still Want to Get on That Train Going "Anywhere"?

Remember the woman in Crystal City who longed to jump on the next express for somewhere better? She needed more than a new résumé and some job-search techniques. She needed direction.

You can't just want out of your present job. You have to have somewhere to go. So take your new, specialized résumés and walk this way. The next chapter is all about direction, whether up the corporate ladder or back into school.

PREPARING FOR TAKE-OFF: How to Get Out If You Want *Out*

PHOTO: JOAN MARCUS

The *Five Lesbian Brothers* in *''The Secretaries''*

The evil stepsisters treated Cinderella like a drudge, but she was really a princess. Everybody picked on young Arthur, until he pulled the sword from the stone and became king. The whole family treated Beauty like a slave, but the Beast shared his castle with her.

What? You don't believe in fairy tales? Well then, listen to this: A Boston law firm's nuclear energy division thought Christine was best suited to typing and washing dishes, yet she finished college at night and went on to graduate school at Boston University. Dave was a legal assistant who couldn't get basic respect, let alone a promotion, until he changed firms and refused to run errands. When he did, he earned a raise *and* a promotion in six months. The staff at a Washington, D.C., news agency ignored Helen and expected her to train her own supervisors. Then a national newspaper began running her features, and her colleagues suddenly started looking at her rather than through her. These three all made it. You can too.

But what should you walk toward? Where will you go? That's what this chapter is all about: direction. There are many choices for you. Most of them are better than what you're doing now. They may not take you to the top of a company, but they will get you into the promotional line. After that, the rest is up to you.

Despite what anyone may tell you at your office, you're as smart as your employers. If you weren't, you wouldn't be working for them. People hire secretaries and clerks who make them look good, who work hard and pour lots of "sweat equity" into improving the boss's career. If you're one of those workers, congratulations: you must be intelligent and capable.

But how do you get anyone to see this? How do you make it count? How do you free yourself from the put-downs, the personal errands, and the sideways mobility that characterize your daily life? How do you cash in on smarts that have been putting money in other people's pockets for years?

First, forget what conventional wisdom tells you. People will try to convince you that you can "eventually" work your way out of a secretarial position. They'll say that you can do this by anticipating your boss's needs or by acting more like an executive.

The truth is, you'll sooner dig your way to China.

Secretaries and receptionists don't get promoted because, like

Cinderella, they are in service-oriented positions that are getting increasingly harder to fill. Bosses? They're the wicked stepsisters and brothers, all too used to having a scullery drudge to wait on them. If you slave away trying to please them, hoping for promotion, they'll dump more and more work on you until you're swamped. Then they'll promote someone else.

Think about it. Can you imagine the stepsisters actually inviting Cinderella to a business lunch or for golf at the country club? Or saying, "Take off that silly apron, you're one of us now"? Well, your bosses are the same way. Once they've seen you in a servile job, they're not going to change their opinion of you just because you work harder. Even when you excel at your duties, or at management tasks, your bosses will just thank you and forget you. If they thank you at all.

I've howled with laughter at books which tell readers to "learn to be a super secretary" or "believe in yourself and others will too." You can believe in yourself. You can also believe in the Easter Bunny. It won't change the fact that bosses dump on secretaries and refuse to promote them. Oh, you'll read crazy things. Books will suggest that you give others credit for your good ideas, so you'll look more like a team player. They'll have you running around in dark blue suits acting like a manager. They'll tell you to offer sales strategies to make yourself look more serious to your boss. All you'll get out of this is a clear shot at office manager, the mother of all secretaries.

✎ Why Being an Office Manager Is Not the Answer

Many firms suggest that assistants and secretaries can one day be promoted to office manager. I don't consider the office manager position a real promotion, because the word "promotion" implies continued upward mobility. Once you're promoted to office manager, there's nowhere to go from there. Office managers are in charge of the clerical staff, it's true, but they aren't expected to move on in the management ranks. They're hired to stay put. When there's a management meeting in a corporation, office managers are usually not invited. If they are invited, it is in a second-class capacity and frequently just for show.

Office managers do a job that's rather schizophrenic. They're supposed to communicate well with administrative assistants, presumably because they once were assistants themselves. But they are also expected to perform as managers, even though nothing about their former jobs taught them to be managers. Stuck in the middle between assistants and management, they have lots of responsibility but no real power. Most office managers, for instance, can't make their own hiring and firing decisions. All they can do is carry out senior management's orders. However, they are expected to absorb the blame for the firing, just as though it was their idea.

By giving office managers the illusion that they have been promoted, executives take care of two nasty little jobs with one stroke. First, they appease the "super secretary" who seeks promotion. By making her an office manager, they shut her up, since they have no plans to promote her to anything else. Second, they create a new workhorse to handle the unpleasant tasks that no real managers want to bother with: ordering office supplies, teaching assistants to do their jobs, moving the office to new spaces, and other detail-riddled tasks.

Being an office manager is also an emotional drain. Office managers frequently have to mediate outbursts from assistants *and* from executives, but they are never allowed to show their own anger or frustration. Instead, they are supposed to act cool and professional at all times. Like administrative assistants, office managers don the "perma-grin" of the perpetual peacemaker and soothe every ripple in the corporate waters, trying valiantly to please everyone. Many office managers bully the secretarial staff in private when this "smile, ladies" rule becomes too much.

And rewards? What rewards? Office managers are expected to work long hours, but they earn no overtime, again under the illusion they are "management." They make only about $5,000 per year more than administrative assistants, but they perform the duties of bookkeepers, personnel departments, labor relations, and galley slaves. When they don the hangman's hood and handle another firing, executives pat themselves on the back for finding such a low-priced alternative to unpleasant confrontation.

✎ Where's the Glass Ceiling? You're Standing Right Under It

The office manager position is poised right at the "glass ceiling" you've heard so much about: that invisible barrier that keeps women and minorities from moving into corporate management.

Where did you think that ceiling was anyway? The thickest part is right over the clerical staff! According to the Labor Department, once women and minorities fight their way into management, they are usually promoted at the same rate as white males. Apparently, there's much more of a battle getting onto a management track than there is riding it to the top. Most people wash out at the bottom, never getting their first opportunity for a serious promotion with a future.

In the lower ranks, men are promoted between 33 and 40 percent more often than women. Companies like WordPerfect, Marriott International, and Georgia Power were 1994's biggest offenders in this category. They had to pay over $600,000 to women and minorities after failing the Labor Department's glass ceiling review. At the same time, McDonald's, Pitney-Bowes, and Canada's Bank of Montreal won "glass ceiling awards" for promoting women and minorities aggressively.

Once you see that the glass ceiling is over you, you'll reconsider that career track leading to office manager. Instead, you can work around this pseudo-promotion trap and land a job that will take you somewhere. Does this sound good? Well, it is good, and a lot of fun, but you'll have to be daring. You can't just wait for someone to notice you. This kind of maneuver requires some calculated risk on your part.

Notice that word—"calculated." I'm not asking you to go without steady employment. I'm merely asking you to start thinking like another type of person. Soon you'll start acting like one.

✎ Come Out, Come Out, Wherever You Are

There's a wonderful, old "Peanuts" cartoon from back when Lucy was still in a crib. She shouted, "I want out! I want out!" and nobody heard her. Finally, she climbed up the sides of the crib and hopped onto the floor. She wandered down the hall shouting, "I want out!" Then she stopped, looked around her, and opened her eyes wide. "Hey," she said, "I *am* out."

And so it is with administrative assistant, receptionist, or clerical work. You can shout, "I want out," until you're hoarse, but no one will hear you. They're not listening. Your bosses and managers are all worrying about their own careers, and they haven't the slightest interest in your upward mobility. If you try simply walking away, however, you'll be surprised. It's not that hard to leave. In fact, all you have to do is start walking *toward* something better, and you can leave your typing woes behind.

If you haven't gone to college, or if you're not ready to return yet, then an easily attainable and highly marketable skill is your best bet for getting ahead quickly. Here are five of my personal favorites:

- Software specializations
- Internet ability
- Customer service on a 1-800 line
- Copier repair
- Paralegal work, if you do plan to go on to college or law school

Here's a rundown on why these are great jobs for people who want to escape the clerical dungeon, along with instructions for how to get them.

✎ Knowing Something They Don't Know: Your Life as a Software Guru

Back in 1906 when Fiorello La Guardia started in stenography, shorthand was specialized knowledge. Only an elite few knew it, and La Guardia's training made him marketable. Now, however, it will simply brand you as an administrative assistant. Today's most flexible specialized office skill is the ability to manipulate computer software. If you master one of the new software packages, you'll have knowledge that companies will gladly pay you for.

Notice, however, that I did not say "learn computer programming." Instead, learn the *results* of programming. Adobe, Claris, Apple, Microsoft, IBM, Corel, and other corporations constantly race each other to produce new software that every executive "has" to have. But managers increasingly lack the time to sit down and learn the latest programs or new releases of older software. Many of them are justifiably worried about losing that all-important edge. They fear that the technological world is leaving them behind.

This is where you come in. If you master one of the popular new software packages, you'll be mighty valuable to one of these executives. And guess what. You won't be typing and filing for a living anymore. Instead, by knowing something the boss doesn't, you'll find yourself qualified for positions with more independence and flexibility.

Watch out for the word-processing trap, however. Master word-processing software only for your own use. If you approach companies as a software guru, but your specialty is WordPerfect for Windows or Microsoft Word, they'll just throw you back in the typing pool. Keep your word-processing knowledge a secret from prospective employers. You'll need it for your own convenience, but advertising advanced word-processing skills may hurt rather than help you. Instead, learn database managers, spreadsheets, graphics, or desktop publishing and emphasize your knowledge of them.

Which software should you learn? It varies year by year, and packages may differ depending upon the professional fields that interest you. One hint: read the Sunday want ads. You'll see some software names repeated often: "Access experience a plus" or "Must be able to use FoxPro and desktop publishing." Community colleges, technical institutes, and short-course schools usually know the most popular software. Call them and ask for suggestions.

Don't bother calling computer stores. They'll try to convince you that what they're selling is what the industry is using. Stick with the applications that you see most often in the papers.

Make sure that you learn the kind of computer software that will put you in departments you find interesting. Although software updates are frequent, businesses are notorious for hanging on to favorite software even when the computer industry moves ahead. The "best" software isn't always the most popular among executives.

This list of popular software packages may give you an idea of what's out there. Remember, though, it's not exhaustive. Check the want ads in your town to find out which software is in widest use.

Databases	*Spreadsheets*	*Graphics/Desktop Publishers*
Access	Excel	Adobe Illustrator
Approach	Lotus 1-2-3	Aldus FreeHand
Dbase	Quattro Pro	Canvas
FileMaker Pro		Corel DRAW
FoxPro		Aldus PageMaker
Paradox		Professional Draw
		QuarkXPress
		Ventura Publisher

Of course, you don't have to choose just one. In fact, you'll be better off knowing more than one. It gets easier as you go, because so many software packages work the same way. Many databases "think alike," as do many graphics packages and spreadsheets. They're not identical, but they follow many of the same rules. You won't have to work as hard to learn a second one as you did learning the first.

For instance, if you go to all the trouble of learning Access, you might want to make yourself a double threat by learning FoxPro as well. Also, companies frequently upgrade to a hot new software package or switch from one program to another. Knowing more than one will enhance your chances of getting a promotion if they change over to a new system. Likewise, landing a job with one software skill and then learning another on the job is the best way to keep your edge.

Paige worked as a secretary for an accounting firm and learned Lotus 1-2-3 and Quattro Pro on the job. Then she interviewed with other firms as a software specialist. An employment agent sent her to an accounting firm that used only Excel. At first she thought they wouldn't hire her, but (to her surprise) the manager did choose her. After all, he reasoned, she'd already learned two important software packages. How long could it possibly take for her to master a third one? The manager was right. Paige learned the new software in less than three weeks and adapted perfectly to the job.

Always think about your own interests when deciding what the market "wants." If you're talented with numbers, learn spreadsheets, but don't force yourself just because someone told you there were jobs in accounting. Perhaps you're more art-oriented, with a good eye for design. In this case, learn desktop publishing and master a graphics package. If you can't decide, learn a couple of databases, since you don't need special abilities in art or math to run them, and almost every company that uses software applications runs a database.

You can find short courses teaching the newest software in most major cities. If you live or work near a good community college or a technical institute, they should offer computer courses on a regular basis. Insist on classes that offer hands-on experience by letting each student work at an individual computer. There's no point going to a class that can't teach you on up-to-date equipment.

But you may be one of the lucky ones who don't have to go anywhere. If you can do it, why not learn new software on your present job? Your boss may let you use your new skills now, giving you valuable practice while you get paid for it. They don't need to know you plan to take these fine talents elsewhere. Look around your office and see what's available, and volunteer to learn it, even on your own time. Then practice, practice, practice, and take whatever advanced courses local schools offer as well.

Bookstores are your best resource for easy-to-understand instructions. Go to any good bookstore with a computer section and read the latest "how to" manuals. These books are often best-sellers because frequently the documentation included with the software is badly written. Make sure you get the book that goes with the release of the software you're using: a manual for Dbase III+ won't help you much if you're running Dbase IV. Many of these books come with diskettes containing useful tutorials and programs. Use them.

Next, start thinking like a software expert instead of a secretary, a receptionist, or a clerk. Once you spend a few weeks learning a software's secrets, you'll be able to apply for a host of new jobs that have nothing to do with filing and making rancid coffee, but you'll have to act the part. As I suggested in Chapter 6, either take the secretarial work off your résumé or deemphasize it. Insist, if asked, that your typing is slow. Software wizards don't have to type fast. They just have to make the software run. Someone else in the company will do the typing, and you'll get to use the latest equipment to create newsletters, design reports, or balance a client's in-house budget.

✎ Hitch Up Your Mouse and Plow Through the Internet

My friend DeVon is a classic example of someone who gets paid to have fun. He became an Internet expert and found a job exploring on-line resources. Now he spends his days browsing the World Wide Web and using netware to seek out new sales opportunities for his employer. He loves his job, and he's earning more than he ever did as a messenger.

Your office may have already supplied you with an Internet connection. If it did, by all means run (do not walk) to the library and check out Internet resource guides, some of which are listed below. Don't confuse E-mail with the Internet, however. Some offices give their employees access to E-mail without a direct Internet link. Use these books to learn what you have and how to use it.

If you do have free Internet, stay late at night and work weekends learning as much as you can about this resource. If your office doesn't give you Internet, and if you don't subscribe to The Well, BIX, Delphi, Portal, America Online, Prodigy, CompuServe, GEnie, or one of the other Internet services at home, then you'll need classes to get started. Fortunately, nearly every city has them.

Again, your local community college or technical school is your best resource for Internet classes. If you look for community colleges near major universities, you'll get the benefit of the university's computer expertise: university graduate students often teach community college courses to earn extra money, and sometimes the professors do too. In fact, the quality of computer courses at the community colleges can be better than at the big university next door, simply because community colleges are willing to spend more money on business equipment. Also, universities tend to be more interested in teaching theory or programming, whereas the community colleges often emphasize software applications.

If you're really stuck and can't find classes, you can try the central branch of your public library. Many libraries participate in community Internet programs and offer classes, sometimes for free. Even if the classes are clear across town, it's worth the drive. Again, don't go to a computer store except as a last resort. Some computer retailers offer Internet classes, but they are usually overpriced and poorly taught.

Here is a short list of Internet books you might want to read. Most are available at the library. Be sure to get the updated versions! Internet guides are useless after a year or two, since the technology changes quickly.

Brendan P. Kehoe, *Zen and the Art of the Internet* (Prentice-Hall, 1994).
Ed Krol, *The Whole Internet User's Guide & Catalog* (O'Reilly & Associates, 1994).
Mary J. Cronin, *Doing Business on the Internet: How the Electronic Highway Is Transforming American Companies* (Van Nostrand Reinhold, 1994).
Tracy LaQuey, *The Internet Companion: A Beginner's Guide to Global Networking* (Addison-Wesley, 1993).
Mary Ann Pike, *Using Mosaic* (Que, 1994).

If this all looks overwhelming, don't despair. Start with the Kehoe and Krol books; they are well-known beginner's guides that explain the major concepts in easy-to-grasp terms. You can then use them and the other books to get more specific information, learning all about on-line library research, for example, or how to search the World Wide Web. You'll learn to use Mosaic, Netscape, or other software that simplifies Internet access. If you're reading these books a year or more after the publication date, then they may have already been replaced with newer ones. Check for updated versions, or look at January issues of computer magazines such as *Byte* and *Infoworld* for best-of-year book reviews.

Once you're comfortable on the Internet, you'll want to specialize in a few standard applications. When you know not only what "http" means but where it takes you, you're ready to get more specific. One woman helps companies set up "home pages" on the World Wide Web. These introductory screens tell Internet browsers more about an organization. Users can even do their shopping on-line through these pages, selecting the items they want just as if they were using a catalogue. She doesn't do the programming herself, but instead she works with a programmer to design attractive, easy-to-use screens. All she needed was Internet experience and a good eye for design. Another fellow helps the law librarians and paralegals in a large firm use the Internet to do legal research.

I recommend Internet specializations to people who are already comfortable with computers and who are ready to explore further. If you're new to computers, start with basic software classes (discussed in the section above), learn to use E-mail, and then move to the Internet.

✎ Dial 1-800-Get-Promoted

Do you want to get senior management's attention? Then stop taking their shirts to the cleaners. Get a new job that makes money for the company, or saves it. Customer service lines do both of these things. If you answer a 1-800 line and take telephone orders, you'll earn money for the company by using selling techniques to boost profits. If you respond to customer complaints, you will save the company money by calming down dissatisfied customers and keeping them from shopping with competitors.

Many companies offer what look like tedious jobs answering their 1-800 lines, often at night on the second shift. These jobs may seem dull at first, but look closer. They usually involve customer service or telephone orders, both of which are vital to a company's financial profile.

If you get a job working for a company's customer service department on the telephone, you begin to learn who their customers are and what they need. By mastering your telephone technique through weeks and months of dedicated service on these "life lines," you will gain valuable experience that can land you better jobs later on. You'll develop good listening skills, and learn to hear what the customers tell you about the company, rather than what it wants to believe about itself. By understanding what customers are saying, you will be able to make suggestions to top executives that even their managers can't give them! You can take customer service to the next step, suggesting catalogue items you think a customer might like rather than just writing down their order. This kind of "suggestive selling" involves understanding your customers as well as your company. Executives are always on the hunt for people who can appreciate the needs of both.

Good customer service departments save corporations money by solving problems inexpensively and by improving consumer confidence in a product or service. Many CEOs personally monitor what goes on in their customer service departments; if you shine there, you may get senior management's attention.

Now, I'm not talking about telemarketing or customer support, which is discussed below. I'm talking about genuine customer service, where the client calls in, frustrated and angry, and you calm them down by treating them with courtesy and respect. If you smile on the telephone, refuse to lie to your customers or become angry with them, and do whatever you can to help them, or at least explain politely why you can't, they will appreciate it.

How do you know you'll do well? That's easy, for lots of customer service clerks are terrible at what they do. I've had customer service representatives tell me that they "didn't care" whether or not my product complaint got resolved. I've spoken with representatives who could not speak enough English to carry on a telephone conversation. My friend Doug was shouted at by a rep who told him he was a "typical middle-class whiner." Alicia tells of the major credit-card company rep who chided her about late payments (her card payments were current, and she had been late only three times in as many years). I have a box of office supplies sent by a chagrined company after I complained in writing to their president. A customer service rep had refused to accept a mislabeled product back for an exchange with the correct product (I didn't even want a refund!). My usual experience with customer service is mediocre to poor, and I expect very little when I call.

If you prove to be the exception to this dismal rule, your customers will remember you. Eventually, someone will remark how capable you are. When customers compliment you, thank them, and then mention that their comments in writing to the president of the company or your supervisor could do you a world of good. Be sure to keep the president's name and direct address close by your telephone for easy reference, especially if the main offices are in a different city from you (this is frequently the case). Ask them to send a copy of the letter to you as well.

If a customer writes a letter to the president or to your supervisor, you will typically get "called in" for a word of congratulations, and then they'll place the letter in your permanent file. If the customer didn't send you your own copy, ask the supervisor for one: say you'd like a souvenir to post at your work station. Store up these letters for later use. Attach them to your résumé when you apply for a promotion or look for a new job.

Don't confuse customer service with its poor relation, telemarketing. Also known as telephone sales, telemarketing is an aggressive business in which only the pushiest survive. Many telemarketing companies are sweatshops, where employees on late-night shifts earn low wages. Some telemarketing companies pay next to no wages, but instead offer employees the dubious promise of "commissions." Well, 20 percent of nothing is nothing; unless you are a super salesperson, you may not even earn a living. Also, many telemarketers don't really train their employees. They follow the "throw 'em in the deep end and see if they float" school of management. If you struggle, they won't care. They have nothing invested in you in the first place. If you fail, they've got nothing to lose: they'll just fire you and move on. Unless you really want to call someone up during the dinner hour and try to convince them to buy Ginsu knives, invest in No-Load Mutual Funds, or spend a fortune on "free" vacations, stay away from telemarketers.

Customer support is frequently confused with customer service, but they're not the same thing. Customer support professionals help clients use something they've already bought from the company. The customer support department at a telephone company might teach customers how to use their voice mail, for example. Customer support at a computer company helps users figure out their software woes. While these may be interesting jobs, they don't make money or save money as customer service does, so you're less likely to get management's attention. When a company is in financial trouble, it may lay off customer support personnel first, while keeping its customer service people. This happened in 1993, 1994, and 1995 all across America.

✎ Do you Copy? Earn a Much Higher Salary Fixing Copiers

Copier repair is another wide-open field for former secretaries. Seriously. Secretaries become accidental experts at the copy machines anyway, so why not formalize those skills by studying copier repair at night school?

Every year corporations hire men in ties to teach bored secretaries how to clear paper jams. Alan Farnham writes about an

MBA manager who couldn't fix a simple copier problem. He begged his secretary to repair the machine. Says the secretary:

> *I hear him in there, wrestling around with it. . . . Five minutes later he sticks his head in my office with this "mama's widdle boy" expression on his face, pleading with me to fix it.* ("Why Your Copier Isn't Working," *Fortune*, May 4, 1992.)

If executives are willing to beg secretaries to fix copiers, then why not become a real expert and earn a higher hourly wage? Any secretary whose company knows her as the "resident de-jammer" is intelligent enough to learn to fix the Canons, Xeroxes, or Konicas of this world and earn a fine salary doing it. You can find courses at technical institutes. Some corporations also have training programs: if a major copier company has offices in your area, call them and ask about classes.

✎ Life as a Paralegal? I Have Good News and Bad News

If you want to go back to college, or if you're considering law school, paralegal work can be much more flexible than other full-time jobs. Your on-the-job research skills will help you in school, and it can be your best bet if you're trying to find a job that will accommodate a student's ever-changing schedule.

The good news is that paralegals make money for law firms, so they're always in demand. Although a typical law firm in a major city pays a paralegal $15 an hour ($8 to $10 in smaller towns), they usually bill the paralegal's time out to clients at $80 to $90 per hour. Yes, you read that correctly. A typical paralegal who logs twenty hours of billable time in a forty-hour week earns about $30,000 per year and brings in nearly three times that for the law firm.

The further good news is that male and female paralegals make about the same amount of money, according to the *ABA Journal* and the *Chicago Daily Law Bulletin.* If you can do the work, you can earn the pay.

Money, however, is also the bad news. While $30,000 a year may seem generous to you, remember that's in a major city, where the legal secretaries might earn a few thousand a year more. Paralegals in small towns typically make $25,000 per year or less. Lawyers claim not to know why paralegals are routinely underpaid. Some argue that paralegal work is an apprenticeship to the legal profession, and part of the ''salary'' in an apprenticeship is the experience you gain. Still, salaries are significantly lower than they ought to be.

The other bad news is that paralegal work has a poor reputation among certain lawyers. Lawyers consider paralegal work a ''satellite occupation''; the paralegal works for a lawyer, who in turn generates business. Just as in ''*Twins* syndrome,'' where a competent, efficient secretary ends up being the stunted side effect while making her boss a professional powerhouse, paralegals suffer from what I call the Worker Bee Effect. Paralegals are trainees, but they don't immediately further their own careers: they put their time, energy, and creativity into furthering their bosses' careers. This may be why paralegal work is underpaid and underappreciated.

We'll start with the worst attitudes among attorneys and work up from there. When I said the word ''paralegal'' to one lawyer, he responded with ''glorified secretary.'' Many lawyers see paralegals as something a little higher than the typing pool and a little lower than the soles of their expensive shoes.

Not all lawyers agree, however. Another lawyer said, ''I don't expect them to type or buy our sandwiches. That would be like using a Porsche to haul lumber.'' While this isn't exactly a ringing endorsement, it at least shows that some lawyers do value paralegals.

When I said ''paralegal'' to a third lawyer, however, she responded with ''law student.'' And, indeed, firms have traditionally hired law students to do paralegal work. The best firms treat their paralegals like future attorneys, according them a measure of respect. In some of the biggest law firms, paralegals even have offices, and they share their own secretary.

What do paralegals, or legal assistants, as they're also called, do? Effective paralegals make lawyers more efficient by taking over routine paperwork. Paralegals can have quite a bit of client contact, signing correspondence, and establishing their own relationships with outside counsel. The only thing a paralegal can't do is advise or represent a client.

Here's a list of typical paralegal duties. Depending on the size of the firm, paralegals interview clients, draft routine contracts, and cite-check legal briefs. Some collect police reports, employment records, and tax returns to prepare for a case. They also manage the discovery phase of litigation, file papers at court, and summarize depositions. Some paralegals even specialize, developing areas of expertise in criminal law, the entertainment industry, and intellectual property, to name only a few. Many paralegals have their eyes on law school.

You can consider the paralegal position a steppingstone between secretarial work and the professional world. Paralegals have better jobs than secretaries, for a number of reasons. First, paralegals develop promotable abilities. They hone their independent thinking, research skills, organizational powers, and writing styles every day. Paralegals research cases and write about them. These skills are integral to higher-level jobs, and you'll never master them if you're busy ordering soft drinks and clearing copier jams.

Second, unlike secretaries, paralegals enjoy job stability during recessions. Even firms that cut back by laying off associates (and, with them, their secretaries) will keep their full paralegal staff on hand, because they earn three times their salaries in billable hours. The Labor Department ranks paralegal work eighth on its list of the country's fastest-growing occupations. There were 83,000 paralegals in the country in 1988, a number which is expected to increase by 85 percent by the year 2005. It's not a perfect job by any stretch, but if you plan to go to college or law school, it can meet your needs as an interim occupation.

✎ Where to Get Paralegal Training

Most law firms train on the job, but many paralegals choose to be certified. Some four-year universities such as Duke offer bachelor's degrees in paralegal studies, but other programs take less than a year. Make certain that any program you attend is certified by the American Bar Association (ABA). Call admissions officers at the universities and community colleges in your area and ask if they offer an ABA-certified degree in paralegal studies. If they don't, keep looking.

Even if you have a certificate, though, most paralegal positions require college, but you can work your way around this. If you don't have a college degree, try getting a paralegal certificate at a community college while keeping your present job. Then transfer your academic credits to a four-year college or university and work your way through school by being a paralegal. You stand an excellent chance of getting a flexible position that will allow you to attend school full-time or three-quarters-time.

Although most employers will say that they only want paralegals with college degrees, many actually hire people who have had law-firm experience, as long as they're working on a degree. This is good news for former legal secretaries. Craft a résumé that puts your law-firm experience and your paralegal training first. Deemphasize your secretarial skills (no typing speeds, please!) and play up your research and decision-making abilities.

Pick apart your duties and experience to find all of the most responsible work you did. Did you draft correspondence? Did you talk to clients and schedule depositions? Did you manage the discovery process? Did you use Nexis and Lexis? These are all important parts of the paralegal position, and you can emphasize them to your advantage.

And certainly take the "secretary" title off your résumé. You can do this honestly by using a "functional résumé" format. A functional résumé lists your duties, not your title, and you are free to leave off anything you'd rather not do again. Consult *The Damn Good Résumé Guide* or *Résumés That Knock 'Em Dead* (see Chapter 6) for advice on making a sharp-looking functional résumé.

✎ By All Means, Go to College or Law School

I'll never forget the night I decided to go back to college. I had just left a good job at a stock exchange to take a better-paying one working for lawyers. They *said* they hired me for my experience. They *claimed* I was valuable to them for my verbal skills. During the job interview no one mentioned secretarial work at all. When I reported to work, however, they showed me to a Dictaphone and asked me to start typing.

Because I didn't know then the things I'm telling you now, I thought that an honest résumé was the way to go. I believed that by telling people I had worked my way up from administrative assistant to statistical specialist at my previous job, they'd respect my drive and ambition. Instead, my future employers saw an overqualified typist, and they tried to throw me back into the swamp I'd just crawled out of.

I wasn't going to let them.

Before the first two weeks were up, I'd had enough. While driving home on Interstate 395 in bumper-to-bumper evening rush-hour traffic, I decided to return to college full-time. The next morning I marched into my boss's office and told him I was returning to college, and he could either keep me on part-time or let me go.

He looked up from the letter he was composing at his desk. I saw his framed diplomas on the wall behind him. He stared at me skeptically, and then said that he thought college would be a big mistake. He said higher education was overrated. He said I might not make it through.

Although he acted calm, he later told the office manager he was infuriated and insulted. After all, why would I ever want to leave a perfectly good job working for him and go to college? He complained that I'd never mentioned college in the job interview. I argued that he'd never mentioned secretarial work either. We were at a standoff, and I was prepared to quit if need be. It was a big scene, and every bit as uncomfortable as it sounds. It was also the best decision of my life.

If you didn't finish college or never started, you may think going back is impossible. People may quote statistics to you, such as "Dropouts never drop back in again." They're wrong. The truth is, most people who drop out of college and then go back do much better.

Adults who begin college or return make 54 percent better grades than people who go directly from high school to college. Plus, they get four times as many scholarships! What's more, they receive the most merit-based financial aid, and they represent over a third of all students who graduate with honors. When adults go back to school they show better class participation, more maturity, sharper study skills, and they are more likely to continue on to graduate education.

These returning students have another advantage over the high school-to-college group: job experience. Even the Ivy League grads are having a tough time finding jobs these days. Positions are scarce, and few employers want to break in a postadolescent who is a four-year expert at the mosh pit and Ultimate Frisbee but knows nothing about holding down a regular forty-hour-a-week job. Adults who return to school already have years of work experience. After they graduate, their diplomas really mean something.

Just three years after that attorney suggested that I didn't need college and, worse, that I couldn't be successful, I finished college and moved on to a graduate program at UVA, his former university.

Everyone talks about what college costs, but let me list a few ways in which college pays you. A bachelor's degree will:

- Increase your confidence
- Improve your work performance
- Qualify you for a better job
- Make you happier

Adult returning students are by far the most satisfied scholars on campus. They aren't there for Mumsy and Dad or because society expects them to be. Instead, they're there for themselves. They study what they want to study. They make superb grades because they care. They're having the time of their lives.

✎ How to Go Back to College While Keeping Your Full-Time Job

It sounds crazy, but you *can* go to school full-time and work full-time or three-quarters-time. If you don't have children, this is your best option for finishing college quickly and successfully. If you do have kids, keep reading. I have advice for you too.

Call the admissions offices at every university in your area—even the expensive, exclusive ones. Be sure to ask for the counselor who works with adult returning students. Do not speak to the adult education counselor. ''Adult education'' is another name for informal night school that doesn't lead to a degree. Emphasize that you are a degree-seeking candidate.

Many universities and colleges have special programs for returning students because they know how great drop-ins are. Any professor can tell you that students who drop back in are the best in class. Don't be apologetic about not having a degree. Be proud that you're an adult who wants to return to college and get one.

Some schools will offer you financial aid, but others won't until they see how you perform. You usually have to complete a semester (normally three classes or fifteen credits) with A-average grades before any school will offer you money. Therefore you will need your job, either for the beginning of school or all the way through.

I was able to carry a fifteen- to eighteen-hour-per-semester course load and work between thirty and forty hours per week. But then I had no kids and very little social life either. If you have children, you'll need to cut this at least in half, perhaps taking six credits per semester. Some working parents find they have time for only one class per semester. Take the maximum number of classes you can while maintaining an A average, or at minimum B's. If your grades slip to C or below, you're doing too much or you're in the wrong program: drop a class and take fewer the next time.

Single parents may think that college is out of reach, but most financial aid officers say it's easier than you think. Single parents, especially working mothers, qualify for more financial aid than any other group on campus! If you are raising children alone, you could qualify for significantly more grant money than parents who have a spouse. Talk to financial aid officers at every major university in your area. If you don't like the answers you hear, keep trying. You can also research grants and fellowships at your local public library.

You may find universities that give you ''life experience credit.'' Others will have special programs just for working parents. Meredith College in Raleigh, North Carolina, has two excellent programs for working women, with or without children, who want to finish college at night. The newest one is ''Meredith After Five,'' offering a four-year degree without making you take time off during the day. This augments their already successful ''A Second Chance'' program, which allows women to complete fifteen hours of credit before being evaluated for potential success. If you'd like to find out more, call Sandra C. Close, director of the Re-Entry Program, at 919-829-8353.

George Mason University in Fairfax, Virginia, offers classes before and after work. Many of their classes start at 7 a.m. Students can go to a fifty-minute class and then drive straight from school to the office. These are just two examples, though, and I found them easily by calling the admissions offices locally. You can do the same, and you'll be surprised at the quality of the schools offering reentry opportunities.

Most universities and colleges are not equipped to handle child care, but Sandra Close says that many Meredith students find an abundance of babysitters on campus, since so many college students need extra money. Once you become familiar with a campus, you may even be able to post babysitter notices on bulletin boards, on the Internet, and in various department newsletters. Some students who can't afford regular babysitters work out a shared arrangement whereby one watches the kids while the other goes to class.

Community colleges can be good starter schools, especially if you had a sketchy record before returning to college. Just make certain that you can transfer all of your credits from a community college to a four-year institution. Don't ask the community college this question, however. They'll try to sell you on their school by saying you can ''transfer anywhere.'' Call the best universities in your area, speak to admissions officers, and ask how they feel about particular community college programs. Ask them if any of their students began at community colleges. Piedmont Virginia Community College in Charlottesville, Virginia, has a strong record of sending its top students to competitive four-year universities as transfers. Not all community colleges enjoy Piedmont's fine reputation, however. You'll want to check with the universities to see how an individual community college rates.

In some cases, a community college degree makes sense. In *U.S. News & World Report* (September 26, 1994), Joannie M. Schrof tells the story of Cheri Wallace, who took an automotive technology program at a community college and got a guaranteed internship at an auto dealer the summer after graduation. Now she's an executive in the auto industry, making over $60,000 a year. Kelly Scott left IBM to fulfill her lifelong dream of being a chef. She took a respected apprenticeship program at El Centro Community College in Dallas. She's now working at a prestigious hotel, and her employer is paying for additional courses. If you wish to work at a specific vocation that includes a set of skills taught at a top-quality community college, then by all means, use that resource.

For someone seeking a more general education, however, I can't recommend community college degrees. An associate's degree from a community college is *not* the same thing as a bachelor's degree from a college or university. If you decide to start at a community college, find out how many credits you can transfer elsewhere and take only that many. Get straight A's. Then show your prime-time record to the big university down the road and watch the doors open.

✎ Are There "Virtual" College Degrees Available on the Internet?

One prediction I hear over and over again is a futuristic promise of degrees by computer. There are whole books devoted to the premise that one day you'll be able to get everything on-line, including your education.

My response? Get real! Ever since the invention of television, pundits have promised that one day we'd sit comfortably in our living rooms and take courses taught by professors in distant cities. These predictions flew when satellites started beaming instant images worldwide, and now, with the World Wide Web sending QuickTime movies and sound bits around the globe, they're promising more of this than ever before.

The people who make these predictions know nothing about university degrees. A college degree is not a mere certificate for hurdles jumped. Rather, it is a school's individual imprimatur. By placing its seal on you, the university is saying, in effect, "This is someone worthy of carrying forth our name. They also paid a bazillion dollars, and we'll acknowledge them as our own." If you only get a degree from a noncompetitive institution such as an Internet university or a correspondence-course school, you may find that it won't take you much farther than your high school diploma did.

Whether you do your coursework by mail or over the computer, you will miss the most important parts of a college education. You'll avoid the very contacts you need to make, because your professors will never see you. You'll miss out on the kinds of interaction that teach you how to act like a college-educated person. You won't learn how to converse with scholars or make persuasive arguments to your peers, because you'll be isolated at home.

The same is true of weekend courses and, to a limited degree, night school. I advise you if it is at all possible to attend a standard four-year degree program at the best university for which you can qualify, even if you have to do it one or two classes at a time. The more competitive your program, the more your degree will be worth after graduation.

✎ How to Break the News to Your Boss and Keep Your Job

Tell your boss about school after it's a done deal. Remember, you're not asking your boss's permission. She or he can go along with your decision and help you, or say goodbye to you, but they cannot tell you "no." I've heard women and a few men say, "I want to go back to school, but my boss would never allow it." You don't need anyone's permission to do something. Choose a quiet time in the day when your boss isn't hassled and break the news in an even voice. If you want to keep your job while going to school, state what hours you will need to take off to pursue your education and what hours you would like to work.

This negotiation phase is where real diplomacy comes in. Once I'd broken the news about returning to school, I said that I'd be "honored" to continue to work at my law firm as a part-timer, thirty hours a week. Was this an exaggeration? You bet. It was hard to mouth platitudes about how pleased I'd be to continue to labor in their sour vineyards. But at the moment I needed some sort of job. It was better to stay where I was and not try to learn a new job while learning a new school system.

✎ What If Your Boss Fires You for Going to School?

Lots of people worry about this at first, but it seldom happens. In reality, many employers value education. One reason bosses treat clerical people so poorly is the "college difference." Many employers divide the adult world into those with education and those without. When you go to college, you identify yourself to them. People often treat you better: lawyers are notorious for this. The more you value school, the more they'll value you.

One interesting exception, however, is the college-educated woman or man who accepts secretarial work. Somehow, people can't see past the "secretary" title to the person occupying the job. If you already have a college diploma and you're working as an administrative assistant or secretary, they won't treat you much differently than if you'd never gone to college at all. I suggest you use the get-ahead ideas in this chapter to change jobs and start over with a new group of workers. The old bunch will have blinders on when it comes to promoting you.

✎ Internships Turn Diplomas into Careers

Although your old job may see you through your first year of college, you might outgrow it pretty quickly. Consider using your summer breaks to work at internships that can prepare you for a new career when you graduate.

Many companies who don't need permanent employees are interested in interns. This is especially true of radio and television stations, publishing companies, museums, and political offices. Although it's true that most internships don't pay a lot of money, it's also true that good internships will make you dramatically more hirable after you complete them. So what if you have to eat peanut butter and live off credit cards for three months? The time will pass quickly, you'll enjoy yourself, and you'll be instantly qualified for much better, higher-paying work once you've paid your internship "dues."

Often you can arrange internships through your college once you are an enrolled student and you maintain a strong grade point average (usually 3.2 and above). Go to the financial aid office and ask about internships as a form of work-study. Also, talk to professors you respect in the Business Department. Say that you want to intern during your summers and see what opportunities are available.

If you call companies directly, you might be able to create

your own internships. Call every company that does what you're interested in and ask. See my advice for cold-calling companies in Chapter 6 and use it to land yourself a great three-month résumé booster. You'll put yourself in the promotion line quickly this way.

✎ An Unembellished "Thank You" Is One Key to Self-Promotion

If you want to get ahead, self-promotion is crucial, and it's your best strategy for breaking the glass ceiling. Self-aggrandizement that would seem egotistical elsewhere is perfectly acceptable and even expected in the professional world. You can relentlessly promote yourself in the workplace, and people will believe you and begin moving out of your way.

Always accept praise when a manager offers it. If a boss ever says "good work," smile, shake her hand, and thank her. Act like you deserve it. You don't have to be arrogant, but certainly accept the praise graciously. Never say, "Oh, it was nothing." Instead, the simple "thank you" (spoken, not whispered) works best.

Has anyone ever taught you to share the credit on projects, suggesting you say things like "Sam really helped me with that report" or "Don't just thank me, thank Vivien and Lorraine too"? Well, forget it. Rather than making you look like a team player, this technique will make you appear weak and even helpless. Instead, practice saying a warm "thank you" with no embellishments. If they offer a handshake, accept it firmly and smile.

Later, you can personally thank anyone who helped you get the job done, but don't rush to tell your superiors how much you owe to others' efforts. Your colleagues have their own jobs to do. They can promote themselves. Emphasize your contributions and leave it at that. If this makes you feel guilty, by all means go out of your way to show your personal appreciation to your friends, alone. When speaking to the boss, however, shine the spotlight on yourself.

Use your successes as a handle to grasp new opportunities. If you do a good job on a legal research project and you want more projects like it, mention this as much as possible. Saying things like "I really enjoyed spending that afternoon at the university law library—do you have other work like it?" is a great way to get the next job. If one lawyer gives you an interesting job to do and it goes well, be sure to mention it to the other attorneys and seek similar opportunities.

The "book trick" is a nifty way to show your enthusiasm without saying too much. To many people you are, to some extent, what you read. The public library or your university library will have good standard reference books on research practice that you can read to learn more about exploring resources. Having these on your desk to read during breaks (instead of, say, Danielle Steel novels) is one way to make yourself appear competent to handle future research tasks.

✎ Let the Doormats Reap Their Own Reward

Once you do get a better job, resist the temptation to backslide into servant habits. It can be tempting to pitch in on kitchen duties or messy, boring jobs when you see a co-worker slaving away, especially if it's a friend of yours. It's hard to watch someone be a doormat, but remember that your friend is an adult who can choose not to be exploited as well as you can.

I call this problem the "former secretary syndrome." Many former secretaries and clerks remember how it felt to be stuck doing dishes, making coffee, fetching lunches, and handling other tasks that individuals in offices should do for themselves. Out of a sense of solidarity and compassion, these people often pitch in and help the beleaguered souls who try to keep fourteen lunch orders straight while answering ten phone lines. Don't do it. Sympathy is one thing, professional suicide is another.

A secretary in one of the law firms where I was a researcher tried to pressure me into helping her with mountains of collation and photocopying for an upcoming case. She offered the famous argument "we all pitch in around here," and her supervisor, a paralegal, agreed with her. Together they tried to pressure my boss into "making" me help with these chores that kept her overtime some nights. I refused. When my boss asked if I couldn't do these things "just for the sake of appearance," I still refused. The secretary and the paralegal were furious. They even called me in for a closed-door session with another attorney to try to force me to participate in the tasks. I held firm, suggesting they hire a temp if they were overworked.

Of course, had I been male, or higher up in the firm, they wouldn't have tried it, but because I was a flex-time hire with some of the skills they wanted, they believed I would eventually cooperate. How wrong they were. Even if my boss had threatened to fire me, I would have refused.

But guess what. He didn't threaten to fire me. He sided with me. After all, he'd found this whole argument beneath his notice to begin with: he just wanted calm and quiet in the office. When I asked him whether *he* would have done these tasks in order to restore peace, he said "no," and laughed.

Then I asked him what my time was worth to him. An hour of my time spent doing a secretary's work was an hour I couldn't spend doing the research he needed. He appreciated the point. After that, he gave me jobs of greater responsibility to show that I was more important to him in other capacities. There are many such unforeseen rewards for turning down "former secretary" duty. The only way to enjoy those rewards is to refuse work beneath your job description and see what happens.

✎ Mom and Dad Were Wrong: Hide Your Typing If You Want to Advance

Perhaps your folks said that you could always "fall back on" your typing and that, with basic word-processing skills, you would be an asset to any company.

They were wrong.

Unless you want to be a secretary, do not, under any circumstances, tell a prospective employer you can type. They'll hire you all right, but you'll never escape typing detail. No matter what job you apply for, they'll always be happy to show you to a chair and get you busy on a pile of typing.

In the office, typing is like hygiene. You can tend to your own, but you should never take care of anyone else's.

If you were hired in a nonsecretarial position, and someone asks you if you could "just this once" type something up, refuse. If you can't refuse, flub it. Make mistakes. Use what I call the

LIBRARY OF CONGRESS

Her pride and joy? Not if she wants a promotion

Dustin Hoffman and Robert Redford typing method, from the opening of *All the President's Men*: point your two index fingers and peck away, slowly. Then shrug and say, "I guess I'm just better at research," or whatever they actually hired you to do. Of course, you should shine in your work duties, but there is no need to demonstrate competence at a skill that can hurt you professionally.

This works just as well for photocopying. My friend Mike Kelly tells a great story from his days as an office temp in Portland, Oregon:

> *Every so often one of the instructors would need some photocopies made, and they always asked me, although it was not part of my job. Soon I got in the habit of*

> *responding to most requests for copies by pointing to the copier that was five feet away and offering to explain how to use it. So they stopped asking, and instead they walked past my desk into Margaret's office to ask her. She would point to the copier and tell them, ''Mike can show you how to use it.''*

Eager young employees hoping for a job often say foolish things to impress employers. Remember that ''I know how to type'' or ''I don't mind making copies'' should never be among them.

If you hope for promotions leading to more responsible positions, then I advise you to stay as far away from secretarial work as possible. This advice especially applies to women. The only way to break out of the pink-collar ghetto is to refuse work you don't want and demand your own terms. If women stop categorizing themselves, and explore the many options available to them, then only the people who truly want to be secretaries or administrative assistants will be, including more men. This will bring more prestige to the profession as a whole.

✎ Maybe You Already *Are* Out!

Like Lucy in the ''Peanuts'' cartoon, you may already be out of your trap and just not know it. If you can imagine yourself doing something else for a living, you're most of the way there. Getting a new job is easy. It's convincing yourself you can do something else that's hard.

Remember that all you need to have a career instead of a mere job is a sense of where you want to go. If you want college, use flexible, preprofessional jobs such as paralegal work to finance your education. If you'd rather get ahead on your present high school diploma or bachelor's degree, then try one of the jobs I've listed here. Relentlessly promote yourself, give yourself a résumé that makes you look like a professional, and, above all, try like the dickens. Don't give up after five attempts. It may take you fifty tries to find the job you want.

Christine, Dave, and Helen are happy now. If these people can break the glass ceiling, you can too.

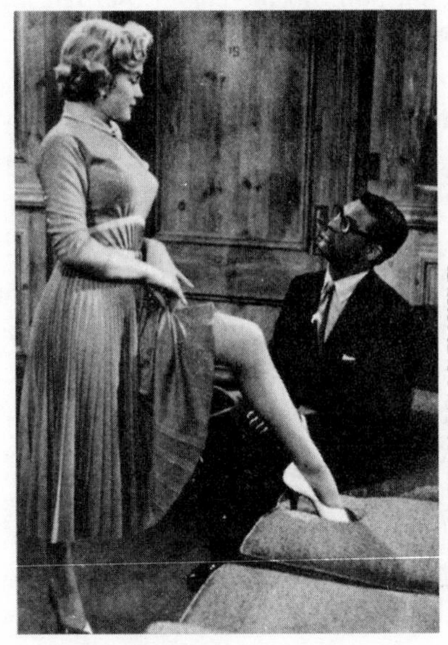

"GOOD HEAVENS, MISS BUXLEY, YOU'RE BEAUTIFUL!": Sexual Politics in the *Support* Staff World

"But do you respect me for the right thing?"
"Sure I do! I respect you for the left *thing too!"*
—Miss Buxley and General Halftrack, from a censored "Beetle Bailey" cartoon

Mort Walker, creator of "Beetle Bailey," still doesn't understand why women are so tired of Miss Buxley. Named for her breasts, Miss Buxley has raised General Halftrack's pulse at Camp Swampy for over two decades. Mort Walker says that Miss Buxley's "godmother" is none other than Marilyn Monroe. This isn't much of a surprise, for Monroe was *Playboy*'s first centerfold and the movies' original dumb blonde secretary.

Shortly after Miss Buxley's 1971 debut, Walker mercifully

exchanged an initial Daisy Mae costume for more realistic clothing, and he boosted her IQ to somewhere above cottage cheese, but that's about all. Twenty-five years later, Buxley still bounces around in tight dresses, the General still salivates, and Walker continues to sort stacks of mail from "those feminists" who object to his caricature of a secretary as tits in a sweater. If Buxley and Halftrack reflect any sort of office reality, and I think they do, then clerical workers are all in trouble. Cultural changes have improved women's prospects in many other areas, but routine office work is still stuck in the 1950s.

✎ Most Bosses Harass Their Assistants, Not Each Other

Thanks to *Playboy*, James Bond, Beetle Bailey, and schoolyard-level boredom, the cheesecake dreams of Everyman sometimes boil down to giving someone a hard time who isn't in a position to complain about it.

I don't have to tell you that harassment is about power. You probably found that out when everyone from the senior partners to the summer associates decided it was okay to stop by your desk and comment on your anatomy. You may have noticed it when an important client and a middle manager joshed about whether you found them attractive, and all you could do was nod helplessly. If you're a clerk, an administrative assistant, or even a paralegal, then you're five times more likely to know what I'm talking about than if you're an executive or a lawyer. The staff gets harassed first, hardest, and worst. If things get bad, it's the support staffer (you) who usually ends up leaving. When you complain about it, few people really listen, usually because no one has been harassing *them*. I've heard managers say such enlightened things as "Sam? He's a family man. I've known him for years. Maybe you just misinterpreted a little joke."

You didn't misinterpret anything. All you've discovered is the Great Office Divide. When Sam is with the managers, he's one guy. When he's with the administrative assistants or the mailroom employees, however, he's someone else. You'll never meet the sociable Sam, who treats people well; they'll never see Sam the Snake, who just wants a quickie and doesn't care who accommodates him.

When someone with the power to fight back gets harassed,

we all read about it in the newspapers. Usually, however, a spokesman for the Old Boys' Network will quickly craft an out-of-proportion response. Hollywood's answer to Anita Hill's testimony and Robert Packwood's misconduct was the 1994 movie *Disclosure*. This embarrassing Michael Crichton blockbuster implied that the scariest thing about sex in today's office is those dangerous women who can't wait to seduce and destroy their male employees. Now *there's* a real problem: hot vixen bosses. Especially since there are so many of them running America's corporations.

But let's be fair. Most bosses don't harass. The average employer starts each day thinking about a lot more than how to victimize the hired help. One man said, "Harassment? Diane? She'd take me apart with both hands! I have enough on my mind just trying to figure out what size ties they're wearing this year." A bored woman, who's been at the same state government job for twenty years with no breaks in her routine, sighed, "When's someone going to sexually harass *me*? I'm still waiting . . ."

If all bosses were animals, if all employees were saints, and if all sexual harassment lawsuits made sense, this chapter wouldn't be nearly so interesting. What complicates matters and makes for dramatic movie plots is how innocently office harassment can begin, and, in extreme cases, how tragically it can end.

Sexual harassment shouldn't happen. When it does happen, however, you *can* choose not to be its next victim.

✎ Two Scenes from the Workplace

Here are two examples of frustrating situations that illustrate how confusing a problem sexual harassment is. In one story, the woman has legal recourse if she can prove the abuse. In the other, both the law and most corporate policies would dictate that she's on her own.

MO AND JULIE

Mo is a managing partner in a San Francisco law firm, and Julie is a summer research assistant, hired to help the associates and paralegals prepare for a big case. At Mo's request, Julie comes into his office.

"Yes?" Julie asks from the doorway. Mo waves her in to

where he stands in front of plate-glass windows overlooking San Francisco Bay and the Golden Gate Bridge.

"You look great today, Julie, really. Is that a new outfit?"

Julie smooths out her tan linen suit and blushes a bit. "Yeah. Thanks." She wishes, however, that he wouldn't always talk about her wardrobe. "What's on the agenda for this morning?"

"We're meeting with the music company people at ten-thirty, and . . . hey, are those shoes Gucci?"

"Pappagallo, Mo. What did you say about Sony Music?"

"I swear my daughter should buy stock in Pappagallo, she spends so much on shoes. Have you ever met my daughter Cecile? She's in law school. You know, you look kind of like Cecile."

"Mo! *Sony*, remember?"

"Oh, right, Sony. We're meeting with them at ten-thirty." He returns his gaze to the skyline, carefully looking away from Julie as he talks. "Say, where do you go to school anyway?"

"I'll be a senior at Berkeley this fall."

"Right. Berkeley. You thinking about law school?"

Julie smiles. "Yes, I am. That's why I wanted to intern here this summer."

"Well, smart girl. You know, I could write you a good letter for law school if you really want to go."

"You'd do that?" Julie is pleased. Mo is a well-known attorney with friends on the Stanford University law faculty. Then she thinks about it for a moment. "You don't know much about my work, though."

"What do I need to know? You're bright, you're beautiful . . ." He turns to her and looks at her body. "You're a delectable young woman with brains to spare. Who wouldn't write a letter for a dynamo like that?"

"Mo, I don't think this is really the place to . . ."

"What? Am I making you uncomfortable?" He steps back three big paces, his hands in the air. "Hey, I'm sorry. I didn't mean a thing by it." Mo sits down behind his desk, well away from Julie. "But if you decide you want to go to law school, you come talk to Mo. We'll go have a drink, and I can put you onto some people who can help you. It's not just brains, you know, Julie. It's friends. You've gotta have friends in this town."

Is this harassment? I say yes, and here's why. Mo has power over Julie. She's only a summer employee, and he can fire her without explaining anything to anyone. His ''offer'' to write a letter of recommendation seems pretty flimsy, when you realize that he doesn't know Julie's work yet. Why would he do this if he didn't expect something in return? Although he's a smart lawyer who knows better than to proposition Julie outright, his comments on her ''delectable'' body and her clothing, plus the offer to meet her for drinks, clearly point to his interest in turning their professional relationship into a personal one.

And don't be fooled because he makes a big show of stepping away from her while apologizing for making her uncomfortable. Mo knows all about harassment suits: a court transcript of his exact words will show that he backed off and didn't come near her again. His behavior is so smooth, in fact, that it's likely someone has accused him of harassment before. Instead, he makes Julie come to him. By connecting something she wants (a law school recommendation) with something he wants (an intimate rendezvous at a bar), Mo baits a trap. Julie would have a hard time winning a case against him if things go too far.

If I were Julie, I'd try the ''slow, straight pitch down the middle'' tactic with Mo. By pretending not to understand or acknowledge his subtext but holding him to his offer of writing a recommendation letter, Julie can effectively embarrass him into doing what he said he'd do (write a letter) without playing along with his game (meeting him for a drink). Executives do this all the time. When confronted with a sleazy offer, including bribes, kickbacks, and other unethical suggestions, many choose to act in a forthright manner while pretending to ignore the illegal offer. They stay above it, but they document the double-dealing in memos to the file and to their attorneys, in case things get ugly later.

Let's say Julie *does* ask Mo for a letter, but she does so at the office instead of meeting him for cocktails. She'll be well prepared if she has carefully documented all of the previous times when Mo connected recommendation writing to a social engagement. Now suppose Mo refuses, saying that she hasn't ''earned'' the recommendation or that she seems shy about meeting him socially. She can legitimately ask if the two are connected. ''Why, Mo, I thought that offer still stood. What on earth would a drink at the Tropicana have to do with it?''

At this point, Julie has baited a reverse trap. If Mo steps into it by spelling out what he wants from her, then he's crossed the line. Julie will have a much easier time making a charge of sexual harassment stick, especially if she has been intelligent enough to have a friend stand nearby but out of sight to hear the whole thing.

LEIGH AND DARIUS

Leigh and Darius are statistical reporting clerks at a Chicago stock exchange. Although they have identical positions, Darius has worked there for three years, and Leigh is a new employee. Darius is in line for a promotion to senior statistical clerk. This will increase his salary, but he won't have supervisory authority. He expects this upgrade in a few months. The vice president has asked Darius to show Leigh around and to take her to a business lunch to talk over her new responsibilities.

"At first you'll work with twenty or thirty brokers, Leigh, and then after the training period we'll give you a normal workload."

"Will you train me?"

"Only if you want me to. After all, I'm not the boss. Anne trained the last four clerks, but I could always tell the vice president you're my personal protégée."

Leigh smiles. Darius seems much more competent than some of the other clerks she's met today, and she knows that he's in line for promotion. Learning from his experience can only help her at this point. She knows that he has no supervisory authority, but she believes he can give her more practical advice than Anne, the manager. "I'd rather keep working with you, Darius."

"Well, good. Let's start off by grabbing a nice, long expense-account lunch, courtesy of the vice president. He asked me to take you out and explain the system."

Darius and Leigh go to lunch, and spend the first hour talking about business. During the second hour, though, before the check arrives, the talk becomes more personal.

"So what's your story, Leigh?"

"Oh, the usual. I went to work on Wall Street, but I didn't want to go to college and become a broker. I guess I just don't consider antacids a food group! I have friends here who told me about the Midwest Stock Exchange, so when a job opened up, I jumped at it."

"What did your boyfriend think?"

"What boyfriend? He dumped me. You couldn't chip Brian

out of New York with a chisel. Oh, he said he'd move, but when it came right down to it, he didn't want to change. We're still friends.''

''And how about here? Have you met anyone new?''

''I've only been here two weeks. I barely have my boxes unpacked.''

Darius smiles and moves a little closer. ''You know, there's a great new comedy club opening up. We could kick off your new social life by going there this Friday.''

Leigh moves away from him a little. ''Who else will be going?''

''I was thinking just you and me.''

''Well, thanks, but for now the group activity thing is more my style. I don't want to seem rude, but I just came off a long-term relationship. Going out on dates wouldn't work for me right now.''

''Hey, whatever. I was just being sociable. This is a friendly department, and we don't get too uptight like they do on Wall Street. If you decide you need a night out, you know who to call.''

Was this harassment? Probably, but a court might not agree. After all, Leigh doesn't work for Darius. Even when he gets a promotion, he will not have the power to fire her. Although he ''knows the ropes'' in the organization and she's a new hire who has more to lose if they get involved, most arbiters would say that Leigh and Darius are professional equals and that he did not put undue pressure on her.

However, Darius *is* acting like a lounge lizard, and his actions are inappropriate. First, he shouldn't be using a business lunch to ask a colleague for a date. Second, since he has offered to train Leigh, she may suspect that dating him could improve her performance reviews, something no professional can afford to imply. It's easy to see how Leigh could feel uncomfortable, since Darius is bringing up the subject of dating so soon, and in a business context. Still, she is independent from him, and she is completely free to reject his suggestion.

These two examples show men and women in situations which, though unpleasant, remain civil. In the first one, Mo is clearly harassing Julie, but she still has some recourse. She can refuse to play his power game, or, if she's up for a little guerrilla warfare, she can bait a reverse trap and catch him in it. It's a shame that she should have to deal with his lechery, but she can probably take care of herself. Similarly, Darius may disappoint Leigh by showing interest in more than her professional development, but she is in no immediate danger of losing her job. He took "no" for an answer, at least initially, so unless something else happens between them, she will probably not find the working atmosphere poisoned by sexual politics.

In either of these situations, the women involved could also take a bit of advice from Katharine Parker, the boss that Sigourney Weaver played in 1988's *Working Girl.* When a creepy fellow executive makes a suggestive comment to her at a cocktail party, Katharine out-innuendoes him. She matches him, nuance for nuance, until he's retreating rather than advancing. But she does so in a manner that's so subtle, he hardly sees it coming. She ends up promising to buy *him* a drink if they get this big deal. He probably won't accept her offer, though, since he's so intimidated by her forceful manner.

Remember when you were a kid and you learned to shake your fist at bullies? Often, bullies run. Likewise in the office, when you make an advance toward someone who's sexually pressuring you, they often crumple. When secretary Tess asks Katharine why she stayed civil with the oaf, she simply smiles and says, "Never burn bridges. Today's junior prick [might be] tomorrow's senior partner."

This worked quite well for me in graduate school when a professor with seniority and power persisted in "joking"; his sexual comments made me most uncomfortable. He never crossed the line into textbook harassment, but he never let up either. Finally I decided to fight back the direct way. I backed him into a corner, gave him my most sultry eye-to-eye look, and said, "How many affairs *have* you had with your students?" He gulped. He looked away. He tried to ease around me and out of the office. He hadn't counted on my calling his bluff like that.

He never bothered me again. We also kept our working relationship.

There are times when the gloves come off, though, and someone in power tries to ruin a subordinate. People lose their jobs every year because of sexual harassment, and most of the time it's the executive who stays on while the clerk, secretary, or receptionist hits the streets to find another job. Here are some basic office sex situations, with suggestions for getting out.

✎ The Boss-Secretary Affair: A Timeless Classic

The libido can play tricks on you. So can boredom. A monotonous office environment is like a sensory-deprivation tank where you can lose your perspective. After you've been in it awhile, someone average may start to look pretty good. If you work next to someone five days a week, twelve months a year, even someone whom you initially found unattractive, you may actually imagine yourself in bed with them. While this usually remains harmless, now and then a boss will play this to advantage by making a move on the secretary. There is little risk for the boss, since bedding the secretary is an accepted executive pastime. For the secretary, however, a fling with the boss is a terrible idea, since the secretary *always* loses public face, self-esteem, and, more often than not, a job.

If you want to see a fine example of how power complicates the boss-secretary affair, rent the movie *Grand Canyon* (1992) and watch Dee, a legal secretary, rescue herself from a real mess. One day over lunch, Dee talks to fellow secretary Jane about whether she should have an affair with her boss, Mack. Mack has already indicated his interest, and Dee thinks she loves him. Jane isn't fooled, though, and she gets to the heart of the problem: "Let me ask you one thing. Do you like your job? Because you can kiss it goodbye. I absolutely guarantee you the thing ends with you losing your job." Jane is right, of course, but Dee doesn't listen. Instead, Dee and Mack have a brief affair, during which they both recite the four major lies that people who cross office and marriage boundaries tell themselves.

The "family fallacy" is first. Dee says, "One of the little things I think is so great about him is how devoted he is to his wife and kids." Jane doesn't fall for this one, countering with "If he's so devoted to his wife, what's he doing messing around with you?" Remember that anyone who will lie to his or her spouse about you will lie to you about everything else. The oldest line in the world is "My wife doesn't understand me, but you do." No matter how much someone may protest to you that they want out of their marriage, if they date you while they're still married, it's because they *choose* to stay married.

Second, Dee and Mack both think they're having a secret affair when in truth there is no such thing. Office affairs are blatantly obvious to most co-workers. Marilyn Moats Kennedy, author of *Kennedy's Career Strategist,* explains:

> *As Lord Peter Wimsey of detective fame noted, ''Love and a cough cannot be hidden.'' If two people who work for the same company get involved, everybody who has any interest in soap opera (100 percent of the people in the organization) knows. (''Romance in the Office,''* Across the Board, *March 1992.)*

The sexual tension between Dee and Mack is evident on-screen; it's just as evident in a real office.

When Dee breaks it off with Mack, he recites the old ''honesty'' line that bosses have used on secretaries for decades. ''I've been honest with you all along,'' he says, meaning he never lied about his marriage or his devotion to his wife. Who is Mack trying to kid? He acts as though his technical adherence to the truth absolves him of responsibility for the affair. Mack was dishonest the moment he used his position of power to attract Dee.

Finally, Mack says, ''I don't want you to go.'' In fact, he will be enormously relieved when Dee quits. He pretends that Dee is a friend and that he will miss her, but he really hasn't treated her like a friend at all. If Mack truly valued Dee as an employee or a friend, he never would have acted on his sexual desire in the first place.

Dee does move on from Mack, but not before she learns, the hard way, that secretaries lose big when these affairs end.

✎ The Only Way Through Is Out

How can you escape? The easiest method is also the most direct. You'll probably have to leave your job, but you can make it worth your boss's while to get you into another, distant department or out the door gracefully, and even with a promotion. Sit him or her down alone, at the office, and say you want to leave but you need help. Your boss may offer it willingly. If he protests that he doesn't want you to leave, tell him that he does not have a choice. He can either write you a glowing letter of recommendation and agree to be a reference for you or you will "go public" about your relationship. Do not worry about being unfair to him. This relationship has been unfair to you all along.

Very few bosses will argue with you about this. Most will help you by writing you a good letter and agreeing to make your transition to another, better job relatively painless. The few who do complain will settle down once they see you are serious about telling your story. Before you announce that you're leaving, however, make sure you have somewhere to go. Read Chapter 6 and consider career alternatives that can improve your professional life.

✎ What's Wrong with Feeling Flattered? What If I Like the Attention?

I've heard this one a thousand times, usually from very young employees who think a sexy older boss genuinely has dating on his or her mind.

Remember the Introduction, where I explained that the folks with MBAs and lots of money are looking for a new servant class to accommodate them? Well, they've got their eyes out for a new hooker class too. They'd be even happier if it was free. I hate to break this to you, but these people rarely look to administrative assistants, receptionists, and other clerks for serious dating material. Most of them won't date seriously where they work, and if they do, it will be with someone at their own professional level. They'll seldom date up the ladder or down it. If a manager is coming on to you, he probably wants sex, not romance.

If you really believe the attention is honest ("Oh, but Jeff respects me and we have so much in common"), then ask to meet his friends and family. That's all. One basic request. If he goes out with you in private and spends other time with his friends, then you can be certain what I've said is true. If you're the one clerk in ten million who is dating a manager, lawyer, or other boss from your company who hasn't stuck you in a separate category marked "Fun and Games," then congratulations. But you're in a very small minority.

✎ It's Tough Being Superman

Don't think only female clerks have problems. Male clerks put up with plenty of sexual harassment, and it's not always easy to guess where the pressure will come from. Statistics indicate that 98 percent of all secretaries and receptionists are women and that only 2 percent are men, but, as we all know, numbers can mislead. I've met lots of men in these support staff positions while writing this book, but few of them called themselves secretaries. Why?

Perhaps because when it comes to sexual stereotypes, the male secretary or receptionist tolerates more than his share. Mike Kelly learned this when he worked as a receptionist in Portland, Oregon. A rather deranged fellow wandered into the office looking for a job:

> *He was harmless and somewhat amusing in the way he talked about his various lawsuits against the government and former employers. He started asking me how I got my job and he commented on how unusual male receptionists are. Then he asked me if I was gay.*
>
> *I then realized most people probably thought that, only this guy was uninhibited enough to ask outright.*

Whatever your sexual persuasion, it is frustrating to have people assume something personal about you because of the job you hold. Male flight attendants, florists, hairdressers, and fashion models all report the same phenomenon. People see them as caricatures rather than as individuals.

Male secretaries also put up with the daily, repeated expectation that they are doing "women's work." They often have trouble obtaining receptionist positions because firms want a female voice and face to greet clients every day. And, of course, the clients expect to hear a woman's voice when they call. Jack, a receptionist in a law firm, says that callers have an exasperating habit of saying, "Who is this?" when he answers the telephone. He responds with his name, and then they say, "Let me speak to the receptionist.'' Even 9 to 5, which claims to speak for support staffers nationwide, bills itself as the ''National Association of Working *Women*,'' and calls all secretaries and receptionists ''she'' and all bosses ''he'' in its literature.

Bosses who should know better often assume that male secretaries are either overqualified for their jobs or incredibly dense, and they put pressure on men to outperform women at clerical tasks. In an amusing *New York Times Magazine* article (June 19, 1994) titled ''Don't Call Me Lucy,'' Art Fazakas writes about the pressures he endured at a New York investment bank:

> *Whatever I did seemed wrong. My lack of expertise in WordPerfect for Windows prompted an ''Oh, God!'' from the female supervisor. I found it hard to immediately absorb two pages of instructions for distribution of financial reports and didn't photocopy a stack of papers fast enough to win her approval. She stood over me as I struggled to handle 15 phone lines, and the pressure compounded my mistakes. No one told me about the fax machine's speed-dial buttons, which were obscured by a plastic flap. In my confusion, I sent a fax to our own number. It was a nightmare. I didn't return after lunch.*

If female secretaries have to struggle against management's assumption that they are stupid, male secretaries have an equally hard time getting supervisors to believe that they need time to master their jobs. Either that or the opposite happens, and managers assume the men are as dumb as rocks and were probably hired just for (here we go again) their sex appeal.

Which is where the harassment comes in. Male secretaries are considered as ''perpetually available'' as their female colleagues. One man reported that plenty of male bosses made passes at him. When he worked as an administrative assistant on Capitol Hill in Washington, D.C., he went into the steam room at the gym, sat down, closed his eyes, and opened them again to find a man's hand on his thigh. It belonged to a married congressman. Just as all male secretaries aren't gay, all married bosses aren't, well . . . let's just say you need a scorecard to know the players.

Although things are improving for men in the clerical world, it's no mystery why so few of them apply for secretarial jobs. My advice for male clerical workers is the same as it is for women.

Learn to ask questions when you don't understand something, instead of letting pushy supervisors assume that you can do twenty things at once without a hitch. Practice the walkout for boorish jokers, especially ones who try to lure you into "locker room" talk that makes you uncomfortable (explained later in this chapter). And prepare yourself for the ritual stereotyping that hounds trailblazers in any profession.

✎ Tales of Terror from the Open Bar

> *I have a head for business and a bod for sin. Is there anything wrong with that?*
> *—Melanie Griffith as Tess McGill in* Working Girl

What do you get when you mix fifty people, a case of scotch, a case of vodka, a keg of beer, and a six-hour party? Generally speaking, at least one ill-advised sexual encounter. After many office parties, somebody wakes up "the morning after" to gaze in horror at the person next to them. As if a pounding headache, a queasy stomach, and clothes that smell like a tobacco factory weren't enough, rolling over to find someone you work with snoring beside you is terrifying. "No, please. Not the budget director. Not the file clerk. Not . . ." (you fill in the blank).

Some people don't even bother going home together after office parties. They have a drunken encounter at work (private offices and the boardroom floor are popular places for this), do the "wild thing," and then stagger away to their respective homes. Then they are left to face each other at the office every day forever after. It can take months for this to fade from memory, and it never completely does. In the better situations, both people agree to forget the whole thing. In worse ones, though, one person remains interested while the other one tries to dodge them at all costs.

If you have one of these flings, the best you can hope for is the blessing of forgetfulness. The grapevine may not let you forget, however. The office wag-tongues will thoroughly talk over every last detail about you and whomever it was you slept with. If you're extraordinarily lucky and the event never leaks "to the press," as it were, you'll still feel foolish for a long, long time.

Christine, an administrative assistant, tells of the night she, her co-worker Jennifer, and a paralegal, Stan, worked late with four attorneys, who took them out dancing afterward to let off steam. Christine says:

> *What's weird is that nobody was really trying anything. There were two men and two women attorneys, plus Stan and us. I'd worked with them all for years, and it wasn't* that *kind of an evening. But then the female attorneys went home, and Stan left, and it was just me, Jennifer, Bruce, and Frank. We danced for a while, and we all got too drunk. Jenn couldn't stop giggling. Bruce put his hand over her mouth to shut her up, and then they started kissing. When Frank and I left them alone and went off to dance, it wasn't long before we were fooling around too. I can't really say who started it.*
>
> *The guys wanted to go to a hotel, and that's when we came to our senses. They didn't argue. In fact, Frank seemed relieved that we said "no." Everybody went home. Jenn and I sat in the car for, like, an hour, going "What* was *that?" The next day the guys were really apologetic. Frank took me aside and said he'd do whatever I wanted to make me feel okay about this. I thought he was going to cry. Honest, it wasn't just him. It was all of us. Jenn and I decided to forget about it, and so did they. But none of us ever really put it out of our minds.*
>
> *It's been three years. Jenn has a different job now, but I still work there. Nobody mentions a thing. We've been at parties after that, but Frank stays on his side of the room and I stay on mine. He got married later, to someone he was seeing at the time. I just try not to look at her.*

This is one of the most frequent office dramas.

If you don't want to wake up one morning wishing you could turn back time, then avoid liquor at office events and keep a discreet distance from intoxicated co-workers. Lavish office parties can overwhelm new employees who aren't used to expense-account festivities. Some employers, particularly lawyers, provide an almost unlimited flow of free alcohol at holiday time. Remember that in the office, as in driving, "if you booze, you lose."

"But why," asked Pam when I shared this advice with her,

"do I have to watch *my* drinking? It's the managers who come on to me, not vice versa." Exactly. The one office reality you have to accept, though, is that the clerical staff will always look like a herd of gazelle to the lions of middle and upper management. The lower you are on the totem pole, the more likely it is that drunken slobs will seek you out at office parties for fun and games. They think you're expendable. If someone "important" catches them chasing you, the consequences will be minimal. Remember *M*A*S*H*, when Hawkeye and Trapper John talked about the nurses as if they were a dumb, available herd of playthings? Well, their carnivorous sentiments are shared by thousands like them (doctors are famous for this). If you're sober, you'll be able to handle the situation, hopefully while embarrassing the manager in the process. If you're tipsy too, however, you might just end up feeling flattered enough to go home with one of them.

My advice differs somewhat depending on the formality of the situation, but the principles are the same. At formal office parties:

1. Notice how much your supervisors drink, and always stay at least two or three drinks behind them. A former boss taught me this trick, and it works. You can go out with friends later if you still want to party.
2. Never drink hard liquor, especially at holiday time when the booze flows. Stick to beer, wine, or nonalcoholic mixers. Scotch, vodka, bourbon, and the like will get you much drunker much faster, especially if there is only light snack food available. If someone important hands you a drink, thank him or her and take a sip. Then dump it when they're not looking and fill the glass back up with soda.
3. Say good night with the "second wave." People usually leave parties in three groups. The "first wave" are parents who have to get home because they've hired babysitters. You don't need to leave when they do. The "second wave," however, are the people who know when to say good night. Leave with them. The "third wave" are the hard-core partyers, and it's one of these folks who might try to talk you (or even coerce you) into doing something ridiculous if you're not careful.

Informal office parties don't require you to be as much on your guard, but there are still traps to watch out for:

1. Beware the open bar. Many people cannot control their drinking, and an open bar is too much for them. An otherwise mild-mannered co-worker can turn into an octopus when the liquor is free. Seek out a group of moderate colleagues and stay with them.

2. Drink much less than your usual limit. If you'd normally have two cocktails when out with friends, sip one slowly, or better yet, just have one beer or don't drink. After all, you are chained to these people because of your job. They'll still think of you as fun and sociable if you only drink a little, or if you don't drink at all. Many top executives refrain from *any* alcohol at office events, because they're afraid of becoming too talkative around the wrong people. They may notice you quite favorably if you do the same.

3. Drive your own car or take a cab, even if it costs what seems like a fortune. Don't depend on a co-worker for a ride home. You may have to be really pushy about this, but never get in someone's car after a late-night party, unless you want an unpleasant confrontation at 2 a.m. Even if the co-worker is a friend, people can change under the influence of alcohol, and you're better off getting home by your own power. Plus, they may not be able to drive safely. Worried about the cost of a cab? You can usually call ahead and get one that takes credit cards. Even if it cost eighty bucks to get home, you'd pay that ten times over to be able to live down a lousy experience with a drunk co-worker.

My friend Rich is quite a partyer among his personal friends. At work, however, although he goes to all the office events, he only sips drinks mixed without alcohol. Daiquiris and Bloody Marys (''Virgin Marys'') look especially convincing in their alcohol-free state, they taste good, and no one catches on. Some bars will even give them to you for free. He reports that, in six years at the same company,

> *nearly everyone has slept with everyone else, except me. I'm the one they come to when they're upset. Folks know that I'm not into all that, and so they tell me stuff. If you like the soaps, this is better than* Days of Our Lives. *They tell me about so-and-so, and I just listen. I like this job. Why would I mess it up by getting involved?*

You can be a wild child on your own time, but you will probably regret it if you use your office as the party connection.

✎ Beware the Welcoming Committee

When you start a new job, especially one in a large corporation, people may stop by your desk during the first two weeks to see how you're doing and to invite you out for social activities. Charming though they may seem, do not be fooled into thinking they're all just friendly folks. Some are. Others are envoys, sent from groups of curious workers on other floors or in other departments, to find out more about you.

One fellow may invite you to Thursday-night softball with the group. This is fine as far as it goes, but remember that he probably has two goals. He wants to find out if you socialize, and he also wants to "check you out" so he can report back to his friends. He will try to learn your marital status, whether you have a steady love interest, your sexual orientation, your interest in/relationship to your boss, and how much of a partyer you are.

Later, some people may suggest that you join a group of co-workers for lunch. Again, they may be looking you over to see whether you are worth recruiting for a social clique. Any information you give these people will go back to their respective groups, for general discussion during lunch and on breaks. It doesn't matter how interesting your life is or isn't: you're new data, grist for the gossip mill.

If you make a common mistake and chatter on about yourself, saying, "Oh, after my divorce I just couldn't handle the stress of living in that house, so I moved into an apartment, but then I started dating this man at work, and things got ugly when I found out he was married, so we broke up, but the office was just *so* small with the two of us there that I called this agency, and they sent me here, and I really like working for my new boss, but she seems a little cold . . ." and on and on, every word will travel throughout the company. People you've never met will say, "What was it like working at United Electric?" when you don't remember telling them about it. They will also know about your affair there, and your divorce, and whether you seem "available" to date in your new environment.

Try this time-tested advice when working for a new company, especially one where you hope to work for years. Form no alliances and make no fast friends for the first six months. Accept people's invitations, and be sure to check out the softball team, the lunch cliques, and the water-cooler discussions, but don't let your co-workers identify you with any one group until you understand who's playing what game. Someone who seems friendly and fun during your first weeks on the job may seem like an idiot when you find out that he makes passes at all the new hires.

At one company, there was a fellow we called the "welcome wagon." He made it a point of pride not only to meet but to bed as many new employees as possible. He loved to brag about his conquests to his buddies, who spread the news everywhere.

Another woman, who had fought a ten-year bitter feud with the company over a management position, would try to convince new hires to take her side in the fight. People who became identified with her faced a tough challenge with management.

In general, the first people you meet are the first people *everyone* meets. By understanding their agenda and staying cheerful but detached, you can spend six months investigating the bigger political picture at your company and forming the kind of friendships that can help you in the long run.

✎ A Conservative Image at Work Can Protect You

In an office, unlike most social situations, you can't always block out offensive people. You're yoked together by a mutual need to earn a living in the same physical area. Therefore a slightly more prudish image, even if you don't really feel this way in private, will screen out 98 percent of unwanted attention from your co-workers. After all, you don't just want to protect yourself from lawsuit material like Mo in scenario one above; you also want to avoid the "shivery" guys who show up at inappropriate moments and who are always ready with a double entendre. The 2 percent your policy doesn't screen out call for a stronger response.

Most sexual harassment chapters make it sound as if all men are slavering, *Hustler*-reading bull toads and all women are Cinderella. In reality, up to a point, much office banter is mutual. I've worked in many offices, and all of them tolerated a certain degree of joking as part of the routine.

In front of the support staff, however, many bosses think that the same rules of decorum which they observe with their colleagues and superiors no longer apply. A commonwealth's attorney once told a lewd joke in front of the administrative staff that he would not have repeated to the lawyers or the mayor. When I complained to the office manager (his assistant), she said that I needed to understand that he was under pressure. She suggested that assistants exist to help diffuse tension in an office and that his ''need'' to tell these jokes was a way of letting off steam.

Horse hockey. I complained to him, and he blushed and apologized. It had never occurred to him that the support staff might have the same sensibilities as his respected colleagues. Although it frustrated me to have to appear prudish just to get the same respect that lawyers enjoyed as a matter of routine, that's exactly what I had to do before this elected official realized how inappropriately he had behaved.

It sounds unfair to ask you to change your behavior to accommodate cretins, but you can take comfort in knowing that most executives do this as well. Every successful executive adopts an image in order to survive in the corporate world. The smart ones act like savvy politicians, going easy on the jokes, and often behaving much more conservatively than they might with family and friends.

✎ But What About Scumballs?

You know who I mean. Every office has them. These are the leering, creepy guys who have to make everything into a sex joke. They never actually come out and do anything aggressive: they just sexualize everything you do or say. Depending upon where you work, some of them may have erotic or even pornographic pictures to show around, and they're always ready to tell you the plot of the blue movie they saw last Friday. Guys who give you the shivers are sometimes a much bigger problem than the textbook harasser who says, ''Sleep with me or lose your job.''

Unfortunately, you will never be entirely rid of these. When I worked 9 to 5, they were there. Then I ''escaped'' to grad school, and there they were again! Some were fellow students who loved to send women pornographic E-mail or talk dirty to them on the computer chat lines. Others were professors who got their kicks out of making the class discuss what many students considered intensely personal subjects. Every population has a ''freak factor,'' as well as two or three people who always seem to be the targets for these clowns.

Never humor them. I worked for a lawyer one summer who loved to come in every morning and tell a sex joke. These jokes weren't merely risqué, they were usually in the poorest possible taste. He enjoyed using graphic terms and watching people's reactions. To my amazement, the women who worked for him (for he only hired women) laughed whenever he told one of these putrid jokes. Some of them were my mother's age. I questioned one of them, Gilda, about it later, and she said the jokes offended her. ''So why,'' I asked, ''do you listen?''

''That's just Larry,'' Gilda responded. ''It's part of the turf when you work for him.''

Larry's joking was a disguised power play: a way to establish his authority at the start of each workday. In a section titled ''What's So Funny?'' from her best-seller *You Just Don't Understand* (William Morrow, 1990), Deborah Tannen explains: ''Making others laugh gives you a fleeting power over them . . . at the moment of laughter, a person is temporarily disabled.'' This is why some people in power like to tell jokes but don't always want to listen to them. Again, as with sexual harassment, power is the key. If these women understood the degree to which Larry forced them into a weaker position with each dirty joke, they wouldn't have laughed at all.

Now, I don't want to make the same mistake other how-to-survive books have made by placing the responsibility on clerks for a boss's boorish behavior. Too many discussions of sexual harassment devote pages of instruction to teaching victims how to tiptoe around abusers, and I'm tired of hearing it. I certainly didn't blame those women for Larry's inability to act like a gentleman in a professional office or for his need to seize power each morning at others' expense. Larry needed to stop. But he wasn't stopping, and these women were afraid of risking their jobs by taking a stand against his anatomically correct humor. I have a solution that disables the joke teller, taking power away from the abuser and giving it back to the support staff.

✎ Public Shunning Works

Shunning is a powerful weapon against creeps. Societies have used it for thousands of years to change deviant behavior. One form of shunning, the walkout, allows you to express your feelings about inappropriate humor without jeopardizing your job. After all, there are many ways to speak out that don't use actual words.

When someone like Larry enters the office with one of his putrid jokes, and you don't want to hear it, walk away. Don't wait for the punch line. Elegantly and quietly leave the room. If you prefer, you can act busy or pretend to go do something that "can't wait." Your insistence upon silently removing yourself from the offending situation will speak volumes to everyone present. This method is especially effective when the offender is a high-ranking executive or lawyer, and you can't say something without starting a no-win fight. Had any one of Larry's employees walked away, especially the women closer to his age, he would have been chagrined, and probably wouldn't have embarrassed himself further by trying it again.

Of course, the jokester is likely to label you a prude. It's really his only defense, and human nature being what it is, he will probably accuse you of Sunday-school manners to lessen his embarrassment over your reaction. When I walked away while a police captain told a lewd joke to a group of female officers, he stopped and said, loudly, "I'll tell this one later when there aren't sensitive ears in the room." Naturally, he tried to make me seem abnormal for not wanting to listen. Yet two police officers stopped by my desk later to let me know they appreciated my doing something. He had been a problem for a long time, and they didn't know how to respond. The joker may pick on you for reacting, but you'll find people siding with you as well.

Similarly, never laugh at a punch line when you don't think the joke is funny. This is especially effective with racial or religious jokes. You don't need to say anything to make this point. Your silence as you return to work will be deterrent enough.

If the creepy comedian tries telling you jokes in private, walking out is still effective. Even if it means leaving your own office or cubicle, do so. Now, I love jokes, and most of my friends know this. However, a stock analyst named Hal used this as an excuse to talk dirty to me. He'd show up at my work cubicle in the afternoon to tell me the latest smutty joke, culled from his collection of porno magazines. These moments were uncomfortable for me. The more nervous I became, the better Hal seemed to like it.

One day I didn't let him even finish setting up the joke. I simply stood up and walked past him out into the office, where I poured myself a cup of coffee. He waited for me, but I didn't return to my desk. When he asked if I was coming back, I said, "Not until you leave." When he tried again later, I repeated the walkout. Eventually, Hal stopped bothering me.

Of course, all office creeps aren't male. Many offices have one or two women who lack dignity and who embarrass themselves or their co-workers. One of these women, Stephanie, gave me a big smile when I showed up for work as a temp one day. "Oh, great!" she cried. "Now you can take over the sexual duties with Fred. I'm all worn out." I didn't know what to say. Fred looked confused as well. Later I learned that she usually "kidded around" like this and that nobody stopped her. One day she pulled her dress up to her waist in front of a group of guys to prove that her panty hose had control tops. (And they say men are the only naughty-jokes buffoons.) Again, walking away from situations like these, without comment, is your best defense. A well-timed "Pardon me," in a straightforward, dry delivery as you leave, helps too.

There's a fine line between creepy, stupid, or inappropriate behavior and harassment, and many people don't know where to draw it. I say that anyone who does anything you dislike even after you speak to them about it or walk away is a harasser. If the above tips don't fix the problem, you may have a more serious situation on your hands. In the sections below I talk about the kind of guerrilla tactics that will instantly identify you as a victor and not a victim. Once the creeps smell that heady combination of triumph and retribution around you, they'll slink off to menace someone else.

✎ When Creepiness Turns Criminal: Navigating the "Gray Areas"

Touching is never acceptable in an office except for handshakes and collegial, Dale Carnegie-style shoulder patting, which should only be used in formal situations anyway. If someone touches you at the office in an intimate manner, you have every right to be outraged and to take appropriate action.

But what should you do? Judith Martin (Miss Manners) has a wonderful suggestion for dealing with touchers:

> *The thing to do is to scream and say, "Oh, I'm sorry, you startled me." Then move away. They don't do it a second time.*

This advice is stronger than it sounds. Remember that you're not alone in most offices, so nothing can go on in secret between you and someone else if you choose to publicize it. Your hearty scream of surprise, however brief, will genuinely frighten most touchers. *Don't just go "eek," scream!* You can be nice and loud on this one, and it will make you feel stronger and less vulnerable to future attacks. People may come running to see if you are all right. You can simply respond that Larry startled you. If they ask what he did, answer with "Why don't you ask Larry."

If this seems overly dramatic to you or even personally embarrassing ("How could I just scream in an office?") remember that it only needs to happen once. Also remember that the toucher will probably not be unknown to his or her colleagues, since harassers usually like to spread their beautiful love around. Everyone will get the picture, without a caption, and most people will be on your side. Touching is a reasonably rare occurrence, and if you try this tactic, it should become rarer still.

✎ Publicize Harassment: There Is Strength in Numbers

When harassment problems cross over from irritating to threatening or criminal, "going public" can make you feel better, and safer. Sometimes your best protection from one guy can be another guy or a strong woman. I'm not physically intimidating, and

ASSOCIATED PRESS

Former secretary Paula Jones and her lawyers

most creeps aren't too afraid that I'll meet them in a dark alley some night. So I've ''recruited'' a little help in the past to get verbal molesters off my case.

I always make friends with the security guards wherever I work. When a co-worker from another department hung around waiting for me to get on elevators alone, I told the guards and their sergeant the problem. One of them chuckled quietly. ''We've heard about him before. We'll talk to him.'' They didn't make a scene; they just stopped him on his way into work for a little chat one morning. Maybe the message had more authority coming from someone in uniform. He left me alone after that.

Another time a female friend of mine (who was six feet two and a bodybuilder) simply showed up early one morning on the doorstep of a fellow we knew. This joker enjoyed saying shocking things to women when he got them alone, and he relied on their embarrassed silence to continue his game. So at six-thirty one morning, my friend banged on his door, knowing full well she was waking him up. When he came to the door, wiping sleep out of his eyes, and peered through the screen, she yanked it open and got in his face. He started to object with an annoyed ''Hey . . .'' but she cut him off. She announced, loudly enough for all the neighbors to hear, that there would be no more problems between him and the women in my department or she would come back, with several friends. Needless to say, the guy was unprepared for this little "wake-up call." He protested, lamely, and cursed a little. Whenever my friend answered one of his questions, she did so in the same loud voice, explaining things not only to him but to everyone else in the community that morning. There wasn't much he could do without starting a fight that he had no hope of winning. He couldn't even complain later on, for how could he tell the story without explaining why she was there in the first place? He stopped bothering us.

Many books recommend that you file lawsuits, call the police, or complain to management. Some of them have detailed instructions on how to make an EEOC complaint. In my experience, these things don't work. EEOC is pretty ineffective, and most of its cases are her-word-against-his matters. Lawsuits are expensive and hard to win, plus they frequently take years. The police won't do anything unless someone actually beats or rapes you. Even if someone threatens you repeatedly, the best the police can offer is squad car assistance if an attack occurs.

Complaining to management does about as much good. You have to give it a try, if for no other reason than to establish a consensus about a particular abuser, but it usually gets you nowhere. I tried telling a managing partner about an attorney who shouted at me, berated me, and threatened to fire me multiple times a day. The partner listened attentively, promised to help, and then forgot about the whole thing the moment I left his office. Some personnel officers simply match the same abuser with employee after employee until they find someone meek enough to tolerate his behavior. Write a memo to document the abuse, and meet with a supervisor to tell your side of the story, but don't expect much unless you're in the mood for a protracted, exhausting, and often fruitless argument.

Of course, you owe it to yourself and your co-workers to try. You just might talk with the one manager in a thousand who has the intelligence and integrity to help you. Also, by talking to management and filing a written complaint, you establish a public record about a harasser. The next person who complains is much more likely to be heard. But don't be surprised if this effort does little to solve your immediate problem.

Instead of relying on these often disappointing tactics, use a device that inventors have been employing for years to protect their rights. If an inventor wants to prove when he had a certain idea, he will frequently type up detailed plans, make several copies, have them notarized, and then send them to himself, his associates, and his lawyer via registered mail. The registered mail system will accurately date- and time-stamp the letters. He will keep one sealed letter on file at home. Should anyone steal his idea, he can sue them and prove that he had the idea first by showing the sealed envelope in court and letting the judge see that it contained a dated, notarized statement.

If a boss or co-worker makes your life miserable because of sexual harassment that you can't prove, document it. Type out four copies of a statement on the day the offense occurs, noting the time, the place, who said what, and why you feel threatened. Have all the copies individually notarized. Send one to a trusted friend, another to yourself, a third to a lawyer, and *send the fourth to the offender with a cover letter*, all by registered mail. In the cover letter, tell the offender that you have documented the abuse and circulated copies. Remind him that the letters will not be opened unless he does something to warrant it. This method works especially well on hard-core abusers, because they know that they are breaking the law but they assume you can't prove anything. How wrong they'll be.

Patricia did this when her married ex-boyfriend, who had also been her boss before she quit, repeatedly threatened to hurt her. She feared he might even try to kill her and she was terrified. The police said they couldn't do anything since it was her word against his. So she circulated registered-mail letters documenting the threat and providing as much information on the fellow as possible. She sent one of these to her ex. The cover letter said, in effect, "You'd better pray for my good health. If anything happens to me, other people, including my lawyer, now have a registered letter on file saying you had something to do with it." She told him that she had instructed a friend to send copies of the letter to his boss, his wife, the local newspaper, and the police if she should have a bad accident or die. Dramatic? You bet, but it worked. He never bothered her again.

✎ Sexual Harassment Is Management's Problem

In sexual harassment situations where the offender has a boss, I blame the harasser and his or her boss equally. People shouldn't act inappropriately in the office. When they do, supervisors should immediately stop the behavior. However, most managers do nothing about sexual harassment. Some don't care, and others are actually afraid of the abusive employee. Many managers you complain to actually think it's fine to sexualize the boss-secretary relationship or to hit on the receptionists. It's funny to them. No matter how seriously they seem to take your complaints, they'll laugh about it once you're out of earshot. ("Hey, Stan, I had another receptionist complain about you. What is this, you're going for some kind of a record?") Whether they admit it or not, managers who tolerate sexual harassment create a hostile work environment by refusing to take action.

Many companies will ignore sexual abuse or harassment in the office until they have no alternative. They'll protest that they have no power over the offender, and they'll put their heads in the sand, hoping the problem will go away. Instead of facing the abuser and forcing him or her to change, they will ask you to change. And they will do nothing to protect other employees who may continue to suffer the abuse without uttering a single complaint.

✎ Things Are Never as Simple as They Are in Books

Unfortunately, although there is only one way to be a lady or a gentleman, there are endless ways to be a boor. Rude and abusive people will never tire of finding ways to make their fellow humans uncomfortable.

Most people put up with office harassment. Most harassers know this. The moment you speak out against office harassment, even if nobody listens, you stop being a victim. By confronting harassers, using Miss Manners's scream technique on touchers, and by complaining *publicly* about inappropriate behavior, you stand a chance of turning office sentiment against abusers.

The modern office is rather like a schoolyard, filled with little boys and girls who do the stupidest things out of sheer boredom.

These childish behaviors can go from harmless to harmful quickly, however. My best advice is to keep yourself above the fray, avoiding the boozy parties, keeping your sex life confined to people you don't have to work with, and adopting a slightly more conservative "public face" than you may actually wear at home.

On this note, a word of caution. Not every abuser is mentally stable. You'll want to decide whether the person making your life miserable is merely obnoxious or actually dangerous. The average harasser is high enough up in an organization to believe that he or she is beyond the rules. Typically, this person suffers from a combination of arrogance, horniness, and poor judgment, but he or she is seldom completely out of control. If you fear that your abuser will harm you physically or seek revenge, don't try to confront him or her alone. Call 9 to 5's support line (1-800-522-0925) and get one-on-one advice.

Will these measures keep you from being harassed? Absolutely not. But they will filter out the pathetic-but-probably-harmless everyday fools who plague us all, allowing you to see who the real troublemakers are. When you isolate them, you'll be able to take more rational action, either by following my suggestions for more serious situations or by using the ideas in this book to land yourself a better job that makes you happier and doesn't wreck your self-confidence every working day.

A CULTURAL HISTORY OF SECRETARIES: A Century of Images from *Television*, Film, *Comics*, and Real Life

"How to Succeed in Business Without Really Trying" (1967)

Secretarial duties haven't always been women's work. Far from it. Would you believe that Fiorello H. La Guardia, New York City's ninety-ninth mayor and the namesake of La Guardia Airport, began his professional life as a *stenographer*? The shorthand course he took cost $7.50, nearly half a week's salary in 1906. He then did steno work at Abercrombie & Fitch, making $80 a month.

He wasn't alone. It may be hard to imagine now, but men had a stranglehold on the secretarial profession until about 1930. Marjorie Wolfe writes that Katherine Gibbs (of the white-gloved secretarial course) began her famous finishing school in 1911 in order to ''smash male dominance of the field.'' Women going to work soon became the norm: they established themselves prominently in the nation's workforce, and after 1945 it would be hard to find a man behind a typewriter again. What happened?

First there was the Depression. Some women went to work as an extension of their suffragist beliefs, but many did so out of economic necessity. To hear Hollywood tell it at the time, women going to the office was some sort of sociological disaster, tearing them away from the debutante balls and fancy honeymoons they might have enjoyed before their families' stocks plunged in 1929. In the 1940 film *Kitty Foyle*, Ginger Rogers looked back on the 1930s and reminisced: ''Then came the Depression, and you had to trade in a few of those dreams for a volume of Gregg shorthand, remember?''

In reality, however, many women found the role of ''white-collar girl'' freeing. They enjoyed earning their own money, making their own decisions, and, for a talented and fortunate few who found advancement opportunities, crafting real careers for themselves.

Joan Harrison was one example. She started work in 1935 as Alfred Hitchcock's personal secretary. Soon, though, she began writing; ultimately she made substantial creative contributions to Hitchcock's films. John Javna notes that Harrison co-wrote such classic scripts as *Rebecca, Suspicion*, and *Foreign Correspondent*. By the 1940s she was one of the few female film producers in the world. In 1955 Hitchcock promoted Harrison again, to associate producer of his successful television program, *Alfred Hitchcock Presents*. Harrison used secretarial work as a logical first step to a rewarding career. If she wasn't exactly typical, at least she demonstrated the possibilities opening up for women as the office began to let them in.

During World War II, most able-bodied men went to war, and many women trained for a variety of positions according to their abilities, not their gender. They helped run American business while the men fought. As more experienced women moved into management, younger women across America packed their suitcases and headed for Washington or New York to be typists and stenographers. In his best-seller *Washington Goes to War* (Alfred Knopf, 1988), David Brinkley describes a typical scene:

> *They came on every train and bus, nearly all of them women, wearing dyed-to-match sweaters and skirts and carrying suitcases tied shut with white cotton clothesline, or cardboard boxes printed with the names of the sewing machines and hair dryers that had come in them. They carried department-store shopping bags already splitting up the sides. They came in response to recruiting advertisements in local newspapers across the country.*

Being a steno for Uncle Sam wasn't just a patriotic job: it was an adventure. If you were a teenager or young woman from a small town who had seen the ravages of poverty in the Depression, you might very well jump at the chance to move to the big city and earn money while meeting new people and helping your country win the war.

So places for women in the workforce grew at two levels. Thousands of clerical jobs opened up at the bottom, and thousands of vacated jobs in the middle and at the top became available to qualified women for the first time, as the men who held them marched off to war.

Then World War II ended, and the soldiers came home. Most of them needed work. Women jumped (or were pushed) out of the more challenging high-level jobs they had held since the war began. The law demanded that any soldier who left a job to fight for Uncle Sam be allowed back into it, and that the replacement worker—usually a woman—step aside. The war left behind it a much bigger federal government, and correspondingly larger state and local governments, plus newly enhanced industries, with plenty of clerical jobs to go around. While the men regained control of the corporate helm, women found their old jobs waiting for them as secretaries and stenographers. If a woman didn't like commanding a Dictaphone after a few years of giving the orders, then she was simply unpatriotic.

The postwar economic boom gave male corporate America the excuse it needed to extinguish a potential rival: *female* corporate America. After all, many economists predicted that the boom might be a prelude to an even bigger depression. Former GIs felt they had enough to fear from Russia and the atomic bomb without worrying about competing with a woman for a job. If Howard, a World War II veteran, can make a fine living as an executive (the thinking went) why should his wife work? Won't she take away a job from another vet who *really* needs the income? What's worse, won't the neighbors think that Howard isn't a good provider? Partly in response to the stigma of being working wives, and partly to allay their husbands' fears about displacement in the workplace, most married women went back home after the war, and stayed there.

During the postwar atomic age, a new sexual freedom affected everyone from the beatniks to the man in the gray flannel suit. Perhaps it happened because the nation needed to "loosen its corsets" after years of living up to a puritan image. Maybe the constant threat of nuclear annihilation gave people the excuse they needed be a little naughty. Whatever the reason, 1950s secretaries found the office atmosphere much more sexually charged.

This was back in the days when the want ads were still divided into "jobs for women" and "jobs for men" (printed on different pages). Companies could legally advertise for employees of a certain race, age, and gender, so bosses naturally asked for pretty, young, single (that is, *nonthreatening*) women to assist them in clerical tasks. Managers enjoyed having a "girl" around to smile sweetly and fetch lunches, and the secretarial role became increasingly decorative.

Hollywood cashed in on this new sexual climate; it gave the working fellow a sly wink and suggested that the secretary was a more interesting plaything than a suburban wife or a downtown mistress. As images of the administrative assistant deteriorated in magazines, in film, and on television, secretarial jobs stopped appearing on the men's side of the want ads. The women who accepted secretarial jobs found their roles considerably dumbed down and sexed up.

A mechanical genius she's not.

She panics at the sight of dials, levers, and rows of buttons. And she still refers to any mechanical object as a "do-hinkie."

Yet it took her only 8 minutes

to learn how to operate her Victor calculator.

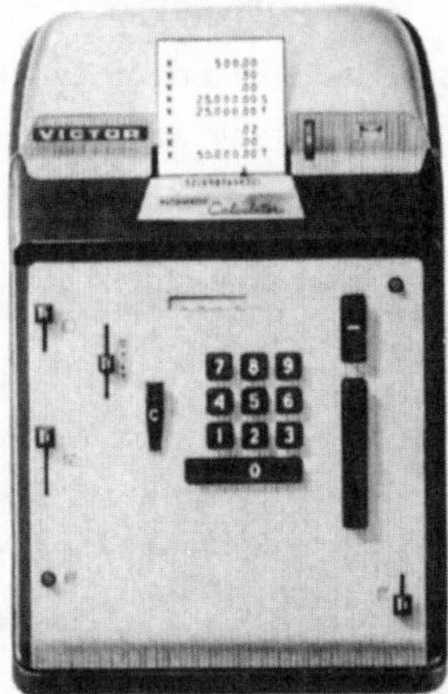

It's all quite simple. One keyboard only; ten lone keys. Touch-system operation, just like a typewriter. Even an easy-to-read printed tape. Give the Victor a tryout in your office and watch your girls become 8-minute wonders.

Put errors out of business with America's most complete line of figuring machines: printing calculators and multipliers, Comptometer calculators, simplex, duplex and wide-carriage adding machines. Victor Comptometer Corporation, Business Machines Group.

VICTOR

3900 N. ROCKWELL ST.
CHICAGO, ILLINOIS 60618

Please send me a free "Problem-Solver," prepared especially for my type of business.

T-75

Name __________

Company __________

Type of business __________

Address __________

City __________ State __________

Playboy, and its founder, Hugh Hefner, made a fortune capitalizing on this new sexual freedom. In many ways, *Playboy* changed the way American men viewed women, and it certainly affected the way women viewed themselves. In the 1940s, stars like Lauren Bacall and Katharine Hepburn wore slacks, made wisecracks, and played up their intellects. In the 1950s, Hefner convinced whole generations of men that they'd rather embrace the Playboy Bunny. He undressed his Playmates and draped them in jewelry and furs, presenting them as accessories to the well-appointed bachelor's life. A pipe dream? Sure, but men across America bought it. They believed that success meant driving fast cars, breaking the bank at Monte Carlo, and bedding all the Bunnies they could handle.

What did this have to do with secretaries? Everything. The first Playboy Bunny was Hefner's private secretary, Janet Pilgrim. She never stripped, but she wore an ermine stole perilously low around her shoulders, revealing deep cleavage. Neale Baxter notes that Hefner asked Pilgrim to pose so often, she reportedly said, "Just once more, but you'll have to buy me an Addressograph machine." The message was clear: Secretaries were no longer working partners. They were potential Playmates.

As popular tastes changed, Hefner offered up tame, innocuous images of women as snuggly Bunnies. Stars like Bacall, Hepburn, Ginger Rogers, and Bette Davis (none of whom ever posed for *Playboy*) had to make room for Jayne Mansfield, Brigitte Bardot, and Sophia Loren (all of whom did). For those men who worried that they might lose their jobs to women after the war, this must have been quite a comfort. *Playboy* and Hollywood helped America create a "place" for women in the office: one where they couldn't do men a bit of harm.

The movies and *Playboy* were so closely intertwined that a young Hollywood starlet agreed to be Hefner's first centerfold. Her name was Marilyn Monroe, and in December 1953 she appeared nude in *Playboy*. On the big screen, just the year before, she'd had a supporting part in the Cary Grant film *Monkey Business*, playing Lois Laurel, a secretary hired for her body, not her brains. Miss Laurel is *so* incompetent at her job that in one scene her boss hands her a memo, thinks better of it, and says, "Find someone to type this." A secretarial stereotype was born.

From Monroe's turn as a dimwit with dynamite legs, it was

a short step to the secretary as a boss-obsessed sexpot, unable to resist manly charms. In 1955's *Kiss Me Deadly* (based on the Mickey Spillane novel), Mike Hammer's secretary, Velda, adores him, desires him, and risks her life to help him. Hammer wouldn't have it any other way. In this detective's world, getting a "dame" like Velda to fall for him means she'll feed him, bed him, and bail him out of jail. When she's not laying a thick, juicy steak on one of his frequent black eyes.

Then came Bond. James Bond: the quintessential Playboy. Author Ian Fleming once said, in a 1963 interview: "I'm sure James Bond, if he were an actual person, would be a registered reader of *Playboy*." James Bond movies in the 1960s and 1970s had M's secretary, Miss Moneypenny, hopelessly in love with him. He responded to her adoration by treating her like a child. In the book *Diamonds Are Forever*, Bond threatened to spank Moneypenny: Fleming reported, "She secretly thrilled to the thought."

Thanks to *Playboy* pinups, Mike Hammer, James Bond, and the like, some men began to gleefully confuse members of their clerical staffs with inflatable dolls. Many women played along, perhaps because they enjoyed the comparative sexual freedom in a puritan era, or perhaps because they needed the money. *Cosmopolitan* editor Helen Gurley Brown, author of the 1962 best-seller *Sex and the Single Girl*, recalled a game called "Scuttle" at one 1950s office in which a man "would select a secretary, chase her down the halls . . . catch her and take her panties off. Nothing wicked ever happened." She claimed that the "girls" wore their prettiest panties to work, in case they should be singled out for this honor (*Time*, November 11, 1991). But what represented liberation to some people was oppression for the rest. The secretarial profession never recovered.

✎ How to Exceed in Sexism, or "A Secretary Is Not a *Boy*"

Respected authors, Broadway playwrights, filmmakers, and television producers all joined in the melee. Shepherd Mead's *How to Succeed in Business Without Really Trying* also appeared in serial form in *Playboy*. It later became a 1961 Broadway hit, winning the Pulitzer Prize for drama.

In *How to Succeed . . .*, Mead follows young J. Pierrepont Finch on his quick rise from the mail room to the boardroom. The articles are witty and even somewhat useful, but their implications for women are chilling. A choice of assistant becomes as important as the proper car or the right scotch. In this scenario, age and looks are everything:

> *You must decide which choice you will make, the beauty or the beast.*
>
> The Beauty. *If you decide on this course, select a girl of ravishing beauty, first making sure that she does not belong to another.*
>
> *Soon your little corner will become a mecca for influential men. . . .*
>
> The Beast. *Some prefer to take the opposite tack. Select the oldest, fattest, and least attractive woman in the building. Leave no stone unturned. With thirty or forty years' experience in the company, she will be able to do all your dull, routine work better than you can. This will leave you free to think, decide, and endear yourself to those around you.*

Men and women hiring administrative assistants still use a variation on this theme when they consider their options. Shall I hire a workhorse who gets things done? Or do I want a sorority-girl type who will flatter my clients? Shall I hire someone intelligent who might quit in a year, or do I want a pushover who will do whatever I say without question?

Office sex jokes reached such a pitch that the showstopper "A Secretary Is Not a Toy" from *How to Succeed . . .* was actually considered witty. The song featured women in candy-colored dresses filing their nails in rhythm, brushing their hair to extreme heights, applying cosmetics, painting on nail glitter, and even giving themselves facials on the job.

✎ H2$ (How to Succeed) in the 1990s

In case you're thinking that was just the 1960s, think again. This chestnut is back, and doing well in a current Broadway revival; Matthew Broderick recently won a Tony Award for his role as

Finch. So how does a contemporary production justify all that stereotyping? The producers just repeat the same tired line. ''But, folks,'' they insist, ''it's satire!''

Few viewers are going along with the ''satire'' explanation. Critic Anthony Tommasini writes:

> *When Rosemary, the good-hearted secretary who falls for Finch, sings her fantasy of life in the 'burbs with an executive hubby (''Happy to Keep His Dinner Warm''), you can argue that the song is just a send-up of the way things were. If so, it's an uncomfortable send-up.* (''Broadway Revivals Dance to New Tune,'' *The Christian Science Monitor*, March 23, 1995.)

When *New York Times* critic Frank Rich reviewed the play, he wondered why nothing had changed in the thirty years since this confection first appeared:

> *Indeed, if some of ''How to Succeed'' has dated since 1961, its view of men and women in the workplace is all too depressingly contemporary. The shock of revisiting the show in 1995 is the discovery that it may be the most timely entertainment in New York right now.*

PHOTO BY JOAN MARCUS

(left to right) Megan Mullaly, Victoria Clark, and Matthew Broderick in Broadway's *How to Succeed in Business Without Really Trying*

> . . . *No wonder the all-male executive meetings at World Wide Wicket still look so familiar; at the top level almost nothing has changed. . . . Three decades later, a secretary is still a toy.* (" 'Succeed' Succeeds Again," March 26, 1995.)

✎ What Does This Have to Do with Your Life at the Office?

Most men and women at the top of today's businesses grew up in the decades before the 1970s. *Playboy, Esquire*, television, comic strips, the movies, and other popular media probably had more to do with how they view the office than anyone's much-touted "glass ceiling" reviews.

If we can't change how certain bosses view administrative assistants, at least we can try to understand them. From the following pop-culture sampler, you'll get an idea of what the typical boss over age thirty sees when he or she looks at the desk in the middle of the office. Of course, these are stereotypes. But they're the ones that bosses commonly think of when they get out a pile of résumés and start interviewing applicants.

THE 1930s

Comic strips were much more popular before television. Several of them starred secretaries. Two of the most famous, "Somebody's Stenog" and "Connie," featured stenographers who were really just flappers waiting for husbands to take them away from office work. On a typical workday, Somebody's Stenog spent most of her time fielding passes from the male staff, eating lunch, and shopping downtown. She actually typed only between 4:45 and 5:00, after which she trudged home, exhausted. Connie was a lovely blond fashion plate who led a charmed office life, despite her co-worker Dolores's attempts to undermine her professional credibility.

Men coined the term "office wife" in the 1930s to describe the closest woman in their lives besides their spouses. Often, however, secretaries became pitted against wives in a psychological tug-of-war over the attentions of busy men who spent most of their time at the office. At the movies, you could see such bedroom/office melodramas as *The Office Wife*, in which secretary Anne Murdock ditched a boyfriend so that she could seduce boss Lewis Stone. In 1936 there was a choice of two office dramas, *More Than a Secretary* and *Wife vs. Secretary.*

The male secretary was on his way out in the professional office, and on the big screen he was all but gone. *Duck Soup*, the Marx Brothers classic, was one of the last films to feature a male assistant. Zeppo Marx played Bob Rolland, personal assistant to Rufus T. Firefly (Groucho Marx). In one scene, Groucho asks Zeppo to take a letter:

ZEPPO: *"Who to?"*
GROUCHO: *"To my dentist. Dear dentist: Enclosed find check for $500, yours very truly, send it off* immediately*!"*
ZEPPO: *"I'll have to enclose the check first."*
GROUCHO: *"You do, and I'll fire you!"*

The movie showed Rolland as a "typical" assistant who was definitely smarter than his boss.

THE 1940s

In 1940, Ginger Rogers got her first Oscar as a secretary. She played Kitty Foyle, a working-class Irish woman who fell in love with her high-society boss, Wynfield Strafford. Just like the earlier 1930s images of the secretary as an office wife and a rival to the boss's marriage, Kitty Foyle walked—or rather fell off of—the fine line between an office assistant and a girlfriend. She was a confusing cross between a competent woman and a cheesecake pinup; in fact, Kitty has her first, accidental interview with Wyn at home when she's wearing only a slip. He gets a good look at her face and figure in this barely dressed state, and he instantly asks her father if he can hire her. Dad sells her skills to Wyn like he's trading a horse, and Wyn immediately makes a deal, since he could use a girl at work to "brighten up the place."

No, wait. It gets better. Kitty starts work at once, and soon she and Wyn are making bedroom eyes at each other right there beside the Dictaphone machine. She tells him he has a lovely voice, "just like Ronald Colman." He tells her she has shapely legs.

Of course, this is the 1940s, so instead of sleeping together they marry, but his family never approves and they finally part ways. The film tries to convince the viewer that this was for the best; that the wealthy bosses of this world should find equally wellborn wives. The underlying message is if you're down, stay down: women like Kitty Foyle must be content with poor but honest fellas from their own social class.

Up until now, married women hadn't worked for a living if there was anything the family could do to prevent it. During World War II, however, the War Department promoted a new image: this secretarial equivalent of "Rosie the Riveter" handled a typewriter much as a man would handle a gun in the war against the Nazis. David Brinkley writes about one 1940s ad which claimed "It takes twenty-five girls behind typewriters to put one man behind the trigger in this war." Brinkley notes that this was of course an exaggeration, since the Army grew to 7.5 million men, and 187 million "girls" would have been more than the total U.S. population. But the point was clear: men *needed* women as co-workers in the office. They came out of a sense of patriotism, and stayed because they needed the money and, often enough, enjoyed the work. Unfortunately, the new freedom of the 1950s that devoured most secretaries' professional hopes wasn't far off.

THE 1950s

Not all 1950s images of secretaries were sexpot cartoons like Marilyn Monroe's portrayal of Lois Laurel. Many 1950s films relied on a stock character: the tough, devoted assistant to a hard-boiled detective. These secretaries were admirable: they were competent professionals who adored their bosses and who would do anything, even die, to serve their men. Let's picture one now, sitting at her desk in front of the private eye's closed-door office. Suddenly the bad guys force their way in and demand to see the chief. She says he's not taking visitors. They say this is an unscheduled appointment he'd be wise not to miss. One of them attempts to move past her and open his door. She blocks his way with her body. "Wait a minute," she cries, "you can't go in there!" You've gotta admire a dame like that; she'd probably take a bullet to protect the big lug.

Television's *Private Secretary* (1953–57) offered Susie McNamara as the professional secretary every girl wanted to emulate. Ann Sothern played the assistant to a theatrical agent who insisted on becoming overly involved in her boss's personal life. The show was a huge hit; secretaries flooded Ann Sothern with mail asking for office tips. An exasperated Sothern finally told *TV Guide*:

> *Look. . . . I am not a secretary. I am an actress. I have been an actress for quite some time now. Acting is the only trade I know.*

In fact, Sothern couldn't even type. The producers had to have a fake typewriter specially prepared so that she could seem to clack on the keys without having to learn the proper form. Sothern didn't choose to be an icon, but her fans wanted to be more like her. An assistant recorded her costume for every show, so that ardent viewers could copy her clothes and trademark eyewear.

Just after Susie left the air, *Perry Mason* debuted, and with it Barbara Hale became a television star as Della Street, legal secretary. Fans now had something else to admire besides a sharp wardrobe and a dream job; they looked up to Della for her connection to the charismatic attorney who never lost a case. Della helped Perry win; she was smart, attractive, and thoroughly devoted.

Oddly, however, even though Della Street was supposed to be smart, many people couldn't see her that way. One director shouted at Hale on the set: ''Just stand there and be quiet and act as though you are thinking.'' Hale never forgot this; no matter how competent and admirable her character may have been, many viewers held the deep-down assumption that she couldn't think independently, if she could even think at all.

For the crowd that so enjoyed seeing Marilyn Monroe's legs in *Monkey Business*, there were great gams on the small screen as well. In 1958, legs were all anybody ever saw of twenty-one-year-old Mary Tyler Moore when she played Sam the receptionist on *Richard Diamond, Private Detective*. Moore left the show when the producers refused to increase her $80-per-week salary. Secretaries now had three things going for them: they were admirable, you could marry them, and they had fabulous, trademark body parts that made them unforgettable.

THE 1960s

If I could sum up the popular view of secretarial work in the 1960s with one word, it would be ''loyal.'' As in ''dog.'' No employee was ever more loyal and devoted than Evelyn Lincoln, John F. Kennedy's private secretary. In a classic photo, Lincoln stands beside Kennedy, looking dutiful and serene in her cat's-eye glasses and smart sheath dress. Her career with Kennedy was no accident either. With her skills and knowledge of Capitol Hill, Lincoln could have worked for any young senator, but she chose Kennedy in 1953 because she thought he had presidential potential. Evelyn Lincoln and John Kennedy were ''*Twins* syndrome'' personified: she sacrificed all to make sure that Her Man made it to the top.

On television, however, this loyal image became a caricature. Actor Nancy Kulp played an equally devoted but utterly ridiculous woman: Jane Hathaway, secretary to Commerce Bank president Milburn Drysdale on *The Beverly Hillbillies.* ''Miss Jane'' had a Vassar education and she quoted Shakespeare, but she found stuffy satisfaction pleasing her wealthy, obsequious boss. Her improbable infatuation with Jethro was a running gag on the show.

True story: Years after she'd retired from television, Kulp ran as a Democrat for Congress in her home state of Pennsylvania. Her opponent, Republican ''Bud'' Shuster, convinced Buddy Ebsen (who had played Jed Clampett on the show) to record political ads denouncing her candidacy. She lost.

Television reviewers focused on Kulp's looks, not her acting ability. One reviewer said she had ''the face of a shriveled balloon, the figure of a string of spaghetti, and the voice of a bullfrog in mating season.'' But Kulp wasn't naturally unattractive: she was costumed to look that way. Her dry delivery and tight-lipped, near-hysterical style were calculated to make her seem as hopelessly old-maidish as possible.

Secretarial work was still 1950s-style admirable, but it also suffered from its silly image on television. Another White House secretary, Geraldine Whittington, made history as the first African-American assistant to a President of the United States. Whittington was also the first American to know that Judge Thurgood Marshall was LBJ's pick for the Supreme Court. (*Jet*, February 15, 1993.) Yet characters like Miss Jane made real-life women like Evelyn Lincoln and Gerri Whittington seem vaguely ridiculous for their loyalty and for taking their jobs and their bosses so seriously.

This may have happened because typical bosses never valued secretarial work in the first place. In secret, bosses looked down on people who took dictation. That these jobs were exclusively

PHOTO BY MARTIN MILLS

Gail Fisher played secretary Peggy Fair on *Mannix*

for women made them twice as inconsequential, since most people didn't place a high value on women's work.

One glance at the want ads from any newspaper of the time will show you what I mean. Under "jobs for women" you could find secretaries, typists, and receptionists right next to ads for maids and nannies. I searched in vain through 1960s ads on the women's page for a job that either paid well or was described in challenging terms.

In the men's section, however, the words changed. Yes, the ads for junior executives and sales representatives were alongside positions for porters, bellmen, and delivery boys, but there was a difference. None of these ads asked for a man with "bright eyes" or a "sunny smile." Few requested that he be "under thirty-five" or "single only": in fact, older, married men were preferable. Women's ads sought pretty, young order takers; men's ads wanted go-getters. Men may have demanded unquestioning loyalty from their secretarial staffs, but they didn't really respect that loyalty. If they did, the position would have been promotable, and it would have paid more. It also might have showed up on the men's page.

Television in the 1960s featured many single women at the office, mostly because working married women were still suspected of having deadbeat husbands, or, worse, of "wearing the pants in the family." Many of the television secretaries from this period were widows, bravely getting on with their lives. Gail Fisher played one of the most poignant single women on the ultraviolent television series *Mannix*. She was Peggy Fair, whose husband, Mannix's friend, was supposed to have been killed in the line of duty. This made Peggy both loyal (she appeared grateful to Mannix for the job) and noble (she was working for all the right reasons). Fisher, a former Miss Black New Jersey, won a Best Supporting Actress Emmy for this role, but she never really cashed in. She didn't get many parts after *Mannix* ended, and she became discouraged with the Hollywood machine.

Commentary of the time made a big deal about Fisher's skin color. This seems gratuitous in retrospect, but it *was* important. In the real world, secretarial work was mostly a white girls' club. In those same newspaper want ads where you could find the women's and men's jobs separated, you could also find the word "white" in the list of requirements. If an ad didn't specify race, eight times out of ten it was for a housekeeper, a nanny, a cook, or a laborer.

In the 1960s, black women could see Gerri Whittington in the newspapers, or Gail Fisher on television, plus Cicely Tyson playing a social worker on *East Side/West Side*, Diahann Carroll playing a nurse on *Julia*, and Nichelle Nichols as Lieutenant Uhura on *Star Trek*. That was it. The rest of the working women both in real life and on television were white, well dressed, and conveniently between husbands.

On *The Doris Day Show,* Day played another single mother, Doris Martin, working at *Today's World* magazine in San Francisco. There was just one teeny problem: Martin's boss (played by McLean Stevenson) didn't approve of working mothers. The show was as squeaky-clean and presentable as Day's trademark daisy-fresh image, and if viewers hadn't known that Doris Martin had a child, they'd swear she was still a virgin. Secretaries, it seemed, never experienced actual, live sex. They just remembered it from the old days or, as in the case of Miss Jane and Jethro, they dreamed about it.

The serious, single-mom types aside, however, the decade seemed to belong to slapstick. Lucille Ball took one look at the American office and decided it was full of opportunities for goofing around with her kind of physical comedy. On *The Lucy Show*, later renamed *Here's Lucy,* Ball portrayed bank secretary Lucy Carter as almost a caricature of Ann Sothern's Susie. Like Susie, Lucy got into sticky situations involving her boss. She was a single mother who had to work, but she did so in such a nutty fashion that she never would have survived in the real workplace.

One of the funniest examples of slapstick was a two-person sketch on the long-running *Carol Burnett Show* (1967–78) in which Burnett played Mrs. Wiggins, secretary to Mr. Tudball (Tim Conway). Neither of them was really from this planet. Mr. Tudball had a strange neo-Italian accent, and he referred to his assistant as

''Mrs. A-Whiggins.'' Burnett's character was inept, again emphasizing how dumb many people believed secretaries really were.

In 1967, moviegoers could see the film versions of *How to Succeed in Business Without Really Trying* and *Thoroughly Modern Millie*, both musical comedies featuring secretaries. *Millie* was a strange film from a boom period in Hollywood musicals; it managed to be cloyingly sexist and scathingly racist in one sweep. Julie Andrews played Millie, a newcomer to the big city who bobbed her hair, flattened her ''fronts,'' and set out to find a man. She announced her plans to marry her boss—any boss—and she ''interviewed'' them to find the most suitable one. But, like the rest of the 1960s secretaries, Millie was doomed to press her nose against the glass, look in at Sexual Fulfillment, and dream.

THE 1970s

You are now entering the Women's Lib Zone. Please return your seat backs to their fully upright and locked positions, burn your bra, and prepare for a strange landing. Women's Lib was the catchword for 1970s-style feminism, and it seriously questioned the role of secretaries in the American office.

In 1972, three days after the Watergate burglary, White House secretary Rose Mary Woods deleted eighteen and a half minutes of a recorded phone call between Richard Nixon and H. R. Haldeman. Woods still maintains that the erasure was an accident, but documents released in 1995 implicate her even further in the cover-up. If she *did* delete that tape, then she becomes an apt icon for a decade of secretarial images that could best be described as ''serious.'' There was little to laugh at about feminism *or* secretaries in the 1970s, unless you're looking backward from twenty years later.

Those feminists who paid any attention to secretarial work at all saw it as something to salvage. Some called it the ''Achilles' heel'' of the women's movement. Others sought to empower the ''sisters'' in the office by challenging the ''coffee, tea, or me?'' image and asking—for the first time—who did this work and why.

The reactions were predictable. Mort Walker responded to feminism by trotting out a big-chested, pea-brained Miss Buxley, who made her first appearance in the World War II-era comic strip ''Beetle Bailey'' in 1971. The legendary television program *M*A*S*H* reached for a similar female image, although it pretended to be more up-to-date. *M*A*S*H* was famous for its scripts, which used the Korean conflict to mirror the Vietnam War. The stories tried to be hip and progressive by putting women and men in nonstereotyped roles (Radar and Klinger typed while the women braved the combat zones), but all it *really* did was substitute nurses for the secretaries of earlier decades. Instead of pinching an assistant's rear end, Hawkeye—the 1950s Playboy in the guise of a doctor—would reach for a nearby nurse.

Some television secretaries found their voices in the 1970s. Marcia Wallace played Carol Kester Bondurant, assistant to psychologist Bob Hartley and dentist Jerry Robinson on *The Bob Newhart Show*. Carol's assertive comic style was a model for how to talk back to your boss.

If only real life had been as amusing. For years, Wallace struggled with her weight, since she portrayed a secretary when they were still considered, as they had been for decades, at least partly decorative. In a poignant 1973 interview she revealed her weight-loss struggles, insisting "there's no such thing as a really funny fat girl."

As this serious decade continued, Diana Ross starred in *Mahogany*, the 1975 film that took her from a secretarial job on Chicago's South Side to the world of high-fashion modeling, where she broke the "color barrier." Meanwhile, in a send-up of *The Maltese Falcon* titled *The Black Bird*, Lee Patrick reprised her role as Sam Spade's secretary, Effie. She complained to Sam Spade, Jr. (George Segal) about how much she hated her boss, thereby striking some sort of retroactive blow against the cultural mores of an earlier generation.

Some movie secretaries seemed to parody this difference between how secretaries perceived themselves and how other people saw them. In *Saturday Night Fever* (1977) Karen Gorney played Stephanie, a secretary from Brooklyn who worked in Manhattan, but who still returned to Disco 2001 Odyssey in her home neighborhood to dance. She was the one being whipped around on that dance floor by a dashing, white-leisure-suited Tony Manero (John Travolta). Stephanie works for agents, and she believes that eventually she'll *be* one, especially since she meets famous musicians and works so close to power. On her first coffee date with Tony, however, she sounds more like an ambitious show-off, pretending to have social skills she actually lacks. She's convinced that she can escape Brooklyn simply by moving away and acting glamorous:

STEPHANIE: *"You know, I'm out of this scene, almost completely, you know, this Bay Ridge scene. I'm moving into Manhattan, I'm getting my own apartment. I'm changing. I'm really changing as a person, and I'm growing, you know what I mean? Nobody has any idea how much I'm growing."*

TONY: *(Laughs) "Why don't you just go on a diet?"*

Although he's crude, Tony seems honest; Stephanie just seems shallow and deluded. She tries to insult Tony by telling him, "You're a cliché, you're nowhere, on your way to noplace," but it sounds like she's merely commenting on her own life.

Feminism didn't appreciate how and why women became secretaries: it criticized women for accepting the very work that, twenty years earlier, had been admirable. Like Stephanie, many of them came from backgrounds where they were never taught how to communicate like a power broker, and they sounded ridiculous when they tried to mimic their bosses.

The sleeper-hit television series *WKRP in Cincinnati* suggested that "feminist" and "secretary" were still mutually exclusive terms, at least in the popular eye. Loni Anderson played Jennifer Marlowe, the front-desk receptionist at a failing FM radio station. She was *supposed* to be bright, but all viewers saw were her Farrah Fawcett good looks. In a *TV Guide* interview, Anderson insisted on Jennifer's intelligence, yet the interviewer remained unconvinced, noting "the jiggle, the wiggle, and the lemon-meringue hair" over her intellectual capacity. After a long decade of secretaries failing at the impossible task of fitting into even a modified feminist scenario, Jennifer succeeded by giving up. She wore tight sweaters and said "Oh, Herb" a lot. Ironically, she was the most famous secretarial icon of the time.

THE 1980s

The yuppie phenomenon hit secretaries hard, and I saw the carnage firsthand. I began in the trenches in the early 1980s, when the Reagan Revolution was in full swing. Our executive director's assistant came to the office every day wearing a dark blue suit, a white blouse, and a cranberry-colored ribbon necktie (remember those?), with a copy of *Working Woman* tucked under one arm.

She made suggestions to her boss about investment decisions, and she wrote memos to managers offering cost-cutting strategies. She wanted a piece of the big money action, but she never got ahead.

To her employers she looked ridiculous. Behind her back those same managers chuckled, wondering just who she thought she was. I listened to their comments, little knowing that their snide opinions probably extended to me as well. I had a crush on a middle manager, but although we were social buddies, he'd never date me. Why not? He wanted a girlfriend at his same "ladder level," or even one rung higher. Upward mobility had its price; you had to plan everything, including your love life, to enhance that all-important Career.

Hollywood and television tried to rationalize *why* secretaries weren't the same as their upwardly mobile bosses: it portrayed them as goofy, incompetent, undereducated, too plump, unmotivated, or any combination of these. Because of these unfortunate (and often incurable) drawbacks, such women naturally couldn't be expected to participate in their employers' fabulous successes and enjoy similar rewards. Yuppie bosses got to drive big Beemers, buy entire wardrobes from Ralph Lauren or Hugo Boss, and go to each other's wine-and-Brie parties. Their secretaries got to be tremendously excited for them.

Many real-life support staffers, from receptionists to office managers, responded to this pressure to Be Successful by getting a financial plan, an IRA, and a Filofax. Publishers offered a slew of dubious secretarial strategy books telling office assistants how to end up wearing a blue suit and a yellow tie with navy-blue dots like everyone else. One book, titled *Not Just a Secretary!*, showed a confident, coiffed woman holding a briefcase and striding through the revolving doors of a big corporation. Another book, *The Working Woman's Report*, quoted every available statistic to try to prove that secretaries were important and respected, just like everyone else. Employers changed the job title to "administrative assistant." Many assistants got business cards.

In 1980, the hit movie *9 to 5* aimed an arrow right at the disenfranchised secretaries who knew these big-bucks opportunities just weren't coming their way. It missed, and missed badly. After a funny first half obviously drawn from real-life experiences (including stories based on the book *9 to 5* by Ellen Cassedy and Karen Nussbaum, Penguin, 1983), the film copped out at the crucial moment by telling secretaries that the best response to an abusive boss was to shoot him with an elephant gun or put rat poison in his coffee.

In the real 9-to-5 world, sexual harassment made national headlines when former church secretary Jessica Hahn accused PTL ministers Jim Bakker and John Fletcher of sexual misconduct. Her charges brought down a religious empire. Apparently, however, her escapades with Bakker and the boys affected Hahn for life. After Bakker went to prison, Hahn packed her bags and moved into the Playboy Mansion to recuperate. A few commercials for No Excuses jeans and a couple of *Playboy* centerfolds later, she graduated to the world of cable TV talk shows and 1-900 chat lines.

Meanwhile, former attorney Greg Howard saw gold in them thar yuppies, and he created a tough working woman for the comic strips, "Sally Forth." Marcie was a secretary who reported to both Sally and her boss, Ralph. She was a real professional with a working woman's wardrobe and a fine rapport with her female boss:

SALLY: *"I can't tell you how much I appreciate you staying late to finish typing this report, Marcie . . . How can I thank you enough?"*

MARCIE: *(Holds up a cup) "A contribution to 'Marcie's margarita fund.' "*

SALLY: *(Reaches into her purse.) "Sounds like a worthy cause."*

MARCIE: *"It is. I'll get you a receipt for your income taxes."*

For the 1980s, it was a terrific image. Marcie never really developed, however. She's still working at the same desk today, and one is led to wonder if she has really had a decent raise. Perhaps Greg Howard should look into it.

The already established comic strip "Cathy" added a new character: Charlene the administrative assistant. Charlene seemed to like her office job, but she was the antidote to Cathy's yuppieism. She was much more interested in clothes, hairstyles, and her new marriage than in getting ahead. Whereas Cathy agonized over her future at Product Testing, wondering whether she'd ever move beyond reporting to Mr. Pinkley, Charlene quietly married one of

Cathy's ex-boyfriends, and seemed content thereafter to be a wife, spending her summers slathering herself with coconut oil for a smooth, all-over tan. While Charlene never appeared stupid, she didn't seem to spend too much time lost in contemplation either. Secretaries, it seemed, were not supposed to buy into the go-go 1980s with the same vengeance. Instead, they existed to help their *bosses* cash in as fully as possible.

It took Susan Ruttan to highlight the gap between office assistants and their bosses, both on-screen and in real life. From 1986 to 1994 she played Roxanne Melman, legal secretary to Arnie Becker, on *L.A. Law*. Newspaper columnist Carol Kleiman reported that when Ruttan learned that she earned less money than the other cast members on the show, she complained. The producers' answer? "You're just a secretary!"

Ruttan became an activist after this, working with national secretaries' organizations to help office assistants get a better working deal. She addressed the American Management Association's secretarial conference in 1993, telling her own stories of being a temp and a receptionist before her acting career.

There wasn't much Susan Ruttan or anyone else could do, however, about throwback characters like ditzy, breathy Ms. Dipesto. Dipesto, *Moonlighting*'s "rhyming receptionist," answered phones at the Blue Moon Detective Agency by reciting jingles like "Amnesia cases are our special today. Finding the real you is our forte." She set popular images of office workers back about two decades.

The big movie valentine of the 1980s for administrative assistants was the New York fairy-tale *Working Girl* (1988). This Melanie Griffith vehicle revisited the "spunky gal climbs the ladder" theme that *9 to 5* could have used but didn't. It was both hipper and wiser than its slapstick cousin, and it's still entertaining nearly a decade later.

The plot, however, was never believable or entirely satisfying. Tess McGill wanted a promotion from secretary to stockbroker. She struggled to finish her bachelor's degree, and she applied, repeatedly, to her company's junior executive program. Her boss gave her the bad news:

> *"The straight shot, Tessie, is they've turned you down for the entree program again . . . You have to remember,*

> *you're up against Harvard and Wharton graduates. What have you got, some night school? Some secretarial time on your sheet?''*

This put-down was actually a challenge, and I wanted to see Tess accept it and fight. Instead, though, she impersonated her new, female boss, and she lied at the highest levels in order to ''prove'' her suitability for a career in mergers and acquisitions. In this sense the film was realistic, since Wall Street is not known for lionizing the most honest among its ranks, but ultimately the film didn't say one thing about how someone like Tess could get ahead in real life.

And, of course, the movie stereotyped Tess as a lower-middle-class loser who changed herself overnight by mimicking a perfect 1980s yuppie. Just as in *9 to 5*, Tess's problem didn't entirely rest with mean old bosses who couldn't spot talent; to some extent it rested with Tess herself. She dressed like the queen of big hair and the $19.99 rack at Loehmann's until she discovered the wonderful world of $6,000 dresses (swiped from her boss's closet). She talked like a cross between Judy Holliday and a telephone date from a 1-900 service. In the movie, all of the other assistants stayed behind typewriters, presumably because they still teased their hair, wore garish eye makeup, and tawlked like New Yawkers (à la Stephanie from *Saturday Night Fever*). Only Tess, who suddenly sounded more high-class, broke free. By now, the story was hopelessly lost in make-believe.

Tess's closest girlfriend, Cyn, put it best. When Tess tried to pass herself off as boss Katharine Parker, Cyn gave her a reality check by leaning over and snidely whispering:

> *''Sometimes I sing and dance around the house in my underwear. It doesn't make me Madonna. Never will.''*

This little film tried and tried to convince itself, and its audience, that, gosh darn it, administrative assistants *could* close multimillion-dollar deals in the 1980s and land Harrison Ford in the sack to boot. The trouble is that no one, especially assistants, believed it.

Hollywood has always let working folks down when it came to secretarial roles. The 1980s proved that the entertainment industry didn't have the first clue about speaking to a mass concern with a measure of wit and intelligence. Assistants, forced to choose between an image of Dolly Parton swinging a lasso and Melanie Griffith modeling garter belts in her boss's closet chose neither, and continued to negotiate their office lives without benefit of any big-screen—or small-screen—dreams.

One real-life executive secretary, Mary Bridget Carroll, watched the men around her climbing the ladder and concluded it couldn't be *that* hard. After her former boss said she'd "never earn" as much money on another professional track as she did typing his correspondence, she proved him wrong. After decades as an assistant, she became a stockbroker. Then she wrote a book, *Overworked and Underpaid* (Fawcett Columbine, 1984), describing her trek from typist to trader. Her secret to success? She did what she *wanted* to do, without asking permission or waiting for a promotion. "When I've seen men move up who shouldn't have," she told *People* magazine, "I've thought if that nerd can do it, so can I."

But assistants wouldn't get any more real help from *Overworked and Underpaid* and *Working Girl* than they would from trying to follow their yuppie bosses up the corporate rungs. Nobody was saying what everybody except assistants knew: that the job was permanently slated for servanthood. Few 1980s bosses could tell the difference between their assistants and their housekeepers, except that housekeepers wouldn't agree to fetch coffee and go "Oh, Marvin, nice Rolex!"

THE 1990s

By the 1990s, bosses and administrative assistants were thoroughly confused about the secretarial role. Thanks to the 1980s message that anyone who didn't make partner, manager, or CEO was a dimwit, nobody knew what the job was anymore or how to portray it on the screen. Stereotype roles were supposedly out, yet directors and screenwriters found themselves reaching for the same stock characters whenever they needed an office assistant in a film. Spike Lee's *Jungle Fever* (1991) was typical. When yuppie architect Flipper (Wesley Snipes) became involved with his blue-collar secretary (Annabella Sciorra) in this odd look at interracial, intercultural love, I didn't know which I liked less:

Lee's portrayal of secretaries or his depiction of Italians. The whole kissing-on-the-drafting-table scene looked like an outtake from Canned Secretarial Roles We Have Known and Hated.

You could call the whole first half of the decade "vague" when it came to administrative assistants. On the television series *Herman's Head* (1991), Yeardley Smith played Louise Fitzer, an assistant who was more like a bright child than an adult. In one scene, Louise wore a white dress and put a bow on herself to present herself (and her virginity) to a suitor. How alluring.

This decade started with an uncomplimentary assumption that anyone still working as an administrative assistant or secretary had to have a screw loose somewhere. At the same time, however, companies squirmed to convince assistants that they were "important" and "respected" nationwide. Federal Express figured out that its most frequent customers were administrative assistants. It launched a new magazine *Via FedEx*, just for assistants, and distributed it to 320,000 readers. Among the items on a wish list that the magazine published were "control tops that don't feel like it" and "lipstick mirrors on the sides of staplers." (*The New York Times,* April 21, 1993.)

Lots of people accepted secretarial work as a steady "day job" while they pursued their *real* careers at night and on the weekends. Actor and comedian Josh Kornbluth was one example. He took his reminiscences of life as a legal secretary to the stage in *Haiku Tunnel*, a one-person show. Kornbluth started San Francisco law-firm life as a temp in the secretarial pool, but eventually the office manager tapped him for long-term duties. His character in *Haiku Tunnel* (named for a Hawaiian tunnel project the secretaries worked on) wrote a novel on the mainframe of the company's computer. He never believed the false "let's be pals" tone that the law partners took with him on the first day, and he spent time trying to understand his bosses (much as one would try to understand a Burmese water python) rather than simply complying with their orders. For example, when he noticed the family photos on his bosses' desks, and concluded that they must have some deep sociological meaning: *The photograph says: I have sex with women and I have two children—a prerequisite for tax law.*

Kornbluth wasn't all that unusual. Increasingly, secretarial work became something you did while you waited for your *real* life to start. Assistants began to look down on their own jobs and make fun of themselves even more than bosses ever did. Most assistants rejected "feel good about your oh so important role" nonsense from earlier generations, and simply concluded that they were stuck.

Having created Secretaries' Day, greeting card companies at long last capitalized on how office workers *really* felt about the event. Hallmark introduced a new card which said, "Secretaries Everywhere Ask: Is it warm in here?" Inside it read, "Or are we, in fact, working in Hell!?" Matt Groening's long-running comic strip "Life in Hell" appeared in office cubicles in record numbers, along with the "Angriest Dog in the World," a comic that showed the same grumpy dog growling on a leash day after day after day. Sylvester the Cat, long a standard fixture on secretarial note boards, now extended his middle finger as he encouraged everyone to take their "silly-ass problems down the hall."

In 1992's *Batman Returns,* Selina Kyle (Michelle Pfeiffer) was a sickly-sweet secretary before her boss Max Schreck (Christopher Walken) threw her off a skyscraper for knowing too much. When the kitties cleaned her up and mewed life back into her broken body, she became Catwoman, and ditched her good-girl image with a vengeance. She returned to her old apartment and ripped the chirpy "Hello There" sign on her wall, until it read "Hell here." Then she went after Schreck with vengeful glee. The original Selina Kyle from the comic books never was a secretary: in the movie, however, it seemed so right to have a happy, cheerful 1950s-style office helper come back from the dead in a B&D leather outfit and bullwhip anyone who got in her way.

Of course, how assistants felt about their jobs depended on who told the story. When a lawyer told it, the tale sounded just like the 1950s all over again. Take 1993's *The Firm*, for example. Holly Hunter played Tammy Hemphill, the secretary to a broken-down private eye (Gary Busey). She was sitting in his lap for a lip-to-lip dictation session just before two killers broke into the office. While she hid under the desk, she became the only witness to her boss's brutal murder. *Best line of the film: Mitch McDeere (Tom Cruise) asked Tammy how she ended up under the desk, and she snapped: "I was vacuuming the rug. Do you want me to draw you a picture?"*

Tammy rented an office and a copier, and helped Mitch catch the bad guys. Again, though, as in *Kitty Foyle*, Tammy was considered better off with Mitch's escaped-convict brother than with Mitch or any other lawyer. This strange role maneuvered Tammy and real-life women like her back to the 1950s, where they played Playtex-cross-your-heart Gun Molls for the private detectives they loved. Tammy was a loyal, trash-talking, blue-collar dream. She slept with her boss and smoked cigarettes off the edge of one candy-red lip, but she was also smart, tough, resourceful, and devilishly brave.

By the time Tammy appeared on the big screen, secretarial work was a scrambled image in most people's minds. Do you call them ''administrative assistants'' or ''secretaries''? Are they decorative playthings or future lawyers and CEOs? *Is* there really such thing as a Tammy Hemphill with a husband named Elvis and the hots for her private eye, or is that just a figment of a former attorney turned novelist's imagination?

Assistants asked similar questions. Why *can't* Tammy Hemphill have a Tom Cruise hunk for herself? What did the television producers mean when they asked Ms. Dipesto to recite jingles into the telephone in a babied-up voice? And who the hell died and made Jane Fonda, who has probably never typed correspondence in her life, the typical secretary? What is the point? Should everyone in the office just go jump off the same bridge at once?

Murphy Brown, that ubiquitous office comedy of the 1990s, seems to think the last suggestion isn't such a bad idea. Creator/producer Diane English swats at two stereotypes with one joke on this popular series. Murphy (Candice Bergen) is the prototype ''impossible female boss.'' Her secretaries, played by everyone from Pee-wee Herman to a crash-test dummy, are dazed, incompetent, noncommunicative, hostile, and everything else you ever heard about support staffers from the boss. The secretarial situation on *Murphy Brown* is complete madness because *that's how bosses view the job.*

In 1994, a group of women calling themselves the Five Lesbian Brothers co-wrote *The Secretaries*, an Off-Broadway play that understood just how silly movies like *9 to 5* and *Working Girl* looked to 1990s audiences. John Simon of *New York* magazine called it ''a camp takeoff on all those nine-to-five-working-stiff movies'':

> *Four girls type away in an office in an Oregon lumber mill; the fifth is their strict supervisor. Their chief extra-*

> *curricular activity is killing off the male employees they consort with by discreetly shoving them into the saws. That, it seems, is the only way of acquiring the guys' lumberjack shirts, which they crave.* (October 3, 1994.)

Forget empowerment and becoming a super secretary. This view, along with programs like *Murphy Brown*, satirized the inevitable: administrative assistant work had become an enduring bit of camp cultural humor.

Meanwhile, the British television series *Absolutely Fabulous* was a huge hit in the United States. Jane Horrocks played Bubble, private secretary to Edina Monsoon. Although Bubble was yet another dimwit, the show sent up the daffy secretary in a manner that was as funny—in its own way—as *Murphy Brown* or *The Secretaries.* When Edina becomes frustrated with Bubble's incompetence, her daughter Saffron tries to justify Bubble's existence:

> EDINA: *''I don't see why I don't just* sack *you.''*
> BUBBLE: *(Begins to sob)*
> SAFFY: *''Oh, don't be silly, Mum. Where else are you going to find someone who makes doing* nothing *into an art form?'' (To Bubble) ''I'm sorry, I* had *to say that.''*
> BUBBLE: *''It's all right. I didn't quite understand what you meant.''*

This portrayal is obnoxious, but it's *so* far over the top that it makes the important point (in its own caustic way) that secretaries and bosses in the 1990s find themselves, ultimately, at impossible odds.

So there you have it: an unscientific survey of office assistant images. Not much has changed, really. Now you understand why I insist that secretarial work is *not* the way to start in a corporation if you want to do something else someday.

When I began as an assistant, I didn't think about Jane Hathaway or Ms. Dipesto. I just wanted a job that paid the bills until I could figure out what was next. What I discovered, however, was a complicated quagmire of sexism and assumptions that made it nearly impossible for me to simply do my job and collect a paycheck. There was always more going on behind the boss's condescending compliments ("very *good,* you write so *well*") and my own growing confusion about my role in the office.

In a perfect world, secretarial work would be either a profession or a steppingstone, depending upon your goals. In the real world, however, it's a tar pit where even the most well-meaning workers can get stuck. Now that you've seen at least a few of the classic stereotypes that most bosses grew up with, you can understand why. This chapter is good for a laugh, but it can also help you walk into the office knowing who many of your employers—even the "enlightened" ones—*think* you are. You and I know better than this, and my mission is to show you how to force bosses to see you as yourself. They can, but you have to *make* them. Left to themselves, they'll try to fit you into one of these popular images and ignore you and your future.

STORIES, STORIES, STORIES:
A Compendium of Clerical Lore

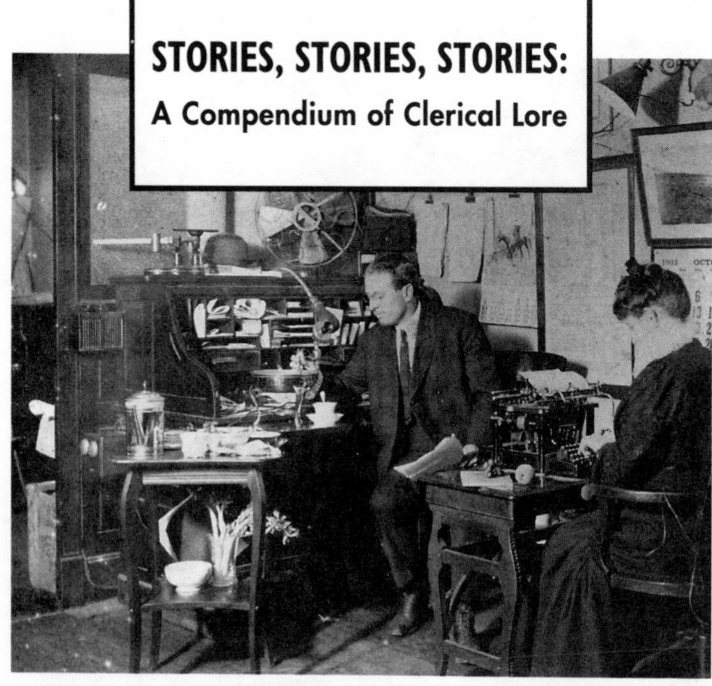

LIBRARY OF CONGRESS

- *Washington Post* columnist Bob Levey publishes an annual support staff column, in which he refreshingly and irreverently attacks the whole concept of Secretaries' Day. He polled his readers some years back and found out that nearly all respondents wanted to trash it:

> *"I've worked as a secretary in Washington, D.C., since 1970," writes "Moving to Florida Next Month." "During that time I've typed his children's homework, xeroxed books for his wife, taken his bird into my home while he was on vacation, driven forty miles round trip to let the electrician into his home, covered his wife's overdrafts at the bank and run her errands while she drove around in her Mercedes, shopping . . ."*

Levey also reported a wonderful list of worst-boss awards that administrative assistants sent in to him. Here are a few of the funniest:

- *A boss asked his secretary to hand-deliver his urine sample to a clinic. The sample was still warm.*
- *A boss ordered his secretary to snip his nose hairs.*
- *A secretary asked for time off to visit a doctor. "Why don't you let me examine you?" the boss replied.*
- *A boss asked his secretary to sew up a rip in his pants—while he was wearing them.*
- *A boss not only asked his secretary to type a term paper for one of his children, he asked her to write it.*
- *A boss demanded that his secretary call his mother and announce that he wouldn't be coming to dinner on Mondays any longer.*
- *A secretary was fired for gaining a few pounds while on vacation.*
- *A suspicious-looking package arrived in the mail. "This might be a letter bomb," the boss said to his secretary. "You open it."*

For his humorous annual columns about administrative assistants, Levey has been dubbed an honorary expert—a designation which still mystifies him since he does his own typing and filing, and says he wouldn't have it any other way.

- Secretaries in Springfield, Missouri, competed for prizes at radio station KGBX by tossing typewriters from fifty feet up. (Raleigh *News & Observer*, 1995.)

- Clerical worker Tammy Kravek takes out her office aggressions by studying karate. ''When I go back to my desk, I feel so much more relaxed,'' she told reporter Lini S. Kadaba. (*The Philadelphia Inquirer*, June 23, 1995.) I think there also may be a useful application here for arrogant attorneys. They might be a lot less prone to hassle a black-belt assistant!

- There are plenty of male secretaries and administrative assistants. Often, however, they call themselves something else so you don't know exactly what they do. Many male secretaries learned their skills in the military. Harvey Gittler writes about two male secretaries, Finley Lanier of Sherwin-Williams, and Jim Ayers, Jr., of Shell Oil, who trained in the Marine Corps and the Navy, respectively. Neither of these men appears in the misleading statistics about secretaries, since Lanier's title is ''lead coordinator'' and Ayers's title is ''office assistant.''

- Deborah Tannen writes of a university president who handed a project to her secretary before going into a conference with a male board member:

> *Before they enter her office, she gives her secretary a piece of paper and says, ''I've just finished drafting this letter. Do you think you could type it right away? . . . And would you please do me a favor and hold all calls while I'm meeting with Mr. Smith?'' Inside her office, Mr. Smith suggests that he disapproves of the solicitous way the head of the college has spoken to her secretary. ''Don't forget,'' he says, ''you're the president!'' (*Talking from Nine to Five*, William Morrow, 1994.)*

- Columnist Steve Twomey reports that several men competed for the job of executive secretary to the Washington, D.C., Board of Education. Forty people applied for the $70,000 position, including lawyer Nate Bush, who didn't get the job.

- After John F. Kennedy's assassination, conspiracy theorists tried to make overmuch of Kennedy's connection with assassinated President Abraham Lincoln, by noting that Lincoln had a secretary named Kennedy, and Kennedy had a secretary named Lincoln.

- Hope Christopoulos Mihalap, former private secretary to Rudolf Bing, general manager of the Metropolitan Opera, remembered preparing his lunch in the early 1960s:

> *As I brought in the tea, he handed me half a bologna sandwich in a little waxed-paper bag. ''Please put this on a plate for me.''*
>
> *When I returned with the sandwich, Bing asked, ''Where is the waxed-paper bag?''*
>
> *''I threw it away.''*
>
> *He said, ''I am not a millionaire. I will tell you when to throw away the bag. Please get it at once.'' I fished it out of the trash and smoothed it, and he kept it going for another three months. Then I knew how the Met ran in the black during his tenure.*

This story comes from *Opera News*, which earns my kudos for publishing a witty and bizarre memoir. You can read more of Hope Christopoulos Mihalap's reminiscences in her book *Where There's Hope* (Granville, Ohio: Trudy Knox Publisher, 1995).

- Journalist Tod Lindberg satirically reminds administrative assistants that they can help promote a free press by leaking important information to reporters. He includes such helpful ideas as:

> *Treat the reporter cordially and exhibit a desire to be helpful. Answer any questions the reporter puts to you honestly and directly. Give him or her any documents he or she seeks. In the case of a document in your possession that is not ready for official release, leave a copy on your desk and offer the reporter a cup of coffee. While you are getting the coffee, the reporter will have a chance to read the document—and you'll still be able to tell your boss that you didn't give the reporter anything. (*Insight, *June 13, 1994.)*

- Lindberg goes on to point out that there is very little difference between an administrative assistant and a journalist:

> *As Lord Beaverbrook, the Fleet Street press baron of yore, once said, journalists need three things: the ability to type; knowledge of shorthand; and low, ratlike cunning.*

This is comforting information for assistants who want to change jobs. Just work a little on your "ratlike cunning," and you should be able to switch over to the American Free Press in no time.

- When offering a bribe to a judge, don't overlook the legal secretary! Corruption among judges in Venezuela is a big enough problem. Many criminals, however, offer the bribes to (or through) the judge's administrative assistant:

> *"People test your capacity to be corrupted with a small gift at the beginning like a bottle of perfume," said one judge's legal assistant. "If you accept, the gifts get bigger," he said, adding that he has rejected bribes "on a daily basis" ranging from cash and a flight to the Caribbean island of Aruba to a hen, bags of fruit, and even half a dozen pairs of shoes. (Andrew Cawthorne, Reuters America, Inc., May 15, 1995.)*

- 1945. New York mayor Fiorello La Guardia does his own secretarial work, to the amazement of the Commissioner of Investigation, Louis E. Yavner:

> *Down the echoing marble corridors came the erratic clacking sound of unskilled typing. Yavner looked at his watch—it was nearly 8:00 p.m. He followed the sound to the office of the mayor's secretary, and there sat La Guardia, pecking away with one finger of each hand and glaring at the keyboard as if it were a political adversary. . . . "Oh, hello, Lou," he said. "I've got these letters to get out and there was nobody else around. Say, can you type?" (*Little Flower: The Life and Times of Fiorello La Guardia *by Lawrence Elliott. William Morrow, 1983.)*

- Debbie Crow, a Kansas City business recruiter, can't imagine why more people don't want to be secretaries: "It is difficult for us to recruit ladies interested in this as a career. Somehow the role of an administrative assistant often isn't properly perceived by people who might be candidates." She didn't mention that secretaries in Kansas City are the lowest-paid in the United States. (*The Kansas City Business Journal.*)

- *The Moscow News* published an interview with politician Konstantin Borovoi, who explains his secretarial hiring criteria:

> *Mr. Borovoi told the popular* Moscow News *in an interview that Marina is not as smart as Lyena and cannot do simple tasks without detailed explanations, which, he adds, is typical for Russian women. But, he said, he prefers Marina over his other secretary, because her "legs were longer, her coffee was tastier, she created a nice climate, and carried out 'diplomatic' tasks well." The day following the interview, according to* Moscow News, *Marina quit.*

I hope Marina becomes a politician and beats Borovoi for his own office. (*The Christian Science Monitor*, August 10, 1994.)

- Nikki Caparn was the real-life secretary to the fictional Sherlock Holmes. She answered the mail that regularly arrived at 221b Baker Street (headquarters of the Abbey National Building Society). Said Caparn of her strange job:

> *Name a country and we've had letters from there. . . . Mr. Holmes has been asked to help with Watergate and Irangate, to solve the murder of Olof Palme, the Swedish Prime Minister, and to find lost homework to prove to the teacher that the student really did it.*
>
> *Many people don't ask for anything in particular. They just want to know what Mr. Holmes is doing now or where he is and they hope he is well.*

Ms. Caparn wrote back to all correspondents on engraved stationery with a silhouette of the famous detective (curved pipe and deerstalker hat), and she claimed that the detective was "retired," not fictional or deceased. (*The New York Times*, November 5, 1989.)

- When Canadian secretary Susan Petersen went to work for top Toronto crime attorney Eddie Greenspan in 1978, he didn't even know her *name* for the first six months of their association. He summoned her by snapping his fingers, and he demanded that she bring him as many as ten cups of coffee a day, along with up to three packs of cigarettes. Things "improved," though, according to Petersen, who spoke warmly of Greenspan for *Chatelaine*, a Canadian magazine, in 1993. They became so happy together that she sang Tammy Wynette's "Stand By Your Man" for him at the law firm's karaoke party a couple of years back.

- How did Petersen interview for her job working for Greenspan? Reports Ann Walmsley: "To ensure she had the stomach for the job before being hired, she was asked to read descriptions of the damage to [a brutal crime victim's] head.'' That sure beats the old typing test as a basis of selection. Maybe more law firms should try it.

- The Haworth Fortune 500 Secretary Study reports that although most administrative assistants are stuck at their work stations for the entire workday, minus breaks, less than half of them had anything to do with the design of those stations. Most work stations are designed to complement office decor, not to help assistants get the job done. Another study shows that most companies spend more time choosing lobby art than they do selecting equipment that support staff will use to keep the office running.

- When legal secretary Marie K. Williams was hospitalized for several weeks following emergency surgery, her boss, Judge Suzanne B. Conlon, demoted her to ''temporary'' status and rewarded her with a pay cut, the *Chicago Tribune* reported (''On the Law,'' April 20, 1993). Williams had a fine work record prior to the demotion. Such behavior is standard procedure in many offices, no matter *what* laws are violated.

- While we're beating on lawyers, I'll repeat a report from the *Chicago Tribune* (''On the Law,'' October 11, 1994) about Christina Tompulis, who proved to a court's satisfaction that the Chicago law firm of Schwartz & Freeman discriminated against her by firing her at age fifty-nine. A partner in the firm reportedly told her, ''Older secretaries make too much money. The imbalance had to be balanced.''

- Jean Stapleton, better known to most people as Edith Bunker on *All in the Family*, used to be Jeanne Murray, an administrative assistant. She changed her name and her profession when she began singing with the Robert Shaw Chorale, shortly before her Broadway debut.

- Shauna Clark of Salt Lake City, Utah, wrote a ''Young Mother's Story'' for *Redbook* magazine (April 1990), describing her maniac boss who ordered her to sleep with him. She didn't comply. In a story that sounded weirdly like a soap opera script she described him screaming, shouting, and threatening to ''blow someone's head off with a shotgun.''

- *Newsweek* reports that Rena Weeks received $7.1 million from San Francisco law firm Baker & McKenzie because it knew a partner was harassing her and did nothing about it.

- *Forbes* (''Slaughtered Secretaries,'' June 5, 1995) reported that twenty-five administrative assistants were fired from the Manhattan law firm Paul, Weiss, Rifkind, Wharton & Garrison in June 1995. The reason? Thanks to computers, fewer people can accomplish more office work in less time.

- (From ''Hotline,'' a column in *9 to 5 Newsline*, October, 1994. Reprinted by permission.) *DEAR HOTLINE: My co-worker sexually harasses me by touching, pinching and grabbing my breasts and my behind. What can I do about it? —Harassed in Houston*

  DEAR HARASSED: Let me be very clear—you are not only being sexually harassed. You are being assaulted, which is a criminal offense. Think about it. If someone did this to you out on the street, you would call the police. The workplace is no different. You can call the police and make a criminal complaint against the harasser. Once you have told your employer about the harassment, they become legally responsible to put an end to it. You should also use whatever channels exist to report the behavior to the company. As in other sexual harassment cases, keep good documentation and seek support. This suggestion ought to be good for at least some ''dramatic relief.''

- (From Judith Martin's ''Miss Manners'' column, copyright 1995 by Judith Martin. Reprinted by permission.) *DEAR MISS MANNERS: Please tell me what to say to my immediate supervisor in the following awkward situation. I do not want to make trouble trying to report him, and it wouldn't do any good.*

  When I wore a pretty blouse, he would keep circling me, looking me up and down and making vulgar, nonverbal gestures. My defense was to ignore the gestures and to stop wearing anything that might excite him. I tried to keep my job by being a plain, very very plain, Jane.

  He then ran around, bringing my appearance to the attention of everyone in the company. He said I did not uphold the corporate image of the company.

  It seems no matter how I dress, I am damned if I do and damned if I don't—thanks to him.

  GENTLE READER: It is exactly this sort of refusal to abide by the decencies of manners that has forced etiquette to turn such shockingly ungentlemanly behavior over to the jurisdiction of the law.

  When your supervisor hears the term ''sexual harassment''—and Miss Manners strongly suggests that you make sure that he hears it soon, from his own supervisor or, if necessary, from a lawyer—he will undoubtedly claim that he didn't see anything wrong with what he was doing.

  He was only (he will protest) joking, or complimenting you, or helping you with your image, or being friendly. How was he to know that you would take it amiss?

The answer is that his mother, his wife, his daughter, and, in fact, the entire society has been trying to teach him that a gentleman does not make indecent gestures to a lady. In recent years, it has also been made abundantly clear that any romantic overtures, even when they are the polite sort that might be acceptable in social circumstances (where the lady could decline further acquaintance without imperiling her livelihood), violate office etiquette.

Miss Manners is sad to say that these etiquette rules have been so widely flouted by scofflaws that enforcement by the gentle restraint of manners could not protect the workforce.

And finally . . .

- *Time* magazine reports (October 30, 1995) that Russian president Boris Yeltsin pinched two secretaries on his way to a press conference.

  "Boris Packwood," *Time*
  "Twin Tweaks," *The Washington Post*
  "Public gaffe puts Yeltsin in a Pinch," *Los Angeles Times*

PHOTO BY ALEX MEYBOOM

Novelist Robertson Davies and his assistant, Moira Whalon

APPENDIX A

How to Fill Out a Government Application Form

The following article originally appeared in *Occupational Outlook Quarterly* (Summer 1993). It's full of good-sense information on properly applying for federal work in any region of the country. Even though most of the information is written for college graduates, there's still plenty of useful information if you haven't gone to college or if you aren't finished yet.

You no longer have to fill out SF 171 for a government job, but it still exists. It's optional now, but many managers are still more used to it. You may substitute a résumé or optional Form 612, but I suggest submitting SF 171 as well, if the agency will accept it. If you must submit Form 612, this article will still help you.

Once you've read this article and learned how to fill out your paperwork, use the job-search resources at the end. There are plenty of Internet and computer bulletin board sites you can consult for the latest government job listings. In fact, almost every available government job is now listed on computer. If you have a computer with a modem, you should be able to check the listings for which you qualify in any state without even leaving your house.

✎ Working for U.S. in the 1990s

by Kathleen Green

The U.S. Government is the Nation's largest single employer. But if you're job hunting, don't think of Uncle Sam in singular terms. About 3 million Federal workers are spread out among more than 100 Government departments, agencies, commissions, bureaus, and boards. You simply cannot send an application to a single Government entity and be considered for every job that exists.

Today's merit-based system of civil service has roots more than a century old. The Pendleton Act, passed in 1883, was the first step toward overhauling the excesses of the patronage system. Congress agreed to reform civil service laws only after President Garfield was assassinated in 1881 by a disgruntled office seeker he had declined to appoint. Until then, jobs went to political supporters, regardless of merit. Now, of the political positions that exist, about 3,000 jobs at the top, are reserved for those who work closely with Cabinet members and the President. So unless you're a friend of the President or a friend of a friend, you'll have to get your Government job on your own.

And there's more than one way to get a Federal job. There's more than one way you can apply for jobs, more than one way you are evaluated, and more than one person doing the hiring. There are affirmative employment programs, cooperative education and other student employment programs, and summer job programs. How you apply for a Federal job depends on your qualifications, the number of vacancies in your field, the number of people applying, where you want to work, the salary you expect, and the kind of job you want. If you are looking for a job with the U.S. Postal Service or are qualified to start above the entry level, you can apply directly to agencies. But if you are a college student or a college graduate looking for a white-collar Federal job, keep reading. . . . This article will help you find your way through the Government's hiring maze.

✎ Learning the Basics

If you're like most Federal job seekers, you don't know where to begin. You might start by learning about the Office of Personnel Management (OPM). Although it does not hire applicants (expect for its own needs), OPM manages employment policy for more than half the civil service. It develops and gives written exams, rates applicants, and refers applicants to agencies with openings. It also publicizes job openings through automated telephone systems, electronic bulletin boards, and printed materials. Most importantly, OPM defines the qualifications required for different occupations and manages the Administrative Careers With America (ACWA) program. (Helpful hint: People in Federal personnel circles refer to this program by its acronym, pronouncing it like the Latin word for water, aqua.)

✎ Do You Qualify? Check *Handbook X-118*

OPM writes qualification standards for the scores of white-collar occupations it regulates. You must meet these minimum qualifications to be hired. . . . For information on other occupations and for more complete information about ACWA occupations, consult *Qualification Standards for White-Collar Positions Under the General Schedule*, generally referred to as *Handbook X-118*. It gives the name of the occupation and its series number, which will prove very useful because jobs are often listed in numerical order. Perhaps most importantly, *Handbook X-118* also gives the requirements for entering jobs at different salary levels.

The Federal Government has several pay systems. About 450 white-collar occupations are part of the General Schedule (GS), which consists of 15 numerical grade levels. College graduates with no experience usually qualify for jobs at the GS-5 level. Even if you are qualified to start at a higher grade, you may need to begin work at the GS-5 or GS-7 level because the agency might be recruiting only entry-level workers. Agencies are not required to hire you at a higher level.

Keep in mind that meeting the minimum qualifications does not necessarily get you a job. Agencies look for the best qualified people. Even though a job such as writer-editor requires no particular degree, employers will look for related experience—school newspaper work, writings, relevant summer jobs—that demonstrates interest and potential for development in this field.

You can find *Handbook X-118* in a loose-leaf binder at personnel offices of all Federal agencies, Federal Job Information Centers, and most Federal depository libraries. Some State Job Service offices, college placement offices, and public libraries also have copies.

✎ A Look at ACWA

ACWA, or Career America, is OPM's job-entry program for college graduates who will, if hired, start at the GS-5 or GS-7 level. College seniors within 9 months of graduation may also apply for jobs through this program. Many of the occupations require a specific degree or completion of certain courses, but you can qualify for others with any degree. No experience is required for any of these occupations, but related experience can always help you compete.

ACWA covers 116 administrative and professional occupations in 7 groups, the first 6 of which require separate exams:

Group 1: Health, Safety, and Environmental
Group 2: Writing and Public Information
Group 3: Business, Finance, and Management
Group 4: Personnel, Administration, and Computers
Group 5: Benefits Review, Tax, and Legal
Group 6: Law Enforcement and Investigation
Group 7: Professional Occupations Not Requiring an Exam

Some of the 100 occupations in the first 6 groups have specific educational requirements, but most do not. All 16 occupations in group 7 are professional and, by OPM's definition, require certain academic coursework.

✎ ACWA Applications

Each ACWA group has a different application form. But, generally, you must pass a written test or show that you have the education required or both. One exception is made for those who qualify for the Outstanding Scholar Program; it exempts from testing college students who graduated in the upper 10 percent of their class or earned a cumulative grade point average (GPA) of 3.5 or above on a 4.0 scale.

To find out which groups you can apply for, visit or call your nearest OPM office or Federal Job Information Center. Ask for each group's Qualifications Information Statement to learn more about that group's jobs, qualifications, and application procedures. You can also call the Career America Connection's automated telephone system at (912) 757-3000. In the Washington, D.C., metropolitan area, call the Washington Area Service Center at (202) 606-2700.

Applications to take the test for most groups can be submitted at any time, but groups 1 and 2 may be closed in your region. For occupations in group 7, you may apply only when openings are announced; hiring is very limited.

Information statements for groups requiring exams include a test scheduling card, OPM Form 5000 AB, as well as application details and a list of OPM offices. Complete the test scheduling form and mail it to the OPM office in the area where you want to take your test. You should also request sample test questions. Within a few weeks of mailing your test scheduling card, you should receive materials indicating the time and location of the exam. Also included is a booklet containing sample questions.

You may take as many different exams as you like, but you may not retake a test within an occupational group for 1 year. You must bring a photo ID for entrance to the testing room.

Each written test has three parts. The first part consists of 12 vocabulary and 13 reading questions. The second part has 8 questions on tabular completion and 9 on arithmetic reasoning. The third part is the Individual Achievement Record, which evaluates how well you have used your opportunities in school, work, or outside activities. The exam takes about 75 minutes: 30 minutes each for the first and second sections and 15 minutes for the third.

✎ After the Test: Ratings and Registers

All exams in groups 3 through 6 for the continental United States are processed at the OPM Staffing Service Center in Macon, GA.

You will receive a Notice of Results within a few days of your test date. Your performance on the exam is boiled down to a numerical score, called a rating. Passing scores range from 70 to 100. (Veterans with a passing grade receive an extra 5 points; disabled veterans, an extra 10 points.) The names of all candidates with passing scores are ranked in numerical order on a list maintained by OPM. The list is called a register or competitor inventory. From this register, OPM makes referrals to agencies filling job vacancies.

Names remain on a register for 1 year. But not everyone on a register gets a job. Currently, only those with ratings in the middle to high 90's are being referred to agencies, and there's still plenty of competition. From October 1, 1992, to February 1, 1993, OPM only referred about 6,400 job applicants to agencies, out of about 70,000 eligible candidates for groups 3 through 6. Of those 6,400 referred, only about 200 were hired. As for the others, according to one OPM official, "the vast majority don't hear and probably won't hear."

Along with your test materials, you will have received a background questionnaire, Occupational Supplement Form B, that you must complete and bring with you to the test. It includes questions on your education and experience, and also has some questions about the kind of position you are looking for. For example, it asks you to indicate up to nine specific geographic locations in which you are willing to work. These can play an important role in whether you are called for an interview, because referrals are made according to candidates' designation for working in the agency's location. The central processing system allows you to be considered for employment in several geographic zones without having to take the same exam in each zone. But don't confuse this with the requirement that you take a separate written test for each *occupational* group that requires one.

✎ Other Jobs, Other Registers

OPM also maintains registers for specialized occupations outside the Career America program. Specialized occupations do not require a written test but do require specific coursework—just as the ACWA group 7 occupations do. Ratings for these registers are based on applicants' education and experience. The specialized occupations include positions in accounting and auditing, biological sciences, engineering, mathematical sciences, and physical sciences. You need to request Qualification Information Statements for detailed information about the specific educational requirements needed. Call the Career America Connection or visit your nearest OPM office or Federal Job Information Center.

The Qualifications Information Statements you will receive for nontest positions do not, obviously, include a test scheduling card. But you will receive Occupational Supplement Form B. For nontest positions, your rating is based entirely on the information you supply on this form. A computer will read your responses, so you must take special care to indicate that you meet the specific coursework requirements for that occupation. For example, with a public administration or other business degree, you are eligible for accountant positions if you have 24 semester credit hours in accounting. But the computer will not recognize that you meet this provision unless you indicate accounting as an undergraduate major (defined by OPM as 24 or more semester hours, or 36 or more quarter hours) on Form B. Read the instructions carefully when completing the form.

All Form B processing is done at the OPM Staffing Service Center in Macon. You should receive a Notice of Rating within 2 weeks of mailing your form. If you are eligible, your rating will be a numerical score from 70 to 100. Currently, applicants referred to agencies to be considered for openings have scores in the middle to high 90's, as is the case with the ACWA occupations in groups 1 through 6. The geographic location you indicated on Form B likewise plays a role in referrals. National registers are maintained in Macon for accountant/auditor and bioscience positions. But engineering, physical science, and math registers are downloaded directly to the specific geographic zones you named on Form B. To be considered for positions in more than one zone, you must submit a separate form for each zone.

✎ The SF 171

For many jobs, filling out an application is part of the hiring process. The Federal Government is no exception. An Application for Federal Employment, Standard Form 171 (SF 171), is required for every Federal employee's personnel file. For many positions, including ACWA occupations, you do not need to submit an SF 171 to take a test or complete an Occupational Supplement Form B. But you will still need to submit an SF 171, prior to being hired. For most agencies, the SF 171 is *the* designated application.

As your prospective employer's introduction to you, the SF 171 is a chance for you to present yourself at your very best. Fill it out quickly and you're wasting your time; thousands of applications are received by Government offices each year, and only the best attract attention. You should spend several hours to complete the application. It may seem tedious, but the time you invest could mean the difference between an interview and a rejection letter.

Blank SF 171 forms are available at Federal Job Information Centers, most Federal agencies' personnel offices, and many post offices, libraries, and State Job Service offices. You can also buy automated programs for producing your SF 171 on a computer.

Before you make any marks on the form, make several photocopies to use as drafts. Then prepare a master copy for each occupation you wish to enter and make photocopies of them. It's acceptable to submit a photocopied SF 171 when applying for jobs. Here are some hints on preparing those masters.

Read the form in its entirety, including the instructions, before you begin completing it. Most of the blocks are self-explanatory, but some deserve special attention.

Item 24, the work experience blocks, can make or break you. This is the section where you are asked to describe your duties, responsibilities, and accomplishments. Duties are the work you perform for your employers, responsibilities involve your independence and judgment, and accomplishments refer to duties performed beyond what is expected of you. If possible, show that you have progressed in each job, and from one job to the next, by taking on more demanding duties or more responsibility.

Note all work experience, including volunteer work related to the position you're applying for. Be specific. You may think everyone knows what a data entry keyer does, but don't stake your future salary on it. If you do not spell out exactly what you did, you may not get credit for any of it. In describing your work experience, use strong verbs, such as "performed," rather than weak phrases, such as "was responsible for performing." Whenever possible, quantify your accomplishments. Present yourself in a positive light, but don't overstate your duties.

Type your work descriptions on blank pieces of paper, leaving room for the heading block at the top of the page and the for-agency-use block at the bottom. Then cut both blocks from a photocopy of the SF 171, tape them in the appropriate places on your typed page, and photocopy the new page. The photocopy of your cut-and-paste page, which will not reveal your tape lines, results in a much neater look than trying to fit everything onto the tiny lines provided. Type your name, social security number, the position title, and the vacancy announcement number on each sheet.

For items 25 through 31, mention all education you have received. Be sure to include seminars, workshops, training programs, and vocational or adult education classes. As mentioned in the Career America discussion, how you specify your major field of study is key in applying for a rating. For some occupations, positions are not limited to a specific major but may require a certain number of course credits. And unless you designate those course credits as your major, your application may be overlooked. As mentioned earlier, for example, accountant/auditor positions may be filled by college graduates with 24 semester hours of accounting credits whose degrees are in related fields such as business administration, finance, or public administration. So if you have 24 semester hours in accounting but majored in finance, list accounting as your major when you apply for a rating as an accountant/auditor.

When you list references for item 36, use names of people who are not related to you who can attest to your working ability. Ministers, doctors, local political leaders, or other character references are of little help in commenting on how you work.

Leave items 1, 48, and 49 blank on your master copy. Item 1 asks what job you are applying for; complete this block each time you apply for a position. Items 48 and 49 are the signature and date certification, and they must be signed in ink on each application. You may wish to leave other items blank on your master copy as well, especially in the section marked "Availability." This section asks questions regarding the lowest pay you will accept, the geographic area where you wish to work, and your willingness to travel. You won't be forced to accept a job that pays less than you would like or would require you to move. On the other hand, you could eliminate yourself from consideration for jobs that you might think about under some circumstances if you fail to choose your responses carefully.

Your master copy will save you time because you won't have to start from scratch for every application you submit. But you may need more than one master copy if you're applying for different kinds of jobs. Even if you apply for the same positions in different agencies, you may find that agencies place emphasis on different skills or abilities. You should get a copy of the vacancy announcement for each job you apply for. (See the next section for a discussion of vacancy announcements.) You need to make sure each application you submit reflects that you meet the qualifications required.

Finally, be sure to proofread your SF 171 carefully before you apply for jobs. And don't forget to fill in the items you left blank on your master copy, including signing and dating the application in ink. Automated SF 171 software is available. According to OPM, at least two private manufacturers have developed programs that produce acceptable SF 171 applications. These are Federal Research Service, Inc., and the Software Den, developers of "Quick and Easy," and "SF-171 Automated," respectively. Contact retail stores for more information.

✎ Vacancy Announcements and Job Listings

Agencies advertise vacancies with brief statements of job information called vacancy announcements or even briefer job listings. Each announcement or listing includes the job title, occupational series number, grade and pay levels, application opening and closing dates (the period during which applications are accepted), number of vacancies, job location, announcement number, person to contact, phone number, and agency name. Announcements, which may run a couple of pages, also spell out specific job duties, both general and special requirements, and application procedures. They even indicate how important each required skill is.

There are many places to find announcements and job listings, although no one place will have every announcement. Regional OPM offices, Federal Job Information Centers, State Job Service or Employment Security Offices, and personnel offices of Federal agencies are all likely to have some announcements. A more comprehensive list of jobs appears in a commercially published magazine, *Federal Career Opportunities Listing*. It is available at many libraries and at many of the offices that have the announcements themselves.

Touch-screen and automated computers, available at nearly all Federal Job Information Centers, also provide vacancy information. You can search these listings—called Federal Job Opportunity Listings—by such criteria as occupational series, job title, or geographic location. The computerized lists are updated at least monthly. They are available at State employment service offices and many college placement offices, as well as through the computers at the Job Information Centers.

Electronic bulletin boards allow you to download job listings on your personal computer. OPM's bulletin board is free (except for the price of the phone call). You can access it by dialing (912) 757-3100 via a modem. There are also six OPM regional bulletin boards.

If you have found only a listing and not the announcement itself, contact the agency advertising the opening, asking that the announcement be sent to you.

For many vacancies, applicants are given only 1 or 2 weeks to submit forms. Be advised that the closing date generally is the day your paperwork must reach the hiring authority, not the date materials must be postmarked by.

✎ Applying to Agencies

Because not all jobs are listed in any one place, you should plan to contact agencies on your own. Each agency's personnel office has the most up-to-date information on its needs and hiring procedures.

You can start your search with a check of U.S. Government listings in the blue pages of the phone book. Call the agencies you think are likely to hire for your occupation. Of course, not every occupation is employed by every Federal agency. On the other hand, you might be surprised at the range of jobs within an agency. For example, you know the Army Corps of Engineers hires engineers, but it employs many other kinds of workers as well. Don't assume that all educators work for the Department of Education or that every librarian is employed by the Library of Congress. Education majors are employed by the Departments of Defense, Interior, Justice, Agriculture, Transportation, and Treasury, among others. Library science majors work in such offices as the Executive Office of the President, Government Printing Office, and Patent and Trademark Office—not to mention the departmental libraries throughout the Government.

Consider visiting Government offices in person to ask about openings. In some Federal buildings, you won't be allowed past the guard desk (though there might be a dropoff box for applications). But in other offices, especially in smaller cities, you might get a chance to meet with someone. Each personal contact you make increases the probability of your getting hired. After all, often the only way you find out about a vacancy is if you're in the right place at the right time.

You might also learn about openings for positions other than the one you're looking for, including clerical and technical jobs. Don't eliminate these outright just because the starting salaries are below those usually offered to college graduates. You may think you're overqualified for some jobs, but they may be good stepping stones to your desired career. Mobility is often easier from within, where you learn more about the agency and have more access to job vacancy information. Many agencies also offer training programs for employees, which can help you gain experience and advance to more responsible positions. Before making a commitment, check out the situation at the agency you are considering working for.

✎ Exceptions, Exceptions

Not all occupations require that you get on an OPM register. In fact, for some occupations, such as those in public safety, you apply directly to the hiring agencies. OPM also grants special authority to some agencies that allows them to hire applicants without prior referral from a register. These special authorities are called delegated case examining, shared case examining, and direct hire authority. There are also excepted positions and agencies that OPM has nothing to do with.

Delegated case examining permits agencies to advertise, evaluate, and hire applicants independently of OPM. In shared case examining, an agency recruits and screens applications before sending them to OPM for final evaluation; OPM then sends a list of the best qualified candidates back to the agency, and the agency makes its selection. Direct hire authority is similar to delegated case examining but applies only to occupations for which shortages exist.

Public safety occupations—which include air traffic controller, deputy U.S. marshal, treasury enforcement agent, and U.S. park police officer—are filled by delegated examining. You must apply directly to an agency to take a written test for one of these occupations. Delegated examining allows the agencies to develop and give their own tests, as well as evaluate applicants and set hiring standards. Treasury enforcement agents, for example, cannot be older than 37 at the time they are hired. The screening process also includes a series of interviews, a polygraph test, background investigation, and drug testing.

Delegated or shared case examining is used to fill most ACWA group 7 occupations. For public safety and group 7 occupations, there is no national register; evaluation methods vary by region and agency. Some agencies accept applications continually and maintain registers to fill openings as they occur. But most accept applications only when they have vacancies for these positions.

OPM grants direct hire authority to agencies for hiring in occupations for which shortages exist. This authority varies by location, occupation, and agency. To find out which agencies have the authority for which jobs, contact your nearest OPM office or Federal Job Information Center. Ask for a list of agencies that have direct hire authority for your field. You can then contact the personnel offices of the agencies on the list to find out about their application procedures. When you call, ask to speak to someone who handles entry-level hiring in your field. If no phone numbers are given on the list of agencies, check the U.S. Government listings in your phone book's blue pages.

Exceptions to the merit system have been established over the years by law, executive order, and regulation. OPM is not involved in any way with the hiring of people for these occupations and agencies.

The excepted positions include the following:

- Doctors, dentists, and nurses in the Department of Medicine and Surgery of the Department of Veterans Affairs,
- Scientists and engineers in the National Science Foundation,
- Attorneys,
- Chaplains,
- Teachers and many other workers overseas,
- Drug enforcement agents doing undercover work,
- Part-time workers in isolated areas,
- Many seasonal workers.

The excepted agencies include such large, well-known ones as the Central Intelligence Agency, Federal Bureau of Investigation, and Tennessee Valley Authority, as well as several lesser-known or smaller agencies. In some agencies, certain occupations are excepted, such as health occupations in the Department of Veterans Affairs and foreign service occupations in the Department of State. Excepted agencies set their own hiring procedures.

✎ Don't Give Up

Federal hiring procedures are constantly changing, but each agency's personnel office should have the most up-to-date information. If there is a best way to look for a Government job, it is to try every method you can for getting a foot in the door. Know your own qualifications and make sure you meet the requirements for getting hired. Visit as many agencies as you can and find out if they're hiring. Leave copies of your SF 171 if possible, even if they're not accepting applications for a specific opening. Keep adapting your strategies to the ones that seem to work best.

And never underestimate the power of your personal network. Ask family members and friends about opportunities that crop up in their offices. Talk to people you know who work for the Government and find out what they do. Meet with people who may have lots of contacts, such as your college professors, and talk to the people they know. Networking is an important tool in the vast Federal work force.

Above all, be flexible. No matter where you look for a job, you can expect setbacks along the way. You're guaranteed to get the runaround more than once, but don't get discouraged. If you are qualified, your persistence will pay off.

✎ For More Information

Reading this article is just the start of your Federal job hunt. Now you're ready to move on. Below is a list of resources to provide you with specific information about tests, job vacancies, and application procedures.

OPM publishes the *Federal Career Directory*, containing general employment and special hiring program information, profiles of Federal agencies, and an index of college majors. You can find the directory at libraries, OPM offices, and Federal Job Information centers. OPM also publishes brochures on topics ranging from the Federal Cooperative Education Program to the summer Employment Program. To receive them, write: OPM Career Entry Group, 1900 E Street NW, Washington, D.C. 20415. To receive *Qualifications Information Statements for ACWA positions and information about job vacancies, special hiring programs, salaries, and benefits*, call the Career America Connection, (912) 757-3000. You can call this automated message service 24 hours a day, 7 days a week. Material requested by telephone is usually mailed within 24 hours. Or write: Office of Personnel Management Staffing Service Center, P.O. Box 9800, Macon, GA 31298-2699. You can also visit any OPM office or Federal Job Information Center.

If you live in the Washington, D.C., metropolitan area, call the Washington Area Service Center's automated phone system at (202) 606-2700 for testing schedules and application materials. The Office of Washington Examining Services schedules most tests on a walk-in basis, and the automated message gives the schedule. You can also follow the instructions on the message to receive the sample questions and Form B for the group for which you would like to take a test.

For exams in groups 1 and 2, and for exams in groups in Alaska, Hawaii, Puerto Rico, and the U.S. Virgin Islands, contact the OPM office in those regions for information and applications. Positions are filled locally, and you may have to file separate applications in each area you want to work.

Telephone Device for the Deaf (TDD) numbers are also available in each region. They are listed on information sheets available through OPM's Federal Job Information Centers.

If you have a personal computer, modem, and communications software, you can access the Federal Job Opportunities Bulletin Board, (912) 757-3100. Information about examinations currently open and vacancy announcements nationwide can be scanned on line or downloaded to your computer. Although not as comprehensive, OPM regional bulletin boards are available in six areas. They are:

(202) 606-1113 Washington, D.C., area
(404) 730-2370 Southeastern States
(215) 580-2216 Northeastern States
(313) 226-4423 North Central States

(214) 767-0316 Mountain and Southwestern States
(818) 575-6521 Western States

Many agencies also publish information about themselves and occupations that are especially important to them. Contact agencies directly to receive these brochures.

(left to right) Judy Fiber, Kim Irwin, performance artist, and Hattie Smith write their autobiographies in "We Are Secretaries" at Cincinnati's Cage, 1993

APPENDIX B

Unions, Professional Organizations, and Other Resources

The Harvard Union of Clerical and Technical Workers/ AFSCME
1306 Massachusetts Avenue, #203
Cambridge, MA 02138
617-661-8289
617-661-9617 (fax)

The union's organizers looked around the wealthy, privileged Harvard campus and knew something was wrong. The professors earned huge salaries. Those students who weren't born wealthy were attending school on scholarships and fellowships. Harvard's endowment had climbed to $5 billion, making it the richest university in the nation. Yet the clerical workers, before they unionized, earned low wages:

> *Some top administrators receive more in annual salary increases than a secretary [at Harvard] takes home in a year. We wonder if the well-being of ourselves and our families is one of the lowest priorities at Harvard University.*

The unionization effort worked. Union workers at Harvard earn a third more than nonunion workers. The union fights for such basic privileges as "child care, elder care and flexibility," along with pay parity and benefits.

You have to work at Harvard to join the union, but you can certainly learn a lot by studying their model. They have an information packet which includes stories of other universities that unionized after seeing how well it worked. Write or call for more information. It's not required, but I recommend that you include a few dollars (around $5) to defray reproduction and mailing costs. This is a good policy for organizations that have to struggle to stay funded and help their members thrive.

9 to 5, National Association of Working Women
614 Superior Avenue NW
Cleveland, OH 44113
216-566-9308
1-800-522-0925

You'll get the lowdown on problems in the day-to-day life of an administrative assistant from this organization. I recommend paying the annual fee ($25 in 1995) and taking advantage of their terrific benefits package that includes prescription drug discounts, free legal consultations, life insurance benefits, a special MasterCard tie-in, dollars-off at Disney World, and more useful premiums. They offer a cornucopia of benefits, and often act more like a club than a labor union.

I've blasted 9 to 5 fairly hard because of its sexist language. If you are planning on administrative assistant work as a career, though, it really deserves a place in your professional life. If you're getting harassed, or if you just want to read about your legal rights for your own knowledge, 9 to 5 has a comprehensive network of resources.

Women's Bureau
U.S. Department of Labor
200 Constitution Avenue NW
Washington, DC 20210
202-219-6652
202-219-5529 (fax)
Director: Karen Nussbaum (formerly of 9 to 5)

You can write to the Department of Labor at this address for a copy of the full report *Working Women Count! A Report to the Nation.* Be sure to include a self-addressed mailing label. I'm not crazy about the ''old-school feminist'' tone, which reluctantly admits that the problems of working women are also those of working *men*, but again, these are useful resources if you're being discriminated against, harassed, or if you are unfairly fired. A partial list of recent Women's Bureau publications includes:

1993 Handbook on Women Workers: Trends and Issues
Women of Hispanic Origin in the Labor Force
Don't Work in the Dark. Know Your Rights
The Family and Medical Leave Act of 1993

Midlife Women Speak Out
Work and Family Resource Kit
A Working Woman's Guide to Her Job Rights (1992, $2.50)

Professional Secretaries International
P.O. Box 20404
Kansas City, MO 64195-0404
816-891-6600

Some employees, especially men, report that certification has made them more employable and competitive. If you're a male administrative assistant who wants to see the support staff ranks change for the better (and fairer), then by all means join PSI. You can earn a professional certification by taking a two-day exam. If you're female, however, then I don't really recommend this kind of certification, since ''secretary'' and ''woman'' are already considered synonymous in some people's minds, and you might just pigeonhole yourself.

The I Hate Filing Club
Margaret DeMonte, President
Esselte Corporation
71 Clinton Road
Garden City, NY 11530
(516) 873-3212 (fax)

Esselte, the company who brought you Pendaflex folders and files, started this group to support frustrated, overworked assistants. You can write to Margaret DeMonte or send her a fax, and she'll put you on the *I Hate Filing* mailing list. She'll send you a package with a membership form, and instructions for earning free premiums like a coffee mug, the Oxford Beaver, tote bags, mirrors, and other items that will tastefully tell your office what you think of the filing chore. This group boasts a whopping 37,000 members, and it even has a thrice-yearly newsletter.

Don't Work in the Dark
800-827-5335

This program of the Department of Labor's Work and Family Clearinghouse provides information on sexual harassment, your rights under the family medical leave act, pregnancy discrimination, age discrimination, and wage discrimination. If you're having a problem at work, or if you just want to know the difference between a good family benefits package and a poor one, you can call them for the latest information.

Black Professional Secretaries Association
3113 Rosewell Road
Marietta, GA 30062-5500
404-578-5005

The Association of Black Secretaries
1212 Broadway
Oakland, CA 94612-1841
510-834-7897

National Secretaries Association
Philadelphia Chapter
1420 Pine Street
Philadelphia, PA 19102-4603
215-545-6400

Texas Educational Secretaries Association
406 East 11th Street
Austin, TX 78701-2617
512-477-0724

RESOURCES FOR LEGAL SECRETARIES

National Association of Legal Secretaries
2250 East 73rd Street
Tulsa, OK 74136-6844
918-493-3540

Austin Legal Secretaries Association
401 West 15th Street
Austin, TX 78701-1665
512-476-5434

Legal Secretaries Association
Salt Lake City, UT 84101
801-531-0577 (fax)

Colorado Association of Legal Secretaries
8270 Louise Drive
Denver, CO 80221-3966
303-428-1044

DC Legal Secretaries Association
Jan Bise, PLS, President-elect
PO Box 65619
Washington, DC 20035-5619
202-296-7881

This chapter offers its members continuing legal education; it hopes to raise the consciousness of lawyers *and* secretaries. Monthly meetings cover everything from doing your job better to tactfully telling ''this highly educated person that his written grammar is poor.'' Part of the National Association of Legal Secretaries.